"Holy Land, Whose  ɔ seeks to understand
the tragedy of contem   ɛe in the Middle East
today."

                                                          Review.

"Without being partisan [Drummond] introduces almost all the players and presents
all the scenes of history that have resulted in the conflict that is causing so much
bloodshed today in the region."

AHARON BEN ANSHEL,
The Jewish Press

"... *Holy Land, Whose Land?* [presents] the importance of the Holy Land to Jews,
Christians, and Muslims without prejudice. The author [makes a] genuine attempt
to be unbiased in that she blames all sides for mistakes made."

ZAINEB ISTRABADI,
*Associate Director of Middle Eastern
and Islamic Studies, Indiana University*

"Holy Land, Whose Land? makes a valuable contribution to understanding a
complex, bloodstained issue...Drummond adds a personal dimension with on-
the-ground observations from her travels..... [This} is one road map that is easy to
follow."

DOUG ESSER,
Associated Press

"Holy Land, Whose Land?, a scholarly yet genuinely personalized account, is both
a description of the present and an explanation of how this tortured landscape has
survived as a religious and cultural mosaic of worldwide significance. Dorothy
Drummond speaks ...with the ease of a gifted tour guide and the presence of a
scientifically grounded, professional teacher. *Holy Land, Whose Land* is both lively
and well-focused."

RALPH K. ALLEN,
The Professional Geographer

"Every serious person wants to have a better understanding of the Middle East
and of the unholy Holy Land, the focal point of international troubles. For the
general reader, there is no better introduction than Dorothy Drummond, *Holy
Land, Whose Land?* Academic books for specialists are not easy; indeed they are
sometimes unpleasant reading. Dorothy Drummond writes in an engaging way
for the ordinary reader. This book should please both the general reader and the
scholar. I urge WAISers either to acquire the book or recommend it to their local
library and schools."

RONALD HILTON
*Hoover Institution, Stanford University
President, World Association of International Studies*

"Drummond masterfully unravels the reasons why these conflicts have developed. *Holy Land, Whose Land?* provides a broad understanding and respect for diversity, a respect that could bring sanity to an insane repeat of history."
                    MARK KANE,
                    Founding Director Institute for Global Education

"A felicitous blend of personal experience, geography and history in a succinct account of the ancient and modern roots of the contest for Palestine."
                    F. ROBERT HUNTER,
                    Chair, Department of History
                    Indiana State University

"{*Holy Land, Whose Land?*] will prove useful long after a first reading, because of the comprehensive series of maps and the several [glossaries]. The book is a source for reference as news reports continue daily. Its uncomplicated style makes for easy reading on a complicated subject."
                    ROBERT J. MARSHALL,
                    President Emeritus,
                    Evangelical Lutheran Church in America

"…The author…does an excellent job of not taking sides in what is a very divisive issue. To get an idea of the history of the Middle East before Israel's independence and even before Zionism, this book is the place to start."
                    PAUL LAPPEN,
                    Under the Covers

"Dorothy Drummond…has written a terrific book…a primer on the Holy Land, interspersed with her own impressions of the sites she visits…all the historical information she presents is relevant to today's headlines. Perhaps most impressive of all is that she… is objective, [giving] equal treatment to the viewpoints of all sides."
                    WILLIAM P. WARFORD,
                    Antelope Valley Press

"There are many, many people who have no idea about the historical significance of the geography [and history] of the [Holy Land]. For these readers Dorothy Drummond's *Holy Land, Whose Land?* should prove enlightening. Drummond is to be commended for undertaking such an ambitious project."
                    NORMAN GOLDMAN,
                    Rebecca Reads

"*Holy Land, Whose Land?* outlines the complex and volatile mix of history, religion and politics that fuels the Israeli-Palestinian conflict…. It covers 4000 years of history and is interwoven with accounts of her travels in the Holy Land. Drummond's book is the story of the people who live in the Holy Land — Jews and Arabs – who bear the weight of ancient injustices and grim everyday realities."

MORGAN JAREMA,
Grand Rapids Press

"Dorothy Drummond [has written] an even-handed primer on the Middle East, its history and the situation there today… *Holy Land, Whose Land?* is packed with information. If you feel uninformed about the Middle East and want to become knowledgeable, this is the place to start… The thirty maps are clear and excellent, and there is a glossary and [annotated] lists of people and places."

SALLY WEEKS,
Champaign-Urbana News Gazette

"The book is a scholarly masterpiece explaining a complicated subject in a clear and organized fashion…It is a good beginning point for the uninitiated and deserves several readings to absorb the many factual details. I highly recommend this book."

BARBARA KELLER,
Centenary Sentinel

"Throughout the book, Drummond is as even-handed as it is possible to be. She leans toward neither the Jews nor the Arabs."

JOHN F. FINK,
Indianapolis Star

"*Holy Land, Whose Land?* is a timely primer for anyone who wants to begin understanding the triggers of the turmoil….She allows readers to gain some clarity about cause and effect in one of the most complex political and religious standoffs in the world today."

RICK FARRANT,
Fort Wayne Journal-Gazette

"In *Holy Land, Whose Land?* Drummond…grips the attention of the reader and holds it through the last page, [as she] deals with the quagmire of the Middle East crisis."

PATRICIA PASTORE,
Terre Haute Tribune-Star

Holy Land, Whose Land?

Modern Dilemma, Ancient Roots

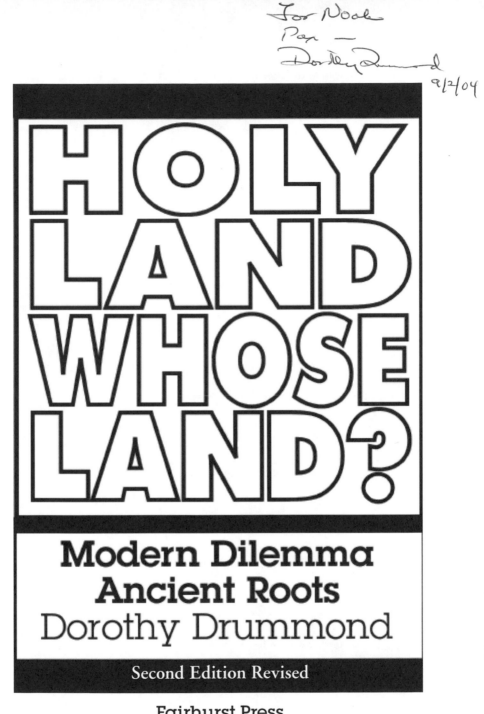

HOLY LAND WHOSE LAND?

Modern Dilemma
Ancient Roots
Dorothy Drummond

Second Edition Revised

Fairhurst Press
Terre Haute, Indiana

Holy Land, Whose Land?
Modern Dilemma, Ancient Roots
by Dorothy Drummond

Published by:
Fairhurst Press
3 Fairhurst Court
Terre Haute, IN 47802
fairhurstpress@verizon.net

SAN: 255-870X

Copyright 2002, 2003, 2004 by Dorothy W. Drummond
www.dorothydrummond.com

Printed and bound in the United States

ISBN First Printing 0-944638-30-9 (Educare Press, 2002)
ISBN Second Printing 0-9748233-1-7 (Fairhurst Press, 2003)
ISBN Second Edition, Revised 0-9748233-2-5 (Fairhurst Press, 2004)

Second Edition Library of Congress Control Number 2003195208

Printed and bound in USA.

Printed on acid-free paper which meets minimum ANSI requirements for printed library materials: ANSI/NISO 239.48 * 1998 (R2002)

10 9 8 7 6 5 4 3 2 1

Publishers Cataloging in Publication Data:
Drummond, Dorothy Weitz.
     Holy Land, Whose Land? : Modern Dilemma, Ancient Roots —
     2nd revised ed. / Dorothy Drummond.
          p. cm.
     Includes bibliographic references and index.
     ISBN 0-9748233-2-5 (pbk)
     1. Arab-Israeli conflict. 2. Jews — History. 3. Palestine — History.
     4. Drummond, Dorothy Weitz — Travel — Palestine.
     6. Palestine — Description and travel. I. Title.

DS119.7.D79 2004
956.94 22
2003-195208

CONTENTS

MAPS

CHARTS

DIAGRAM

PHOTOGRAPHS

Acknowledgments

No work begins in a vacuum. It is the outgrowth of ideas accumulated, often subliminally, over a lifetime. Nevertheless, I want to acknowledge especially those persons who have been influential in the making of *Holy Land, Whose Land?* My interest in the Holy Land started when I was on a Fulbright fellowship in Burma, more than forty years ago. At that time, I met Dr. Daniel Hillel, an Israeli agronomist temporarily detailed on an advisory mission. He had grown up in Israel before World War II and many of his friends were Arabs. I never forgot our long conversations, nor my subsequent experiences as a guest in his young country the year that Israel celebrated its tenth anniversary. He went on to become a world-renowned soil scientist, something I could have predicted from his brilliance, his energy, and intensity, even then. I am grateful to my friend Jane Hazledine, who headed me in the direction of the Hashemite Kingdom of Jordan nearly a decade ago. That experience initiated my research on the Decapolis and led me to want to return to Jordan, and to Israel as well, at an early opportunity.

My interest in Middle East history is long-standing, but for a focus on the history of the Holy Land, and of the Biblical accounts that are critical to its understanding, I credit author Thomas Cahill, whose two books, the *Gifts of the Jews* and *Desire of the Everlasting Hills,* gave me a new way of seeing. Also immensely helpful was Karen

Armstrong's *A History of God.* I think, however, that my intense interest in the Biblical accounts, and their relationship to the Holy Land today, began with weekly discussions on the Book of Genesis led by Dr. William Dando, who saw all the comings and goings of the Patriarchs through his geographer's eye.

Through the years, I have been blessed with friends who on a personal level have given me insights into the Israeli/Palestinian dilemma. Friends in my town travel often to Israel to visit their families, and I have come to know the grief and anxiety and outrage that they feel. A Holocaust Museum is in my town, the personal creation of a remarkable woman, Eva Kor, who as a young twin survived the vicious Auschwitz experiments of Dr. Josef Mengele. She has traveled widely to bring her message that one can live to overcome bitterness. An arsonist torched her museum late in 2003, destroying her carefully gathered collection. Yet even in the face of this ugliness, she refuses to give in to despair. Years ago, I shared discussions with Elsie Mayyasi, whose Palestinian husband was working in my town as a chemist. Through Elsie and her husband, I began to sense what it meant to be uprooted and stateless. But it was Irmgard Fuchs who, in New York City in the early fifties, first introduced me to the horror of forced displacement. She wore a concentration camp tattoo on her forearm. In the 1980s, a Palestinian geographer colleague in Iowa, Dr. Bashir Nijam, spoke and wrote about the Palestinian tragedy at every opportunity, but at that time few were listening, and he died before the full impact of what he was saying revealed itself. At Indiana State University another colleague, Dr. Akhtar Siddiqi, sharpened my awareness of Arab contributions to scholarship through his publications on Muslim geographers of the Middle Ages. Dr. Siddiqi was loyal to his Muslim roots, but alas he too died before I could have the talks with him that would have helped me in writing this book.

Three authors who most helped me to understand the volatility of today's Holy Land wrote more than a decade ago, but their accounts seem fresh today: Thomas Friedman, *From Beirut to Jerusalem;* David K. Shipler, *Arab and Jew: Wounded Spirits in a Promised Land;* and Father Elias Chacour—an Arab, a Palestinian, a Christian priest, and an Israeli citizen—whose aptly titled *We Belong to the Land* gave me a sense of what it means to be part of an aggrieved minority. Bernard Lewis has published extensively on the Middle East and on Islam, and his clarity and insights have focused my thinking. Edward Said, the Palestinian historian who was teaching at Columbia University at the time of his death in 2003, once wrote that "the intellectual as exile tends to be happy with the idea of unhappiness." Said's voice was the voice of the dispossessed Palestinian, and his writings consistently and often brilliantly reflected the bitterness he felt toward the West. With his death Palestinians lost an effective spokesman.

I cannot possibly do justice to the magnificent effort put forth by a thoroughly knowledgeable and sensitive Israeli guide named Yossie Weiss, as well as by John Reitan, whose itinerary maximized coverage in a limited time frame. I appreciate the willingness of my sister, Arlene Weitz VanderKlomp, and our mutual friend, Karen McCullough, to harbor me as a triple in a succession of rooms meant for two, and I treasure the conversations we had that ultimately triggered this account. I owe a debt to my three daughters, Kathleen, Gael, and Martha. It was so they and their husbands could share my Holy Land experiences that I set out originally to write a modest journal, and it was they who first urged me to expand it.

I am especially grateful to my friend the Rev. Arthur Simon, founder of Bread for the World, who early had faith in this book and gave encouragement at every step. My editor on the first edition, Ms. Marianne Van de Vrede, helped give form to substance but tried valiantly not to impose her sense of style on mine. The creative stamp of artist-mapmaker-designer Jeff Reynolds is on every page. In addition I am indebted to the Rev. Joseph H. Chillington, Dr. Christine Drake, Dr. Mark Kane, the Rev. Barbara Nolin, Dr. Elizabeth Westgard, Dr Samuel Schnitzer, Dr. Zaineb Istrabadi, Carol Rueckert, Jonnee Western, Margaret Bruning, Lou Petrulis, and Connie Ratcliffe, all of whom have given valuable critique and/or encouragement.

Alert readers will perceive omissions in my attempt to link the present to the past, but they may realize, too, that I have made no attempt to be exhaustive. I offer my book as a primer, a place where one can start the process of understanding. In researching and writing this book, I have gained a world of understanding. It would please me to know that the reader may feel likewise enriched.

Foreword

The idea that grew into this book seemed simple enough on first resolve. It was late March of the millennial year. I was sitting on Suleiman's Wall, overlooking the Old City of Jerusalem, on the last day of my most recent visit to the Holy Land. As I was churning over in my mind how to condense my experience so that I could both retain it and share it, I realized that this was not going to be an easy task. I would first have to dig into the past to make sense of the Holy Land as it is today. I resolved to do so. Soon after, the urgency of the Intifadeh and the collapse of the peace process placed an added layer on my resolve.

On the Wall I was idly musing, "How did it happen that the land holy to three faiths can be kept secure only at gunpoint?" Today this question is irrelevant, for soldiers and firepower no longer guarantee peace. They only serve, as guns always do, to inflame. Why is the Holy Land–today again, as so often in the past – a cauldron of conflict? Seeking answers, I have had to delve deeply. What started as a simple account of my travels has become far longer and more complicated than I had originally intended.

The Holy Land has a complex story, played out in a varied landscape, where the past is continually intruding into the present. Piecing it together has taken me more time than I had anticipated. Many lights have gone on in the process, leading my research continually in new directions. But the story of the Holy Land has not yielded easily to generalization.

This account is no longer centered on my travels. It is the story of the Holy Land, with my own experiences interspersed in italic. I offer it now to anyone who may be contemplating a journey to the Holy Land or who may simply want to understand the complicated story – both sacred and profane – of this unique, beautiful, and tortured land.

January 22, 2002

FOREWARD TO THE SECOND EDITION

This second edition extends the Present to May, 2004. In revising I can record some change, in direction if not in substance. There has been periodic escalation of violence, but little or no progress in negotiation. The United States and European countries, with a Roadmap, continue to be involved in diplomacy to nudge the Israelis and Palestinians toward a peaceful solution. But Israelis and Palestinians continue to contend, without a clear path out of the dilemma. Sharon and Arafat are two years older, both past 75, but the vitriol is still in their bellies, and they continue to distrust and cancel out each other's overtures. Palestinian terrorists continue to infiltrate Israel, followed by Israeli military retribution.

Seeing no end to terrorism, nothing to be gained by retribution, and no progress in negotiation, Israel is now embarked on a unilateral solution: it is building a security barrier, part wall, part barbed-wire-and-berm, that snakes into Palestinian territory to encompass all West Bank settlements near the Green Line. Israel is also beginning to talk about abandoning settlements, in the Gaza Strip and those beyond the barrier. As a deterrence, the barrier is beginning to work (two-thirds of it remains to be completed), but disruption to daily life has only worsened for Palestinians. Most of the world views the barrier as another roadblock to peace. In the larger world, to which the

Holy Land dilemma is inextricably connected, Sadaam Hussein has been captured, Osama bin Laden remains at large, and international terrorism remains a threat. But a new generation of non-government peacemakers reflects the longing of people on both sides of the Green Line for peace, and some see hope on the horizon.

Dorothy Weitz Drummond
Terre Haute, Indiana
May 20, 2004

Prologue:
From Suleiman's Wall

On a warm spring day at the start of the third millennium, I am leaning against a shaded niche on the parapet of the Wall that Suleiman the Magnificent built five centuries previously to enclose the Holy City. My most recent travels in Israel and Jordan, the land where Abraham, Jesus, and possibly Muhammed walked, are nearly at an end. I am thinking of the millions who have come before me, pilgrims of three faiths and of no faith at all, drawn like iron to the magnet of Jerusalem, this ancient city at the crossroads of civilizations.

I try to recall bits and pieces of the long history of empires and armies that in the past four thousand years have struggled for control of the Fertile Crescent passageway at the eastern end of the Mediterranean Sea: the Egyptians, the Hittites, the Philistines, the Hebrews, the Assyrians, the Babylonians, the Persians, the Phoenicians, Alexander the Great, the Romans, the Byzantines, the Arabs, the Crusaders, the Seljuk Turks, the Ottoman Turks, and the British. Below me, interspersed among the crowd thronging every passageway in the Old City, I can see Israeli soldiers, Uzis slung over

1

their shoulders, guarding intersections. They remind me that most of the Holy Land is now under control of a new and continually wary power – the modern state of Israel – committed to guarding and protecting all pilgrims who come to its land, of whatever faith.

I am thinking, too, of the peoples of the past who were caught in the continual upheavals as superior forces invaded their territories: the Canaanites and Hebrews in the central highlands, the Philistines and the Phoenicians on the coast, and the peoples of Moab and Edom on the plateau rising starkly east of the Jordan River. Currently, the most tragic are the stateless Palestinian Arabs who lose their homes as Jewish refugees from the Holocaust flood into the Palestine Mandate after World War II and into the new state of Israel after 1948. One human tragedy begets another, and yet a third: As Arab countries react with anger to the founding of the new state of Israel, Jews resident in Arab lands for a thousand years and more are told they must leave; many are resettled in Israel. How to address the grievances of the displaced Palestinians is no closer to a solution today than it was in 1948. As the Jews keep the memory of the Holocaust alive, so the Palestinians cry out that they too are the victims of injustice. The Palestinian issue has pitted Israel against the Arab nations. It has involved the United States time and again as broker in the peace process. And, as I write, it is still confounding the efforts of good people on all sides to bring about peace. Only now, the urgency is all the greater, for nuclear weapons are positioned in the region.

On this day, however, there is peace in Jerusalem. Pope John Paul II worships the day before at the Church of the Holy Sepulcher, and he is shortly to conclude his own intense and difficult pilgrimage to Holy Land sites. Israelis, Palestinians, Jordanians, and Egyptians have spared no security efforts, and the visit has been without incident. Armed Israeli soldiers stand guard to protect the thousands of pilgrims who have come for the millennial year. They protect Pope John Paul II as he prays at the places holy to his faith, and they protect the pilgrims loyal to other Christian traditions. They protect the Jews who come to the Western Wall to bewail the fate of their twice-destroyed Temple; they protect Muslim pilgrims who come to the Haram al-Sharif to pray at the Al-Aqsa Mosque, where the outer courtyard of the Temple once stood; and they protect visitors like me. I doubt that I need protection, for the tightly packed crowds here today are peaceful. But the city is volatile, no less today than in the past, and the Israelis are determined that the shrines of this Holy City shall be kept open to all who wish to visit.

The story of the Holy Land that follows is not intended to answer the question posed in the title of this book. Rather, by shedding light in dark corners, it attempts to bring understanding. The story is in three parts: The first details the present Israeli-Palestinian conflict and puts it into modern context. The second surveys the roots of conflict in the Holy Land, traveling four thousand years into the past to unravel the tangled web of religion, conquest, and politics that has made the land unique and its future consequential far beyond its borders. The third takes a broader worldview, examining how and why the conflict has been co-opted, and why there is no alternative to negotiation. In all three parts, I use the present tense to give an immediacy to all that has happened, for in truth, the past is always present in the Holy Land.

Holy Land, Whose Land?

Part I
The Present:
Turmoil in
the Holy Land

The Holy Land, holy to the world's three monotheistic faiths—Judaism, Christianity, and Islam—must be defined geographically. Broadly speaking, it encompasses most of the territory where events chronicled in the Hebrew Scriptures (foundational to the faith of Jews, Christians, and Muslims alike) and the first five books of the New Testament take place.

The heartland of the Holy Land is the region known historically as *Palestine*, a name given to it by the Romans in the second century. West to east, Palestine extends from the Mediterranean Sea coastlands through hill country rising to 3,000 feet, then plunges to the geological trench occupied by the Sea of Galilee (Lake Kinneret), the Jordan River, and the Dead Sea. North to south, it extends from the source of the Jordan on the southern slopes of Mount Hermon to the Negev Desert where the Wadi Arabah terminates in the Gulf of Aqaba at Eilat. In the time of Jesus and before, there was no such named region. Instead, there was Galilee in the north, Samaria in the center, and Judea in the south, all governed by Rome. Because Biblical narratives take place not only in Palestine but also on the plateau east of the Jordan River and the Sea of Galilee, southward within the Negev and Arabian Deserts, and west of the Negev Desert

7

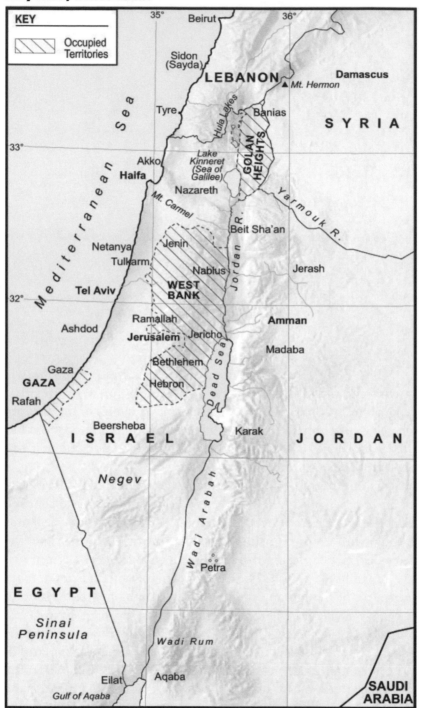

KEY

/// Occupied
Territories

Beirut

Sidon
(Sayda)

LEBANON

Damascus
▲ Mt. Hermon

Tyre

Banias

SYRIA

Hula Lakes

Mediterranean Sea

Akko

Lake
Kinneret
(Sea of
Galilee)

GOLAN HEIGHTS

Haifa

Nazareth

Mt. Carmel

Beit Sha'an

Yarmouk R.

Netanya

Jenin

Tulkarm

Nablus

Jerash

Jordan R.

**WEST
BANK**

Tel Aviv

Ramallah

Amman

Ashdod

Jerusalem

Jericho

Madaba

Bethlehem

Dead Sea

Gaza

Hebron

GAZA

Rafah

Beersheba

Karak

JORDAN

I S R A E L

Negev

Wadi Arabah

E G Y P T

*Sinai
Peninsula*

Wadi Rum

Petra

Eilat

Aqaba

Gulf of Aqaba

**SAUDI
ARABIA**

Map 1. The Holy Land today.

8

	Area (Sq. Mi.)	Population Mid-2003	Capital
Israel	8,019	6,700,000*	Jerusalem**
Occupied Territory*			
West Bank	2,262	2,300,000	Ramallah†
Gaza	130	1,300,000	Gaza City†
Golan Heights	447	38,000	
The Holy Land also includes portions of the following countries on Israel's borders:			
Jordan	35,637	5,500,000	Amman
Syria	71,498	17,500,000	Damascus
Lebanon	4,016	4,200,000	Beirut
Egypt	386,662	72,100,000	Cairo

* Includes also Israelis settled within the Occupied Territories.
** Embassies of foreign countries are located in Tel Aviv.
*** Territory occupied by Israel since 1967, following the Six-Day War. Excludes Jews settled within the Occupied Territory– ca 207,000 in the West Bank, 173,000 in East Jerusalem (which has been annexed by Israel); 7,400 in Gaza; 20,000 in the Golan–who are counted within Israel's population.
† Palestinian Authority headquarters exist both in Ramallah and Gaza City.

Chart 1. Political entities in the Holy Land.

into the Sinai Peninsula, the Holy Land traveler hopes to traverse these lands as well.

Defined in this broader sense, the Holy Land today is under the political jurisdiction of six entities. It includes all of Israel and that part of the Occupied Territories governed by Israel, all of the fragmented territory governed by the Palestinian Authority, the coast of southern Lebanon, southwestern Syria, western Jordan, and Egypt's Sinai Peninsula. The threads of religious heritage could well weave this region into one, but the Holy Land has never been more fractured politically.

Today, one cannot travel between Israel and Lebanon or between Israel and Syria. At this writing, however, one *can* travel between Israel and Egypt and between Israel and Jordan, but only by using selected border crossings. Even travel within Israel and the territories that Israel occupies is restricted. For the most part, visitors are still free to travel everywhere within Israel and the Occupied Territories.

9

Technically, Israelis are also, but they are not welcome in the cities governed by the Palestinian Authority. Palestinians in the West Bank and Gaza essentially cannot travel. A figurative Green Line separates Israel proper from the territories it has occupied since 1967. Since the beginning of the present Intifadeh, Israel has given permission to cross the Green Line only to those Palestinians who can display difficult-to-obtain work permits. The permits are often suspended. And only with greatest difficulty can Palestinians move through Israeli barriers from one part of their fragmented Authority to another.

The first time I am in Israel I look over a wall into the Old City of Jerusalem and stare into the muzzle of a Jordanian gun. That is in 1958, the year Israel celebrates its tenth anniversary. The most fervent wish of Israelis in that anniversary year is for all of Jerusalem to be part of Israel. In another nine years, this wish is fulfilled. More than forty years later, I wonder again about the future of the Holy City.

1
Birth of a Jewish State

Had the Arabs accepted partition, Israel would have ended up with considerably less territory than it gained through their rejection. [The Arab armies] provided the Jews with the most severe motive in battle: survival.
David K. Shipler
Arab and Jew

Although its roots are deep and immemorial, the young State is foredoomed to many grave trials.
David Ben-Gurion
The Call of the Spirit in Israel

Desperate for a place to settle at the end of World War II, Holocaust survivors are languishing dazed and weak in makeshift refugee camps in Europe. Young Jews from the British Mandate of Palestine, healthy and bright-eyed, visit the refugees. "Come to the Promised Land, Eretz Israel," they say. "We will help you get there, and you can help us build a new Israel." The young Jews are operating illegally. They represent the underground organization known as *Haganah*, dedicated to bringing Holocaust survivors to Palestine. The British do not want any more Jews in their Mandate. Over the preceding sixty years, Arab Palestinians have seen more and more of their farmland purchased by Israeli

1945-1946

11

settlers. Since the Nazis came into power, Jewish immigration into the Mandate has swollen. The Arab Palestinians are feeling threatened. For the past twenty years, intermittently, a Palestinian underground has been harassing Jewish settlers, and the Jewish underground has been retaliating. The settlers keep arms close at hand. The situation is volatile. The British determine to continue their policy of limiting Jewish immigration.

The British Dilemma

Britain is in a quandary. It is tied by its Mandate to protect the rights of Arab Palestinians and to maintain order. At the same time, when the Mandate is established after World War I, one of its goals is to further Jewish settlement, in accordance with a British government policy (the Balfour Declaration) that dates from 1917. It is clear that if masses of Holocaust survivors settle in Palestine, Arabs will be displaced. Already a trickle of Arabs is beginning to flee. As the first wave of refugees reach Palestine, militant Jewish settlement groups intimidate and harass Arab property owners. The militants want the Arabs out of the Promised Land, and they make no secret of this. Not all Jewish settlers share this view, however. Most hope for a Palestine in which Arabs and Jews can live peacefully, side by side.

Jewish Zionists from Europe have been coming to Palestine since the late 1870s. Zionism wants a national homeland for Jews in the land that gave birth to Judaism, the Promised Land, Eretz Israel. With early financing from Zionists in England (soon also from Jews and some Christians in European countries), more and more Jewish pioneers come to Palestine. They buy land from the Arabs and begin to farm. They set up shops in the cities. Slowly they prosper. The Jews are European; the Arabs are Middle Eastern. Their ways are different. By the end of World War II, 300,000 Jews are living in Palestine. Although Arabs still constitute the majority of residents in the British Palestine Mandate, they fear that the onslaught of Jewish refugees will change Palestine forever, and Arab Palestinians will be a minority in their own land. The Arabs look to the British for support. The British try to hold back the tide, preventing boatloads of refugees from landing, for the landings are indeed illegal. But the landings continue. The Haganah has learned to work around the British.

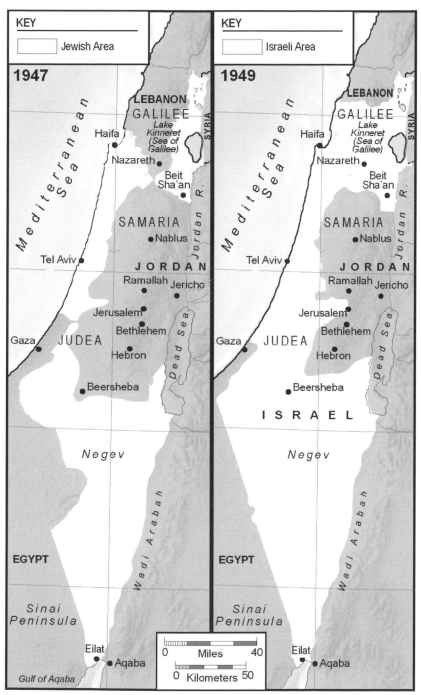

KEY

☐ Jewish Area

1947

KEY

☐ Israeli Area

1949

Map 2. U.N. Proposed Jewish State, 1947 (left), and Israel following Armistice, 1949 (right).

Meanwhile, within Palestine, leaders of a militant Jewish underground organization called *Irgun*, formed originally to protect settlers from Arab militants – and to make life so uncomfortable for Arabs that they will leave Palestine – now realize that for the time being their enemy must be the British. They do all they can to disrupt the British, going as far as blowing up the King David Hotel in Jerusalem. The flood of refugees continues, Arab indignation rises, the Irgun destroys British headquarters, and the British in the end can do little to stop the violence. They seek help from the United Nations.

Independence and the First Arab-Israeli War: 1948

In November of 1947, the United Nations (UN) passes a resolution partitioning Palestine into a Jewish state and an Arab state *1947* (See Map 2). Jerusalem is to be a UN protectorate. All Arab countries oppose this resolution, but a majority of other countries support it. Official partition is to take place in September of 1948. But the Jewish settlers in Palestine – whose very presence is by this time vehemently opposed by the surrounding Arab states – act unilaterally. On May *1948* 14, 1948, they proclaim Israel as an independent country. At the same time, the British give up their troubled Mandate over Palestine.

A day after Israel proclaims its independence, its Arab neighbors declare war. The Israelis anticipate this action. The territory they were to receive under the UN partition includes only a portion of "Eretz Israel," the land of the Zionists' dreams. It is not even enough, Israelis say, to serve as the basis for a viable state. If they are to gain more territory, indeed if they are only to keep what has been granted them in the partition, they must fight. Units of the Haganah and Irgun, bolstered by the seasoned veterans of the Jewish Brigade that volunteered to fight with the British in World War II, form the core of a hastily mobilized Israeli army. As Arab forces enter the territory of the former British Mandate, they are determined to push the Israelis into the sea. The Jordanians, with their crack British-trained Arab Legion, fight well, advancing across the Jordan River to take the land known today as the West Bank. Israeli troops, harassed from all directions, are held to the borders shown in Map 2.

14

Egypt takes the Gaza Strip, and Syria retains the Golan Heights, overlooking Lake Kinneret (the Sea of Galilee). The Israelis make their strongest stand in Jerusalem; there the Jordanians are able to take only the eastern half of the city. But this half includes the Old City and, above all, the Temple Mount, where Solomon's Temple once stood. The Temple Mount has not been a site of Jewish worship since the Roman destruction of the rebuilt Temple in 70 CE (Common Era). Now called the Haram al-Sharif by Muslims, the former Temple Mount contains the Dome of the Rock, the third of the three most holy sites of Islam (after Mecca and Medina in Saudi Arabia). Nearby is the Western Wall, the only portion of the Temple complex that escapes Roman destruction. Now the Jews of Israel will no longer have access to this sacred site.

UN-Brokered Territorial Settlement: 1949

The UN brokers a peace settlement in 1949. Under this settlement, Israel begins its life with fifty percent more territory than it would have had under the UN partition plan. It has control of the *1949* entire eastern Mediterranean coast south of Lebanon (except for the Gaza Strip), the northern (Galilean) and southern (Judean) portions of the bordering hill country, and the western portion of Jerusalem. Samaria and the northern part of Judea (the area subsequently called the West Bank) is in Jordanian hands, as is almost the entire Jordan Valley. Egypt controls the Gaza Strip and Syria the Golan Heights. Southward, Israel controls the southern and drier part of the Judean hills, and beyond Judea the Negev Desert, from the southern part of the Dead Sea westward to the Sinai Peninsula and southward to the Gulf of Aqaba. But its spiritual heart, the Old City of Jerusalem, remains in Arab hands.

War and Israeli Territorial Gains: 1956 and 1967

In 1956 Israel's position with regard to its neighbor Egypt becomes untenable. Egypt blockades the Straits of Tiran, Israel's only outlet to the Red Sea, cutting off its access to petroleum. *1956* Meanwhile, Egypt is aiding Palestinian raids into Israeli territory. Israel takes action, coordinating planning with Britain and France.

15

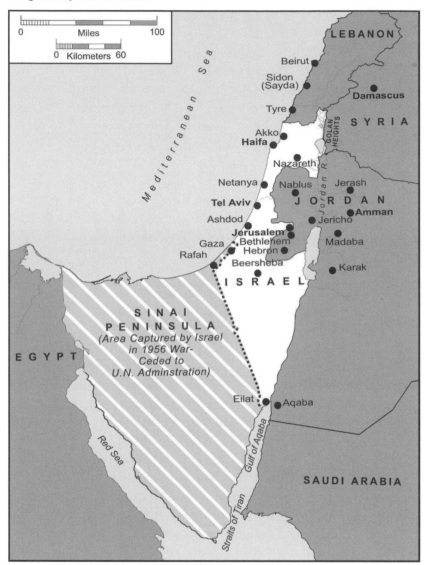

Map 3. Israel following 1956 war.

As Israel invades Egypt, racing across the Sinai Peninsula for the Suez Canal, British and French troops invade Egypt and attempt to take back the Canal which Egypt has nationalized. A full scale war is averted by urgent international diplomacy, at the height of the Cold War. Britain and France pull out of the Canal Zone for good, and control of the Sinai Peninsula and the Gaza Strip goes to a United Nations Peacekeeping Force.

16

Map 4. Israel following the Six-Day War, 1967.

In succeeding years the Egyptians refuse Israel the use of the Suez Canal, move troops into the Sinai, and demand the withdrawal of the U. N. Peacekeeping Force. From Egypt on the west, Syria on the north, and Jordan on the east come cross-border raids on Israeli settlements, in a continuing Arab attempt to redress the grievances they feel: that hundreds of thousands of Arab Palestinians are languishing in refugee camps, and that an independent Jewish state

17

has been created in what they feel is Arab territory. Meanwhile, from the Golan Heights Syrian artillery is shelling Israeli towns and settlements in Galilee.

1967   In early June of 1967 armies of Lebanon, Syria, Jordan and Egypt are massing on Israel's borders, preparing for a united effort to defeat their enemy state. On June 5 Israel preempts the war, simultaneously striking targets in Egypt, Jordan, and Syria. In six days of hard fighting, Israel once again takes the Sinai Peninsula, conquers all Jordanian territory west of the Jordan River (the West Bank), takes over all of Jerusalem, and occupies the Golan Heights. Palestinian refugees are again caught in the middle. Thousands more flee eastward and northward, joining those who leave Palestine in 1948.

1973   The war lasts for just six days before all parties accept a UN Security Council cease-fire (See Map 4). Israel immediately occupies all the territory it has conquered. In 1973 Israel and Syria war briefly, and the easternmost part of the Golan Heights reverts to a UN

1979- Peacekeeping Force. In 1979, urged on by the carrot of U.S. aid,
1982 Egypt makes peace with Israel and against all odds the two adversaries establish diplomatic relations. In 1982, as the agreement requires, Israel hands back the Sinai Peninsula. But the rest of the gains of what has come to be known as the Six-Day War of 1967 remain under total or partial control of Israel to this day.

2
OCCUPIED TERRITORIES

Only through the [1988]
intifadeh did the West Bankers
and the Gazans really emerge
as a nation in the fullest sense.
The intifadeh transformed [them] from
Jordanized and Egyptianized Palestinians
into Palestinians—period.
Thomas L. Friedman
From Beirut to Jerusalem

On most maps created outside Israel, including United Nations maps, the West Bank and Gaza are separately designated as areas of disputed ownership, or *Occupied Territories.* Their status, the status of the Golan Heights, and the status of Jerusalem are thorny issues that no peace initiative has been able to resolve.

The West Bank

At first, after Israel wins the Occupied Territories in 1967, a liberal Israeli government leaves the West Bank more-or-less alone, with the exception of a military presence. Ruled by Jordan *1967* since 1948, the West Bank is economically underdeveloped, for the young country of Jordan is overwhelmed by the influx of Palestinian refugees on its soil. Nevertheless, the West Bank

19

Photo 1. Irrigated farmland in Israel, along the Jordan River.

has a relatively efficient administrative infrastructure. Its people are Jordanian citizens, free to work in Jordan and continue their links with Jordan, even using Jordanian currency. A few Israeli kibbutz settlements are built in a lightly occupied strip along the West Bank of the Jordan River, keeping a relatively low profile.

As I pass northward in the West Bank along the Jordan Valley, I see how Jewish settlers are making the land highly productive by combining technology with hard work. Only later do I realize that the irrigation water they are using, the result of a huge Israeli investment in water development, is often denied to neighboring Arab farmers.

A conservative government follows. Its members consider that the Occupied Territories are part of the Biblical Promised Land and must be absorbed. Israeli settlements soon spread to the Samaritan and Judean hill country, and the West Bank is linked economically with Tel Aviv. The conservative government is determined that the West Bank shall be an integral part of the Jewish state.

Jewish Settlements

By 1970, the Israeli government is confiscating land and building homes in the heavily settled areas of the West Bank. Palestinian villages and neighborhoods are being bulldozed to make way for new construction, and olive groves are being uprooted. The settlement program makes it clear that the intention is not only to create new settlements, but also to destroy evidence of previous Palestinian occupancy. Although some Israeli settlers come for ideological reasons, to help give permanence to Israeli occupation, most are attracted by the favorable terms (low taxes, low-interest loans) under which they receive housing and land. Serving a defensive purpose as well as providing housing, most West Bank settlements are sited on hilltops, overlooking Palestinian villages or towns. As the planned settlements grow, they reach outward in the direction of the settlement on the next hill, with the intention that eventually the two will merge.

About 207,000 Jewish settlers now live in the West Bank. Most live in 128 separate settlement "towns" that range in size from two hundred to several thousand inhabitants (See Map 5). But about 20,000 settlers live in some 115 enclaves or "outposts" too small to be called towns. The rate of Jewish population growth in the West Bank, over eight percent per year, far outpaces Israel's 2.5 percent average rate of growth.

From time to time the Israeli government agrees to halt the building of new settlements except in the vicinity of Jerusalem. But in actuality, settlement building, as well as maintenance of the settlements now in existence, continues unabated. [At this writing, in the spring of 2004, the Israeli government is proposing abandoning more-remote settlements, but no time table has been set, and the wrath of displaced settlers is a factor that could well destabilize any government that attempts to implement withdrawal.] The Israelis have built a network of high-speed roads by-passing Palestinian towns to connect the settlements with each other and with Israel proper. Settlers use the by-pass roads to get to their jobs in Israel's cities, but Palestinians are not allowed to travel on these roads. The roads separate Palestinian villages from each other as effectively as interstate highways, cutting through cities in the United States, once tore apart urban neighborhoods.

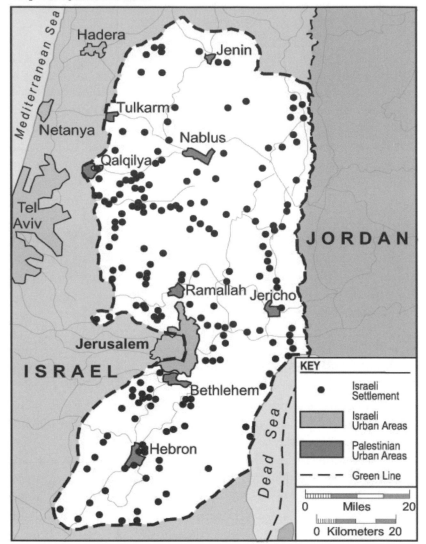

Map 5. Israeli settlements in the West Bank.

To build the settlements, the by-pass roads, and the military installations dotting the West Bank, Israelis confiscate land from Palestinian owners. Israeli law requires payment for land confiscated, but Palestinians are generally denied building permits to replace the homes the Israelis destroy. Many villagers have been separated from their farmland by a by-pass road. If they try to put up a building on their separated plots, so that they can once again farm their land, the building permit is denied. But if the land remains idle for three years, it can be confiscated. Rarely is a building permit issued to a Palestinian; yet if he goes ahead and builds without a permit, and many do, he risks having his structure torn down. In ways such as this, the Israeli settlement program sends a message to West Bank Palestinians: This land is ours, we intend to stay, and you may leave if you wish. More than ten percent of the total West Bank population is now Jewish. The settlers are among the most militantly anti-Arab of Jewish voters.

The settlements require military protection, an infrastructure of schools and medical care, water and sewer lines, as well as connecting roads. The settlers receive water rights denied to Palestinians. Palestinians are denied access both to the settlements and to the infrastructure that serves them. By contrast with nearby Palestinian villages, the West Bank settlements appear conspicuously affluent. Their occupants are employed and prospering. Their presence is deeply resented by the Palestinians.

To protect the settlements, Israelis have set up roadblocks and checkpoints, which have now been given a measure of permanence, with steel bars and metal grating delimiting the areas where people must queue. Palestinians must endure frequent security checks if they wish to travel between their own communities. Settlers, by contrast, are waved through checkpoints as they travel between settlements or out of the Occupied Territories into Israel proper. The Jewish settlers and the Palestinians have almost no communication. They speak different languages, and their children learn different histories and different religions in separate school systems. Distrust and mistrust prevail.

Jerusalem

Israel does not consider East Jerusalem to be part of the Occupied Territories. In all other areas, except for Jerusalem, the Occupied Territories represent the land won by Israel in the Six-Day war of 1967. But the Green Line does not run through Jerusalem. Instead, it runs east of the city. Shortly after the 1967 armistice the entire city is placed under Israeli civil administration (in contrast with the West Bank and Gaza, which are under military administration). In 1980 the Knesset, Israel's parliament, explicitly annexes East Jerusalem, despite a host of UN resolutions censuring Israel for doing so. Israeli policy toward Jerusalem is twofold: 1) to guarantee the security of all religious structures and those who worship there; and 2) to increase the percentage of the population in East Jerusalem that is Jewish in order to validate Israel's claim to the entire city. On both policies Israel is succeeding. As far as worshippers are concerned, of any faith, Jerusalem is an open city. But as far as the Palestinian population is concerned, life in Jerusalem presents a host of difficulties.

Although Palestinians in East Jerusalem represent thirty percent of the city's population, they are allotted only ten percent of the city's municipal services budget. They are crowded into an area where forty percent of the houses are substandard, but they are not allowed building permits to upgrade their housing. They are given identity cards, which can be revoked. On the northern, eastern, and southern outskirts of the city, where municipal boundaries have been expanded, there are now ten major Jewish settlements, housing more than 200,000 settlers. To build these settlements, one-third of the Palestinian-owned land in east Jerusalem has been confiscated. Payment is made for land confiscated, but building permits are not issued to build new dwellings. The ring of settlements effectively separates Palestinian residents of the Old City from Palestinians in the West Bank. In terms of population, Jerusalem – now a city of more than 800,000 – is becoming ever more a Jewish city.

What about the future of Jerusalem? Israel's position is that there is no room even for negotiation; the entire city must be the capital of Israel. (No country except Israel itself recognizes Israel's claim to Jerusalem as its capital. All embassies are located in Tel Aviv.) The position of the Palestinian Authority is that Jerusalem should be an Open City, but that administration should be divided between Israel and Palestine, on pre-1967 boundaries; East Jerusalem must be the capital of Palestine. But remembering the years between 1948 and 1967, when everyone from Israel is denied access to the holy sites in the Old City, and Jewish graves and holy sites are desecrated, Israel is determined that never again shall the city be divided. The European Union, and many world statesmen, support the idea of Jerusalem as an international city, as proposed in the 1947 United Nations partition plan – a city that would be administered by a governing body separate from either Israel or Palestine. Meanwhile, for now Israel's control is defacto and absolute.

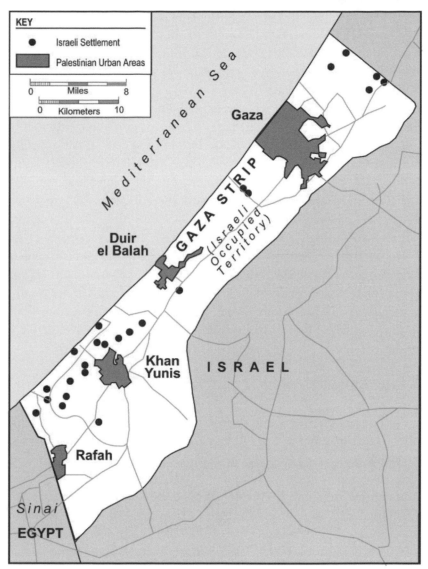

Map 6. Israeli settlements in the Gaza Strip.

The Gaza Strip

When the Israelis take over the Gaza Strip from the Egyptians in 1967, it is already one of the world's most crowded areas and is seething with discontent. The people of Gaza, most of whom lost their homes in Israel, had not been granted Egyptian citizenship, nor had they been allowed to work in Egypt. In effect, more than half were

25

(and one-third still are) wards of the UN, living in crowded refugee camps. From the first, Israel imposes harsh security measures in Gaza to quell unrest. Now, with a population of more than 1.3 million, three times its 1967 size, the Gaza Strip has a density averaging more than 10,000 people per square mile. Eighty-nine percent of the working force is unemployed. Yet, unbelievably, a few Israeli settlers have been enticed to live in the Gaza Strip. The majority of Israeli settlements are on the rich agricultural lands of the southern coastal plain, where land was confiscated (See Map 6). The 7400 Jewish settlers form half of one percent of the population, but their landholdings and the security measures needed to protect them include thirty percent of the Gaza Strip. This includes a security zone along the border, in which no building is permitted (See Map 8). There is little reason in Gaza for tempers to cool. At this writing, the Israeli government is suggesting the possible withdrawal of all Gaza Strip settlements except those tangent to Israel proper, leaving the Gaza strip almost totally under Palestinian administration. But settlers are protesting. And many Israelis fear danger from a Gaza Strip that already is effectively under the control of hard-line Palestinian terrorists

A "Hot Button"

The presence of the settlers in the West Bank, East Jerusalem, and Gaza is one of the "hot buttons" that Palestinians keep pressing, knowing that Israelis themselves are divided on whether the settlers should remain. Sixty percent of all Israelis now feel that settlers and Israeli military personnel should be withdrawn from the Occupied Territories (but not from Jerusalem). However, the Israeli government is a democracy run by coalition, and the controlling votes in government, the "swing votes," are those of the ultra-Orthodox religious right. To the extent that the religious right is in control, Israel can be viewed as much a theocracy as a democracy. For the religious right, Israel's very justification for existence is based on the Hebrew Scriptures. Eretz Israel – post-1967 Israel – is the ancient Promised Land, and the Palestinians are the Canaanites who must be expelled. Until recently there has been little prospect that the government will willingly abandon the settlers. But a Security Barrier, already one-third finished, is gradually separating Israelis from West Bank Palestinians. (See Map 31) Where it runs through crowded areas with a high security risk, the fence is a concrete wall, twenty feet high and topped with barbed wire, reminiscent of the wall that divides Jerusalem between 1948 and 1967 (See Diagram1). The barrier is snaking beyond the Green Line to incorporate those settlements nearest Israel. When completed, it will allow Palestinians to enter Israel only at certain highly guarded checkpoints. In this way the Israeli government hopes to protect not only Israel proper but about 75 percent of West Bank settlers as well. The rest of the settlers may soon face a choice: either pull back or live within a new Palestinian state.

A "Land-for-Peace" Solution?

United Nations Security Council Resolution 242, adopted on November 22, 1967, presents a "Land-for-Peace" solution that Palestinians say they can support. It calls for the establishment of a *1967* just and lasting peace based on Israeli withdrawal from territories occupied in 1967 in return for the end of all states of belligerency, respect for the sovereignty of all states in the area, and the right of all people to live in peace within secure, recognized boundaries. In effect, the resolution commits Arab countries to the acceptance of Israel as a sovereign state. The dangling carrots of peace and acceptance have led many Israelis to favor this resolution, with the caveat that Jerusalem is non-negotiable. But they point to Palestinian statements in the printed media and on the Internet that decry the very existence of Israel, and they say the Palestinians are not sincere. Palestinians, on the other hand, point to the Israeli settlements within the Occupied Territories and the commitment of the religious right to the expansion of Eretz Israel as proof that the Israeli government has no intention of leaving, ever.

Since September 2000, Palestinians have responded with the pent-up fury of stone-throwing, mortar fire, and suicide bombing that is known as the *Intifadeh* (an Arabic word meaning "shaking off the dust and burden"). The Israelis have answered with force. The death *1988-* toll mounts on both sides, but it is far heavier among the Palestinians. *2000* The first Intifadeh lasted from 1988 until 1993. Now a new wave of violence exists in the Holy Land, far more deadly than its predecessor. At this writing some 3500 coffins have been filled, three-fourths of them Palestinian, one-fourth Israeli. No end to the violence is in sight.

3
Arafat's Islands

*To end the occupation and all that has gone with it is a
clear enough imperative. Now let us do it.*
Edward Said
Al-Ahram Weekly, January 11, 2002

*Hamas does not recognize the right of Israel to exist. Its
long-term aim is to establish an Islamic state on land
originally mandated as Palestine.*
Martin Asser
BBC News, December 3, 2001

I n the recent past, there have been measured steps toward
peace. Today there is a Palestinian Authority with jurisdiction
over fragmented portions of the Occupied Territories that skeptics
call *Arafat's Islands*. The steps that lead to the creation of the Palestinian
1979 Authority begin in 1979 when United States President Jimmy Carter
brokers a peace between Israel and Egypt (called the Camp David
Accord), followed by Israel's return of the Sinai in 1982.

In Oslo, Norway, in 1993, following two years of delicate
negotiations in Madrid and Washington, the Israeli government and
1993 the Palestinian Liberation Organization reach enough of an agreement
that they can sign a common document, called the Oslo Accord.
This hopeful first step in resolving the Israeli-Palestinian dilemma
recognizes both Israel's right to exist and Palestinian rights to the

Occupied Territories. It calls for an end to building settlements, an end to Palestinian terrorism, gradual self-government for Palestinians, and future determination of such knotty problems as the status of Jerusalem and the rights of Palestinian refugees. The signers are Israeli Prime Minister Yitzhak Rabin and PLO leader Yasser Arafat, who in 1994 jointly receive the Nobel Peace Prize for their breakthrough *1994* agreement.

Many Israelis and many Palestinians are not pleased with the Oslo Accord. Yitzhak Rabin is subsequently assassinated by an ultra-Orthodox Jew trying to scuttle the agreement. A right wing government in Israel determines to continue building settlements. And terrorist organizations among the Palestinians continue as before, some aimed at getting Israel out of the Occupied Territories and others at destroying the Israeli state.

Arafat leads the Palestinian delegation to Oslo as head of the Palestinian Liberation Organization. The PLO, which Arafat helps to organize in the 1950s, consolidates two formerly clandestine organizations, Fatah and the Popular Front for the Liberation of Palestine, whose aim is to oust the Israelis from all of Palestine. Arafat's group, Fatah, still exists within the PLO, and he commands its military wing, Tanzim. Openly employing terror to achieve its goal, the PLO becomes an international pariah especially after the 1972 Olympics, when almost the entire Israeli Olympics team is murdered by PLO operatives. Pariah or not, Arafat is the only Palestinian with enough leadership credentials to represent the Palestinian side at the Oslo negotiations, and after Oslo the PLO is legitimized. Before Oslo, Arafat is the unofficial spokesman for all Palestinians everywhere. After, he specifically represents Palestinians in the West Bank and Gaza Strip, and in 1995 he wins his leadership by popular election. *1995*

The first benefit to Israel is the establishment of diplomatic relations with Jordan in 1994. The Palestinians see no benefit until a year later, a benefit granted by the Israelis only after prodding from U.S. President Bill Clinton and a further Oslo II Accord brokered in Washington. Israel begins withdrawing its military forces from all West Bank cities in 1995. At the same time, a *Palestinian Authority* is created. As the Israelis gradually withdraw from West Bank cities, the Palestinian Authority, headed by Arafat, takes over governance. In addition, the Palestinian Authority begins to govern in some of the rural areas where many Palestinians live, but in these areas Israel

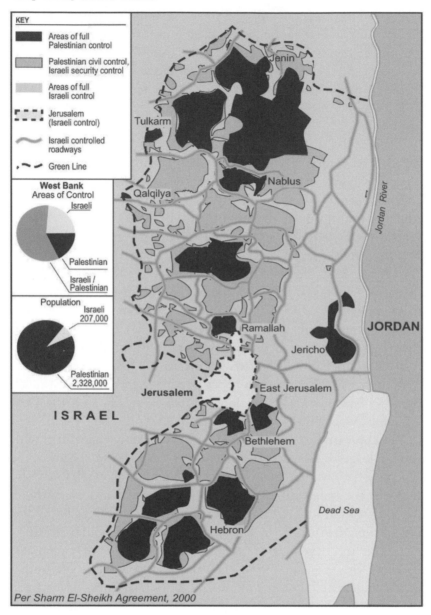

KEY

- Areas of full Palestinian control
- Palestinian civil control, Israeli security control
- Areas of full Israeli control
- Jerusalem (Israeli control)
- Israeli controlled roadways
- Green Line

West Bank
Areas of Control
Israeli
Palestinian
Israeli / Palestinian

Population
Israeli 207,000
Palestinian 2,328,000

Per Sharm El-Sheikh Agreement, 2000

Map 7. West Bank administrative areas.

retains security responsibility. By Oslo Accord terms, at first only three percent of the West Bank (the urbanized area) is to be placed under total Palestinian control, but gradually the area under total Palestinian control is to increase greatly. The object of the Accord is an independent and viable Palestinian state.

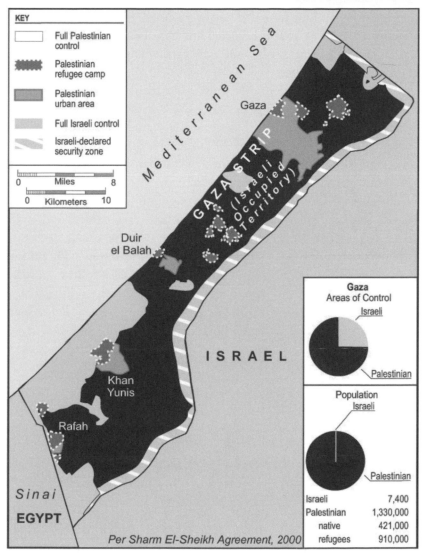

Map 8. Gaza Strip administrative areas.

A Broken Framework

On the other steps provided for in the Oslo Accord – negotiations over shared sovereignty of Jerusalem, the status of Palestinian refugees, further territorial withdrawal, security arrangements, and disputed boundaries – there is little progress. A conservative Israeli government in power since 1996 opposes the Oslo Accords on principle and drags its *1996* feet on further negotiations. The Palestinians, wary of Israeli objectives

31

and insisting on East Jerusalem as their capital, likewise stall. Neither Palestinian terrorist attacks on Israel nor Israeli retaliation measures let up. As the Israelis furiously build new settlements in the West Bank, the Palestinians feel betrayed.

The five-year period after Oslo, allotted for the achievement of Palestinian independence, passes by in 2000 without accomplishment. Nevertheless, diplomacy continues, most with no results, but some with *2000* measured success. In March of 2000 the Sharm el-Sheikh agreement increases to 18 percent the amount of West Bank territory over which the Palestinians have sovereignty and reduces to 24 percent Israel's area of absolute control. Control over the remaining 58 percent is to be shared, with the Palestinian Authority to have civil control and Israel to be responsible for security. The majority of the Israeli electorate is convinced that Israel's security will be compromised with further concessions. Not only do no additional concessions follow, but the Intifadeh that begins in September of 2000 effectively nullifies many of the original concessions, as Israeli tanks enter cities in the Palestinian Authority to counter Palestinian suicide missions. The Oslo Accord has failed. The Palestinian Authority's governance of a fragmented portion of the Occupied Territories is the only part of the Accord that remains.

The Palestinian Authority

In all cities of the Occupied Territories, the Palestinian Authority is sovereign in local matters. It regulates civic affairs, and its police force is in charge of security. These cities occupy a fragmented and noncontiguous area of the Occupied Territories, creating the almost ungovernable territory termed by some as Arafat's Islands. In the towns and villages of the Occupied Territories the Palestinian Authority handles civic affairs, but Israel is responsible for security. That leaves total Jewish sovereignty over nearly one-fourth of the Occupied Territories including East Jerusalem (which Israel does not consider to be part of the Occupied Territories), most of the Jordan Valley, and all of the Jewish settlements. This, say the Palestinians, is unacceptable. To which the Israelis answer that the security of their settlers and their capital of Jerusalem are at stake. The differences seem unbridgeable.

The cities in the West Bank and Gaza now governed by the Palestinian Authority include places sacred not only to Jews and Christians but also to Muslims, who share ancient traditions with Jews and who

32

consider Jesus Christ as a major prophet: Bethlehem, the birthplace of Jesus; Hebron, where Abraham is buried and where David assumes the kingship; Nablus (ancient Shechem), where Abraham first camps when he reaches the Holy Land and where the Israelites later crown their kings; and Jericho, the first Canaanite stronghold taken by Joshua and his Hebrew soldiers. Other cities within the Palestinian Authority are Ramallah, Jenin, Tulkarm, and Qalqiliya in the West Bank, and Gaza, Rafah, and Khan Yunis in the Gaza Strip. At the outskirts of all these cities today, Israelis have erected barricades and have sometimes positioned tanks. Significantly, the Palestinian Authority has no jurisdiction over Jerusalem, the city both Palestinians and Israelis claim as their capital.

Hebron, one of the largest cities in the West Bank, is an exception to the Oslo plan. With a small but militant Jewish population, Hebron exists as a divided city. Palestinians have control over eighty-five percent of Hebron, but Israel retains governance of the fifteen percent where 400 ultra-Orthodox Jewish settlers, almost all from the United States, have established their homes. When trouble breaks out between the two factions, the Israeli authorities inevitably impose a curfew on the Arab population, but not on the Jewish settlers, heightening Arab resentment.

Terrorists or Freedom Fighters?

Once Yasser Arafat signs the Oslo Accord and commits himself to negotiation with the Israelis, the extremists among Arabs in the West Bank and Gaza (those who feel that the Palestinians will never receive justice so long as Israel exists) begin to view him as a traitor. They ally themselves instead with the two underground organizations that are committed to Israel's demise: Hamas and the Islamic Jihad. Hamas and the Islamic Jihad are termed "terrorist organizations" by Israel. But to Arabs, their members are "freedom fighters." Both organizations receive support from sympathizers in Arab countries. The Islamic Jihad is closely related to militant Islamic fundamentalist counterparts in Egypt. Because Hamas is homegrown, and Islamic fundamentalist as well, it has a somewhat more popular following than the Islamic Jihad, whose main base of support is in Gaza. Leaders in both organizations have trained abroad, some under Osama bin Laden in Afghanistan.

For Hamas and the Islamic Jihad the fight against Israel has become a Jihad, a Holy War, fought in the name of their religion, Islam. Although they are Muslims, a new term has now come into use to describe Muslim extremists: *Islamists*. Islamists believe that the Quran tells them to fight non-believers, and especially Jews, and they believe they are acting in the name of their faith. They want to weaken Israel's resolve to remain in the Middle East, a cancer, as they see it, among Muslim states. They employ terror in their efforts to destabilize Israel and to thwart any attempts at negotiation between Israel and the Palestinian Authority. But both organizations also provide social services for people in areas where the chronically under-funded Palestinian Authority does not reach, in line with their commitment to Islam and to its mandate to perform acts of charity. In this way they gather support and loyalty from increasing numbers of Palestinians. Towards Palestinians whom they suspect of collaborating with Israel, Hamas and the Islamic Jihad are brutal. If and when Palestine becomes a sovereign country, they intend to provide its leadership and direction. To this extent they are a threat to Arafat and his somewhat more moderate PLO.

As violence escalates, Arafat responds to the threat to his leadership that Hamas and the Islamic Jihad pose. Increasingly he embraces the militant version of Islam that is energizing the followers of his political adversaries. In 2001 he organizes a militant terrorist organization within his own ranks, an organization known as the Al Aqsa Martyrs Brigade. Suicide missions to Israel are now as likely to be sent out by the Al Aqsa Martyrs Brigade, over which Arafat has absolute control, as by Hamas or the Islamic Jihad. It is young Palestinians inspired and directed by these three organizations who blow themselves up in Israel's cities, on buses, in shopping districts, in cafes, or wherever they can most effectively sow terror.

Another threat to Arafat's leadership comes from within, from the party that once joined with Arafat's party, Fatah, to form the PLO. Just as Arafat has kept Fatah alive, has retained its loyalty, and still controls it and its military wing Tanzim, so also has the leadership of the Popular Front for the Liberation of Palestine kept its organization intact. PFLO leaders question Arafat's leadership and would quite willingly supplant it.

Unable or unwilling to stop acts of terrorism toward Israeli civilians, Arafat has no credibility with Israelis as a partner in any peace negotiations. Most Israelis believe that Arafat himself is a terrorist. Nevertheless, because Arafat is the elected leader of the Palestinian Authority, technically he is the one with whom Sharon must negotiate. Sharon refuses. The distrust that the two bear for each other is a long-standing one (Chapter 26).

With the growing strength of Palestinian terrorist organizations, and Arafat's seeming reluctance or inability to quell terrorist activities – indeed, his participation in them through the Al Aqsa Martyrs Brigade – Israelis seem determined to hold on to their military presence in the Occupied Territories and to exert force as they deem necessary.

The Al Aqsa Intifadeh

At the turn of the millennium, Arafat declares publicly that in September of 2000 Palestinians will proclaim their fragmented territory as an independent country. This does not happen. Instead, September of 2000 marks the beginning of the Al Aqsa Intifadeh. *2000* Feelings by this time are running high. Palestinians are frustrated that negotiations for a sovereign state the previous summer have gone nowhere. At Camp David, outside Washington D.C., Arafat refuses what on the surface seems like a magnanimous Israeli offer of withdrawal from 93 percent of the West Bank; but the offer keeps Israeli control over Palestinian roads, and it does not give the Palestinians full sovereignty over the Haram al-Sharif. For both sides, retaining control of the Haram al-Sharif/Temple Mount is non-negotiable.

Towards the end of September, 2000, Ariel Sharon, at this time Israel's defense minister, organizes a provocative walk on the Temple Mount, to make the statement that he has a right to be there. Technically he does. (In 1967 at the end of the Six-Day War, when Israel has conquered all of Jerusalem, Moshe Dayan, then the country's defense minister, gives authority over the Haram al-Sharif to the Waqf, the Islamic organization responsible for its maintenance. The only condition Dayan sets is that all persons should henceforth have access to the mount, to which the Waqf agrees.) Sharon knows the effect his walk will have, both on Orthodox Israelis and on Palestinians. He publicizes his walk well in advance, in the cities of the Palestinian Authority as well as in Israel. Probably he expects to trigger violence. Palestinian leaders seize on this opportunity to unleash pent-up frustration as negotiations for a hoped-for Palestinian state collapse. They urge Palestinian youths to be present for a confrontation. As some 1500 Palestinian youths assemble, they find piles of stones ready for throwing. The Israelis send 1500 police to accompany Sharon and other government ministers on the "walk". Stones fly, a few Israeli police are injured, but on the day of the walk there are no deaths. These happen the next day, when stone-throwing continues, Israeli police answer with bullets, and four youth are killed. The Al-Aqsa Intifadeh (named for the mosque on the Haram al-Sharif) is underway. Violence escalates. It intensifies with each suicide bombing, with the wailing at each Palestinian funeral, and the cry for revenge that follows each attack.

Israeli tanks enter Palestinian cities and bulldoze houses of suspected terrorists, disregarding the accord that gives the Palestinian Authority sovereignty over its cities. Much of Jenin, in particular, is leveled, and there are civilian casualties. The Arab world now speaks of the "Jenin Massacre," and in Europe Israel loses sympathy, despite Sharon's claims that Israel acts only in self-defense, and that efforts are made to minimize civilian casualties. What Arabs claim are hundreds of civilian casualties in Jenin are later revealed in a UN investigation to be thirty-eight. But any civilian killed is one too many.

Sharon requires seven days without violence as a precondition for negotiation. But it is in the interest of Hamas and the Islamic Jihad that violence continue. Sharon is well aware that his terms may not be met, and he suspects that Arafat is neither willing nor able to stop the violence.

Thoroughly distrusting Arafat, Sharon refuses to negotiate with him. Arafat, for his part, refuses to share power with ministers whom he appoints to speak in his stead. President Bush joins with other western countries to offer a Road Map to peace, but the road map requires that both parties come to the table. This is not happening. Meanwhile, the Israelis seem to have given up on the prospect for coming together. The thorny questions of the Jewish settlements, compensation to Palestinians for seized property, resettlement of Palestinians in Israel, and the status of Jerusalem seem beyond resolution. Moderates on both side want peace. But in Israel it is the reactionary Jewish religious right who call the shots; in the Palestinian Authority, it is, de facto, the radical Islamic extremists. Seeing no solution, the Israelis are now building a security barrier to keep Palestinian militants out.

The Security Barrier: Solution or Further Irritant?

Until recently Israel's conservative party, the Likud, has insisted that all of the land conquered in 1967 belongs to and must remain an integral part of Israel. The Jewish settlements in the West Bank, the Gaza Strip, and the Golan Heights are a reflection of this policy. But as violence persists and there appears to be no effective military solution, conservatives in Israel confront a demographic reality that is causing them to change course. Arab women, on average, bear five to six children; Israeli women two or three. If Israel continues to include all of the land taken after 1967, then as early as the year 2010 Jews will be a minority within their own country. They must then either rule as autocrats, a minority forever suppressing a majority, or – in a democracy – abandon the idea of Israel as a Jewish state. This reality, plus the decreasing likelihood that negotiation will bring an end to violence, prompts Sharon to shift directions. No longer will he depend only on a military answer to Palestinian terrorism. No longer will he look to negotiation as the only pathway to peace. Instead, he embraces the idea of a security barrier.

As originally proposed by the liberal Labor party, the security barrier would run along the Green Line. With all movement between the West Bank and Israel funneled through checkpoints, the barrier would minimize the threat from terrorists. It would also be a defacto acceptance of Israel's pre-1967 border and a defacto recognition of Palestinian territory. At first Israel's conservative party, the Likud, wants nothing to do with a security barrier. But now, with the inevitability of demographics, Sharon sees the barrier as an instrument of revised Likud policy, a two-state policy. When finished, the barrier will be 425 miles long (See Map 31). It follows the Green Line in part but also snakes into the West Bank to include 75 percent of all settlers within its protection. The Palestinians lose nearly 15 percent of West Bank territory in the process. In cities the barrier is a concrete wall, 20 feet high. But for most of its length it is a thick mass of barbed wire, fronted with a plowed berm. Sharon calculates that the more than 85 percent of their West Bank territory the Palestinians retain will be adequate for them to form their own state, particularly if Israel withdraws its settlers from all of the Gaza Strip and from West bank areas beyond the security barrier. He sees a future with two sovereign

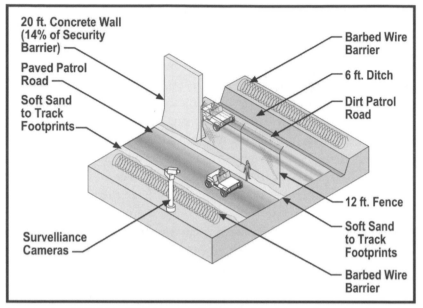

20 ft. Concrete Wall (14% of Security Barrier)

Paved Patrol Road

Soft Sand to Track Footprints

Barbed Wire Barrier

6 ft. Ditch

Dirt Patrol Road

12 ft. Fence

Soft Sand to Track Footprints

Survelliance Cameras

Barbed Wire Barrier

Source: Israeli Ministry of Defence, Israeli Ministry of the Interior, Palestinian Central Bureau of Statistics, CIA World Factbook, BBC website.

Diagram 1. Aspects of Israel's Security Barrier.

states side by side, cut off from most communication, and doing no harm to one another.

Outcries against the security barrier come from all sides: from the Palestinians, who protest that they are being robbed of territory; from Palestinian sympathizers world wide, who decry the barrier; from Israelis on the far right, who insist that no settlers be abandoned; and from the 25 percent of settlers who will have to give up their homes and insist they will not do so without a fight. But most Israelis, tired of a conflict that has no end, support the security barrier. Sharon firmly declares that the barrier does not mark a political boundary, and that once terrorism has ceased the barrier can come down. Palestinians, either supporting or unable to control the terrorist incursions that have led to the barrier's construction, are dismayed and disheartened.

Economic Woes

The places governed by the Palestinian Authority today are under-funded, lacking in economic opportunity, and a breeding

Photo 2. Visitors at the Church of the Nativity in Bethlehem.

ground for frustration and recruitment of young men into radical movements.

My experiences in the Palestinian Authority are positive but also indicative of the contrast between Israel and the Authority. The day I visit Bethlehem, in March of 2000, my view is totally blurred by the thousands of tourists who come to the city of Jesus' birth on the day following the Papal visit. But human and automobile movement carries on apace, and the Palestinian Authority in Bethlehem seems to be coping. Not so its Arab citizens, however. I talk with a man in suit and tie who convinces me that, despite working two jobs, at the end of the month there is nothing left to pay for much-needed dentistry, to send a cherished three-year-old to nursery school, or to replace a frayed shirt with a new one. "No matter which way I turn, I feel I am in a box," he tells me. Driving through Jericho in early evening, I find the streets poorly paved, the storefronts shabby, and the overhead lights dim to save on electricity.

The Palestinians claim that what they most need is investment in industry. But few investors are willing to commit to Palestine until both peace and the rule of law are certain. Nongovernmental organizations, representing the gamut of religious and political affiliations, give much-needed help. In addition, before the present

Intifadeh, there were encouraging examples of Israeli and Palestinian businessmen working together on an individual basis. Although in general the private sector is steering clear of Palestine, there is one notable exception: Until the outbreak of the Intifadeh in 2000, work was progressing on a luxurious casino in Jericho, privately funded by Palestinian and Israeli investors. There is as yet no other in the Holy Land, and if the Jericho casino should some day attract hordes of Israeli gamblers, as the Palestinian Authority expects may yet happen, the taxes, they say, will go into the public coffers.

I do not enter the Gaza Strip, but I have one unforgettable encounter with an Arab woman from Gaza. An attractive young woman, she and her three sickly children are sitting in the lobby of the Jerusalem hotel where I am staying. Through an interpreter, I learn that she is twenty years old, from Gaza, and that her husband has beaten her. Her parents will not shame themselves by letting her come home, so the Israeli police have taken her to the hotel as a safe house for one night while her husband cools off. When she returns, she expects to be beaten again. She has no money, no food, and it is obvious the children are sick. I share what food I have with her, but the feverish children only nibble on it. In the morning, I search for her, to give her some money, but the police have already taken her back. She still haunts me. Before the present Intifadeh the Israeli and Palestinian police are cooperating. I doubt if such cooperation is possible now.

Israeli national statistics do not include the West Bank and Gaza as an integral part of Israel. On the one hand, this is an admission that the areas are separate from Israel proper. But there may be another reason. By all measures, the Palestinian Authority ranks among the world's poor nations. Its birth rates and death rates are high, its national product per capita is less than a tenth of Israel's, and its infrastructure is little-developed. With the exception of the Jewish settlements, Israel has paid scant attention to the welfare of these lands under its jurisdiction since 1967. Many Palestinians in the Occupied Territories formerly found work in Israel. Now, with strict imposed security measures, Palestinians find it almost impossible to get to their former job or even get around roadblocks from one city to another. The economy of the Palestinian Authority, never strong, is plunging. In Gaza, more than eighty percent of the population is unemployed. With high unemployment and a rapidly decreasing tax base, Palestinian Authority coffers are nearly dry.

Although the armed struggle of the Palestinians is costly, much of the cost of arms for the Intifadeh is borne by sympathizers in other countries. In 2002 the Israelis intercept a ship in the Red Sea that is bound for a port in Gaza. The ship, captained by a Palestinian member of the Fatah organization, is carrying a large shipment of arms manufactured in Iran, financed privately by a Saudi citizen or citizens, and destined for the Palestinian Authority. Sporadic non-military aid also reaches the Palestinian Authority from both Arab and western countries and also from non-governmental organizations. But Arafat is accused of channeling aid funds to his personal accounts, and many Palestinians feel that the Palestinian Authority is corrupt in its financial dealings.

Syria and the Golan Heights

Syria is ready to establish normal relations with Israel in return for Israel's full withdrawal from the Golan.
Hafez al-Assad
late president of Syria at conference with
U.S. President Bill Clinton,
October 27, 1994

S yria wants Israel to return the Golan Heights, the area north and east of the Sea of Galilee (Lake Kinneret). The Golan is not included in the original 1947 UN partition plan, for it is Syrian territory. At the end of the first Arab-Israeli War, the Golan remains in Syrian hands. Across the border Israeli and Syrian troops continue to skirmish. Israelis covet the Golan and the farmland and water resources it represents. From the Golan Heights, in the years *1948-1967* between 1948 and 1967, Syrian guns shell Israeli water-control projects in the lowlands north of Lake Kinneret. Syrian guns are also turned on Israeli settlements in Galilee.

In the northern town of Beit Sha'an, I speak with an Israeli woman who remembers the frequent nights in her childhood spent in terror, huddled in a reinforced basement while Syrian shells explode overhead.

Israel takes control of the Golan Heights in the 1967 War. It quickly dismantles Syrian gun emplacements and effectively ends the

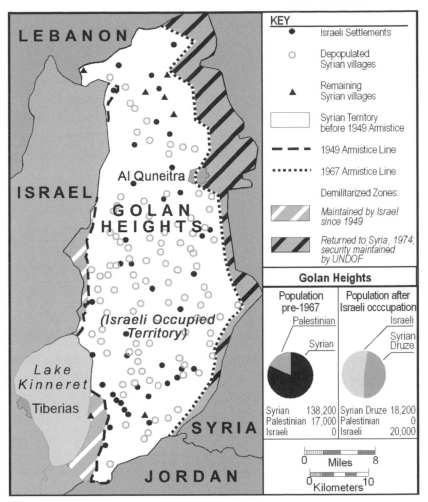

KEY

●	Israeli Settlements
○	Depopulated Syrian villages
▲	Remaining Syrian villages
☐	Syrian Territory before 1949 Armistice
– – –	1949 Armistice Line
·····'	1967 Armistice Line

Demilitarized Zones:

Maintained by Israel since 1949

Returned to Syria, 1974; security maintained by UNDOF

Golan Heights

Population pre-1967		Population after Israeli occcupation	
Palestinian		Israeli	
Syrian		Syrian Druze	
Syrian	138,200	Syrian Druze	18,200
Palestinian	17,000	Palestinian	0
Israeli	0	Israeli	20,000

0 Miles 8

0 Kilometers 10

Map 9. The Golan Heights: depopulated villages, Israeli settlements and administrative areas.

threat from that quarter. Then it begins the systematic destruction of Syrian villages, forcing their occupants to flee to other parts of Syria. Estimates of the number of Syrians displaced vary, from 70,000 (Israeli estimate) to 150,000 (Syrian estimate). Also fleeing to Syria are some 17,000 Palestinians, who now are refugees for the second time. The Syrian nationals are given temporary housing in apartments in and around Damascus. The Palestinians are housed in UN refugee camps, joining their compatriots who reached Syria in 1948.

One group of Syrian nationals who neither flee nor are forced out in 1967 are the Druze, of whom 18,000 continue to live in

43

Photo 3. Eastern shore of Lake Kinneret (Sea of Galilee) from Hippos archaeological site at the western edge of the Golan Heights.

their Golan villages. The Druze are an Arab people who practice an offshoot of Islam.

Most of the Golan is now given over to fruit orchards, commercial grazing and dairy enterprises conducted by some 20,000 Israeli setters who live either on kibbutzim (collective farms) or moshavs (cooperative farms). Israel now gets much of its beef and dairy products from the Golan.

In 1973 Syrian and Israeli armed forces clash once again over the Golan. The United Nations subsequently sets off a strip varying
1973 in width from six to fifty miles along the east side of the Golan, which has since been patrolled by some one thousand members of a United Nations Disengagement Observer Force. Israel vacates this territory but not before leveling the town of Quneitra, the former chief city of the Golan. Syria decides not to rebuild Quneitra but to leave it as evidence. The strip has since been resettled by some of the Syrian villagers who originally fled the Golan.

In 1981 the Israeli parliament formally annexes the Golan Heights. This action receives no international recognition, but
1981 because the Golan is now considered a part of Israel, many Israelis have incorporated it into their perception of what constitutes their

country. They know that most of the tributary streams flowing into the Jordan River and Lake Kinneret originate on the Golan slopes, and they feel that only an Israeli presence in the upper basins of these streams can insure their continued westward flow. Before 1967 Syria was attempting to divert Golan streams southward and eastward into Jordan.

Syria wants the Golan back. Its claim to the Golan extends to the northeast shore of Lake Kinneret, as recognized under the never-implemented 1947 UN partition plan. Many Israelis are willing to give back the Golan Heights if these heights are demilitarized and if the new border remains well away from Lake Kinneret. But further they refuse to go. They point out that all of Lake Kinneret as well as the Golan Heights was a part of the original British Palestinian Mandate. But in 1923 the northeast portion of the Palestinian Mandate is transferred to the French Mandate of Syria as part of a Franco-British agreement. When the Syrian-Israeli armistice is negotiated in 1949, the Golan, extending to the northeast shore of Lake Kinneret, remains in Syrian hands. But Israelis have never forgotten that originally the Golan Heights was a part of Palestine, and they point to ancient traditions of Hebrew settlement in the region as recorded in the Jewish Scriptures.

"No way," growls the Israeli taxi driver, as he tells me what he has heard on the evening's radio concerning Syria's demands. "Kinneret is ours, shore to shore." He will give his vote to whichever party vows to keep Israel intact.

During my travels, I traverse the beautiful Golan Heights area, as well as the land bordering Lake Kinneret. The view from the Golan toward snow-capped Mount Hermon to the north, the Jordan Valley below, and Lake Kinneret to the west is unforgettable. But the double rows of barbed wire fencing protecting the border and the concrete bases of pre-1967 Syrian gun emplacements convince me that a peace settlement in this area may still be a long way off.

The future of the Golan Heights will probably bring change. Israel wants to establish additional settlements there, despite strong Syrian objections. Early in 2004 the Ba'athist President of Syria, Bashar al-Assad, lets it be known that Syria would like to restart *2004* negotiations with Israel over the future of the Golan, and Israel is willing. The end result could be a compromise on the eventual borders, and Syria's recognition of Israel. Or, like the negotiations between Israel and the Palestinians, talks between Israel and Syria over the Golan Heights could drag on for years with no resolution. Israel for its part will insist that the Syrians withdraw their support from Palestinian terrorist organizations and also from Lebanese Hezbullah guerrillas, who regularly cross Israel's northern border to harass kibbutz settlements. The Palestinian refugee population in Syria has increased to nearly 500,000, of whom nearly thirty percent remain in UN refugee camps. Although the remainder have become integrated within the Syrian economy, none have been offered Syrian citizenship. Syria will insist on the refugees' right of return to their former homes in Israel.

5
Palestinian Refugees

*Refugee camps are no longer the makeshift tented structures
of the early years, but 50 years on are densely-packed and
crowded fixed constructions. Consequences of chronic
density [are] poorer housing, greater physical and mental
health problems, increasingly poor study habits among
children, and a sense of powerlessness
among the population.*
Oxfam Report, March 1999

Between 1947 and 1949, about 750,000 Arabs leave their
homes in Palestine, pushed out by the Jewish military and/or
fleeing in panic, depending on the chronicler. They go mainly *1947-*
to the West Bank, then under control of Jordan, and to the Gaza *1949*
Strip, Lebanon, and Syria. After the Six-Day War in 1967, another
300,000 Palestinians become refugees as they leave the West Bank *1967*
for Jordan, unwilling to live under Israeli rule. Technically, a Refugee
is someone who has been uprooted from his/her home. A Registered
Refugee is one who has sought UN assistance. Today, more than a
half century later, two-thirds of the dispersed Palestinians still remain
Registered Refugees, uprooted and in need. Since 1948, the question
of Palestinian refugees has been a core issue in Arab-Israeli relations.
The refugees want to return home, to the land now ruled by Israel.

Any final settlement between Israel and the Palestinian
Authority must eventually deal with the Palestinian refugees who
wish to return and have not accepted (or been offered) citizenship
elsewhere. Yet, resettlement of Palestinian refugees is not currently on

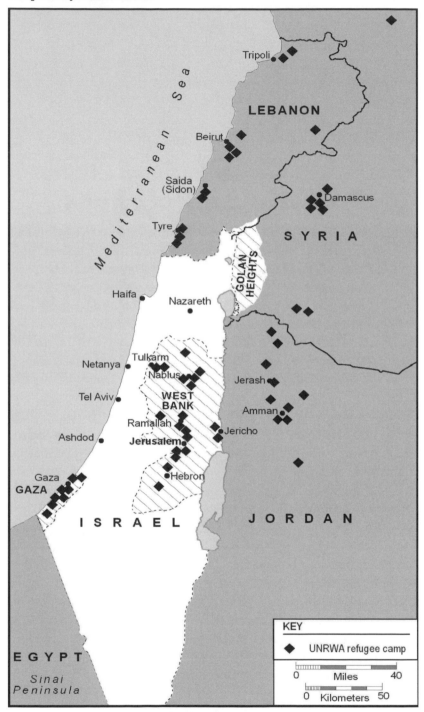

Map 10. UNRWA Palestinian refugee camps.

the negotiating table. The issue festers. And it concurs with the strategy of Israel's Arab neighbors, Jordan excepted. None of them has offered citizenship to the Palestinian refugees or contributed measurably to their well-being. It better serves their long-term anti-Israel policy that upwards of a million-and-a-half refugees remain wards of the UN, unsettled, dispirited, and angry, reminding the rest of the world that they have a right to return home.

What begins as a displaced population of three quarters of a million people in 1948 has now reached more than six million, all of whom have an intense emotional claim on the land they, their parents, or their grandparents left. Most have spent a lifetime consumed with one objective: to return "home."

The largest number of refugees live in Jordan, Gaza, and the West Bank, with Lebanon and Syria also having sizeable numbers (See Chart 2). The rest are spread throughout the Arab and Western worlds. The lucky few, the highly educated, have found professional niches in countries of Europe, North America, and the various Arab states.

Since 1948, the United Nations Relief and Works Agency (UNRWA) has been charged with providing at least minimal living accommodations for the refugees who require it. Even today one-third of all Registered Refugees (those who apply for aid) remain in UN camps. In the West Bank, it is one-fourth, and in Gaza, it is fifty-five percent. In effect, the refugees living in camps are stateless, unable to leave, and unable to work. Jordan has offered citizenship to its Palestinian population, and some 600,000 have accepted. Hundreds of thousands of others have found a way into the Jordanian economy and are now refugees only in name. In Jordan, only fifteen percent of Registered Refugees remain in camps.

An independent Palestinian state, if and when it does emerge out of the Occupied Territories, will not solve the problem of the refugees in camps in Lebanon, Syria, and Jordan. The Palestinian state would be hard-pressed to find room for them. Israel does not want them back and has worked to keep resettlement out of any peace negotiations. (Palestinians, however, point out that there are portions of far northern Galilee where Israeli settlement is light and farming today is done by imported foreign workers. There is still room in Israel where Palestinians could be resettled, they say.) Meanwhile, in the crowded refugee camps, most Palestinian refugees still harbor the notion that someday a united Arab force will push Israel into the

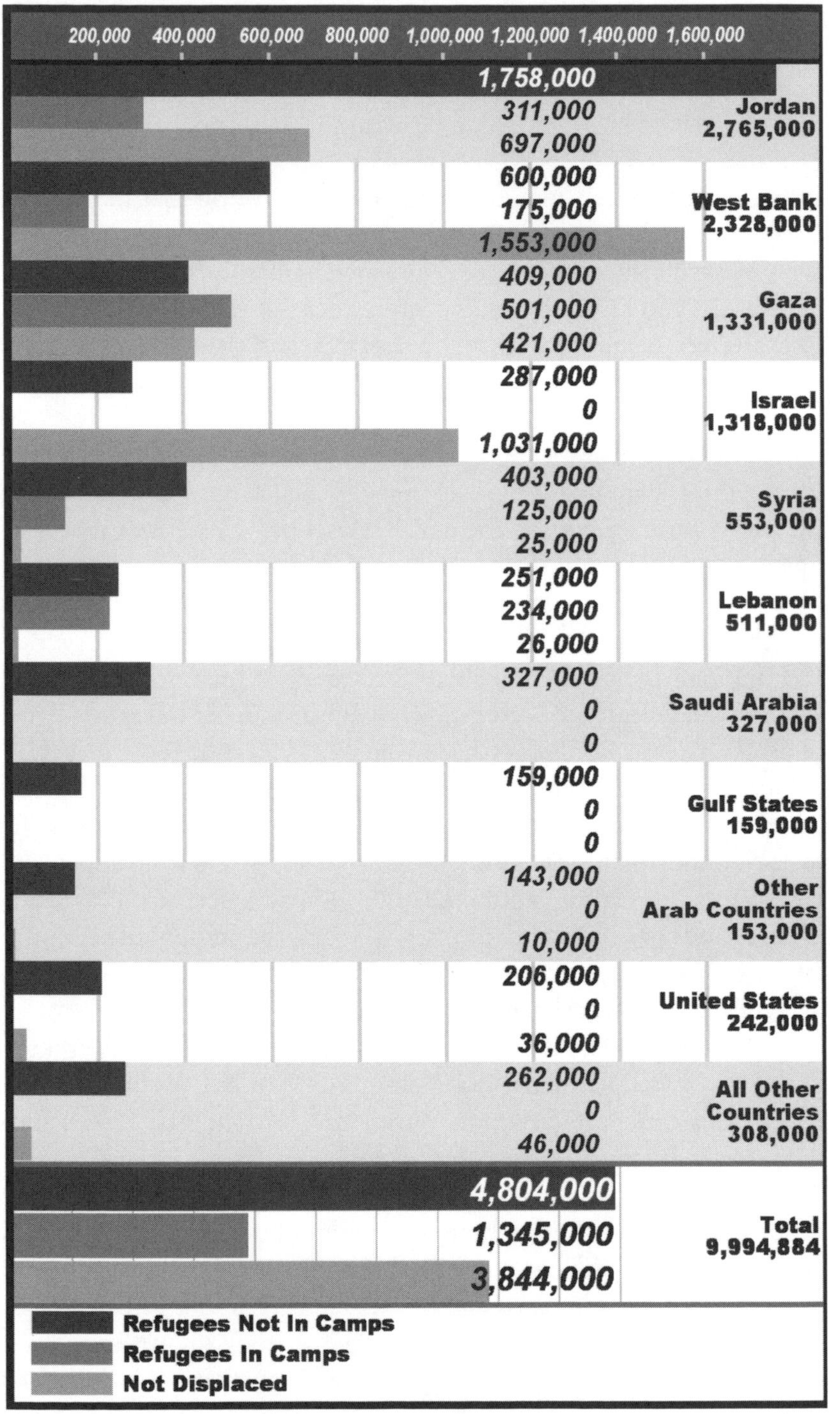

	200,000	400,000	600,000	800,000	1,000,000	1,200,000	1,400,000	1,600,000	
						1,758,000			
						311,000			**Jordan**
						697,000			**2,765,000**
						600,000			
						175,000			**West Bank**
						1,553,000			**2,328,000**
						409,000			
						501,000			**Gaza**
						421,000			**1,331,000**
						287,000			
						0			**Israel**
						1,031,000			**1,318,000**
						403,000			
						125,000			**Syria**
						25,000			**553,000**
						251,000			
						234,000			**Lebanon**
						26,000			**511,000**
						327,000			
						0			**Saudi Arabia**
						0			**327,000**
						159,000			
						0			**Gulf States**
						0			**159,000**
						143,000			
						0			**Other Arab Countries**
						10,000			**153,000**
						206,000			
						0			**United States**
						36,000			**242,000**
						262,000			
						0			**All Other Countries**
						46,000			**308,000**
						4,804,000			
						1,345,000			**Total**
						3,844,000			**9,994,884**

■ Refugees Not In Camps
■ Refugees In Camps
■ Not Displaced

Chart 2. International distribution of Palestinians.

sea. At the least, they pray just to return home. Their grandchildren play soldier and fantasize themselves as avengers, and their young men, recruited by Palestinian extremist organizations, act out these fantasies.

Not all Palestinians are refugees. Some 1.3 million Palestinian Arabs live in Israel and are Israeli citizens. Of the 2.3 million Palestinians in the West Bank, two-thirds are not refugees: They lived in the West Bank in 1948, and they live there today, although without the rights of Israeli citizens. The Gaza Strip is another story: Only thirty-two percent of its 1.3 million people are native to Gaza. In Jordan, those who have accepted Jordanian citizenship are no longer classed as refugees.

People of the Holy Land

The wonderful hospitality,
the authentic longing for Zion,
the naïve messianism are perhaps beautiful things
to one who loves such things, but for me they are not
the symbols that I want to see in the society
[of western culture] that my spiritual fathers
and I fought to establish here.
Ammon Dankner
Columnist for the liberal
Jerusalem newspaper Haaretz,
cited by David K. Shipler, Arab and Jew

Immersed in the swirling countercurrents of competing
images of the Jew as alien, as superior, as illicit,
as powerful, the Arab [in Israel] learns
the special techniques of staying afloat.
David K. Shipler
Arab and Jew

Various terms are used to categorize the people of the Holy Land: *Israeli, Jew, Arab, Palestinian, Druze, Jordanian, Bedouin.* Defining and categorizing these terms leads inevitably to overlaps. Nevertheless, defining also helps to clarify. To consider these terms with finer precision, here are some guidelines:

- All citizens of Israel are Israelis, and seventy-six percent of Israelis are Jews.
- Almost all Jews have their cultural roots in Judaism. but at least half would describe themselves as secular rather than religious.
- Before 1948 *Palestinian* meant a person (Arab, Jew, or other) who lived in the British Palestine Mandate. Since 1948 *Palestinian* has come to mean persons of Arabic language and culture who live or once lived in the territory of the former Palestine Mandate.
- A few Jews have always lived in Israel, but the vast majority of Israeli Jews are first, second, or third generation immigrants.
- Of Israeli citizens, 1.3 million are Palestinians, whom Israelis prefer to call Arabs.
- An Arab citizen of Israel is both an Israeli and a Palestinian.
- Druze are members of an Arabic-speaking ethnic group who follow an offshoot of Islam and maintain a separate identity. Israel has 268,000 Druze citizens.
- Most Palestinians are Muslim; about five percent are Christian.
- A Bedouin is an Arab with tribal affiliation who presently lives (or in the fairly recent past lived) in arid regions as a nomad.
- All Bedouin are Arabs, but most Arabs are not Bedouin.
- Jordanians are citizens of the country formed from the part of the British Palestine Mandate that was east of the Jordan River.
- Palestinians make up almost half the population of Jordan.
- Most native-born Jordanians have Bedouin heritage; most Palestinians do not.

Arab and Jew

Who is an Arab and who is a Jew? In ancient times, both came from the same Middle Eastern Semitic stock and used similar languages. By tradition, both are descended from a common ancestor, Abraham, with the Arab branch stemming from Abraham's firstborn, Ishmael, and the Jews from the second son, Isaac. The origin of this deeply ingrained tradition is covered in Part II. For now, it can be said that an Arab is easier to define than a Jew, for most Arabs speak Arabic as their mother tongue. (However, not all who speak Arabic as their mother tongue are Arabs, for in past centuries Jews and other non-Arabs in Arab countries grow up speaking Arabic as their first language as well.) Probably, but not necessarily, an Arab is a Muslim, for Islam claims the allegiance of more than ninety percent of all Arabs. His/her ancestors may or may not have been Bedouin nomads from the Arabian Desert, with a traditional way of life centering on animal husbandry.

Palestinians, who are Arabs, are the descendents of the various non-Jewish people who lived in the Holy Land over thousands of years past. In the latter years of the Byzantine Empire, most were Christian. Their ancestors were absorbed into Arab culture when the faith of Muhammed reached the Holy Land, beginning in the seventh century. Many, but not all, eventually adopted Islam. Most Palestinians do not have roots in the desert, but some do. Most Jordanians, by contrast (excluding the Palestinian newcomers), are but two or three generations away from their nomadic and tribal Bedouin past. Few Palestinians can name their tribal affiliation; most Jordanians can.

Unlike Arabs, Jews cannot be defined on the basis of their mother tongue, for Jews now in Israel have come from more than 100 countries, including Arabic-speaking countries. Nor does he/she have to be a strict observer of Judaism to be an Israeli Jew, for many in Israel think of themselves as secular. Israeli Jews believe their cultural roots are in the Holy Land, and for this reason they choose to live there (or have come because they can no longer live in the land of their birth).

Because the cultural roots of Palestinian Arabs are also in the Holy Land and Arabs are living in the Holy Land when immigration of European Jews begins, Jews in Israel must deal with the fact that they have displaced prior inhabitants. They also are aware that through two and a half millennia Jews in the Holy Land have often been displaced (but never totally) through expulsions. Jews of ultra-nationalist or ultra-Orthodox religious persuasion believe that their occupation (for them, re-occupation) of the Holy Land is destined and God's will; a radical minority are convinced that the occupation will not be complete and successful until all Palestinian Arabs are gone or subjugated. Israelis of more moderate or liberal views (formerly a majority, but now shrinking) feel that Jews and Palestinians can live together, in equity and justice, in the Holy Land and that Israeli policy should work toward that end.

Part II tells the story of ancient Israel that is meaningful to all Jews, observant or not. It also tells the story of the coming of Christianity and then Islam to the Holy Land – a story that has put indelible ethnic and cultural stamps on the land that Israel now controls.

Israelis

Of all the countries within the Holy Land, Israel has the most well-developed tourism program, as well as the majority of sites associated with the Bible. As a result, some visitors to the Holy Land perceive that the Holy Land and Israel are one and the same and that most people of the Holy Land are Hebrew-speaking followers of Judaism. But the Holy Land extends beyond Israel to include parts of the four countries on its border, all of whose people are Arabs. It is true that the great majority of Israel's 6.7 million citizens are Jews and that almost all Israeli Jews learn to speak Hebrew, the resurrected ancient language that is now the *lingua franca* of Israel. But nearly one-fourth of Israeli citizens are Palestinians whose mother tongue is Arabic, whose children go to Arabic language schools, and who worship either as Muslims (the vast majority) or as Christians.

The first Christians were Jews, and today a small community of Messianic Jews combines both ancient Jewish traditions and Christian beliefs. Representatives of many branches of Christianity live in Israel and care for ancient or modern churches, seminaries, hospitals, and schools started by others of their faith in years past. Many of these institutions serve Arabs and Jews alike and provide venues where dialog can take place. Although most Christians strive to remain as neutral as possible, some tend to make common cause with the Palestinians, others with the Israelis.

Israel's Jewish population is ideologically fractured as they consider how to deal with the Palestinians they have displaced. Israelis are fiercely democratic, and the Knesset, Israel's parliament, is split into a score of political parties, representing the full range of opinion within the country. The ultra-conservative far-right, the religious and ultra-nationalist parties, never command a large segment of the electorate, but without their alliance, no party can gain a majority. The far-right currently controls the Knesset.

Tourists quickly learn to abandon any pre-existing stereotypes regarding Jews in Israel. Although Israel's Jews share a common religious heritage and now speak a common language, they are a blend of all the cultures and ethnic strands that immigration has introduced. To absorb its newcomers, Israel has had to blend cultural and genetic threads that Jews acquired in centuries of Diaspora in Asia, Africa, and Europe. Of Israel's 6.7 million people, seventy-six percent consider themselves to be Jews (of the balance, twenty percent are Arab, four percent Druze). A strong Semitic appearance has persevered through the centuries; nevertheless, Israeli Jews differ vastly in appearance. People seen on the streets of Jerusalem can range from a green-eyed, fair-skinned Slav whose Jewish ancestors might have come from the Russian steppes to a dark-skinned, black-eyed Ethiopian whose Jewish ancestors lived in highland East Africa.

Although small numbers of Jews live in Palestine throughout the past two millennia, Jewish immigrants begin coming from Europe to Palestine in the latter part of the nineteenth century. The largest number of Jews in Israel come originally as refugees, uprooted and stateless. They come because they cannot live any longer in the land of their birth. Survivors of the Holocaust reach Israel in the late 1940s and 1950s. In the subsequent three decades, many Jews come to Israel from Arab countries, where their ancestors have lived for centuries. In the past two decades, the greatest migration has been from Russia. For most of these immigrants, their move to Israel is an act of desperation. Some Israelis, however, have voluntarily uprooted themselves, mostly from Britain, North America, and Australia, to be a part of the Jewish "in-gathering" and "nation-building" that has created the modern state of Israel. Three million immigrants have come to Israel since the country was founded in 1948; of these, one million have come since 1990, mostly from Russia.

Most Jews in Israel would agree that the main reason for Israel's existence is to provide a nation where Jews can work out their own destiny in their own country. This reasoning requires a country where the overwhelming percentage of the population is Jewish, which has been true for Israel ever since the country's founding (Chart 3). The low rate of natural increase of the Jewish population is similar to that of the world's industrial countries. But through immigration (most recently, from countries of the former Soviet Union), the annual rate of population increase is around 2.5 percent. The rate of natural increase among Israel's Arab population, by contrast, is 3.5 percent. This ratio guarantees that unless immigration is increased, the Arab citizens of Israel will form an ever larger proportion of the population. This situation underlies Israel's steadfast refusal to consider allowing Palestinian refugees the "right of return" to Israel that they seek. It also underlies Israel's continuing efforts to encourage Jews all over the world to make their home in Israel.

Immigrants to Israel form three broad groupings based on their geographical origin, and these groupings tend to mark their cultural outlook, the people with whom they associate, and the way they vote: the Ashkenazim, or Jews who come to Israel mainly from central and eastern Europe but also from North and South America, South Africa, and Australia; the Sephardim, who are forced from Spain and Portugal during the Inquisition and scatter throughout North African, Eastern Mediterranean, and Balkan lands; and Eastern, or Oriental Jews, who descend from ancient communities in Islamic lands of North Africa and the Middle East.

Most immigrants arrive with little or no knowledge of Hebrew. Once settled, they are no longer considered refugees but Israeli citizens. They learn Hebrew and are integrated into the life and economy of their new country. Children learn quickly in schools. For young people, mandatory service in the military is the great integrator. For adults, integration is not always so easy.

I am a guest in the home of a family of Jewish immigrants from England. The home is culturally familiar. There is a piano, and on it a Mozart sonata. The bookshelf holds volumes I too have read. Dinner features ham, for the family is not religiously observant. Their loyalty is to Israel, and they have come to help build this nation. After dinner, I join the family in attending the final-day festivities for their daughter's fourth-grade class. There is music, dancing, and recitation. But nothing is familiar — not the oriental minor key and halftones of the songs the children sing, not the dances they perform, nor the recitations in Hebrew. Afterward, back at their home, I realize that the children are talking with each other in Hebrew, while the parents converse in

English. Communication between generations is stilted. In immigrating, the parents have retained much of their own culture, but their children are absorbing another. The parents must swallow their frustration, subverting it to their pride in their children's rapid assimilation. It is the poignant, bittersweet dilemma of all immigrants everywhere.

Many immigrants enter Israel with a good education, and Israelis value learning. Their universities and research institutes are excellent by international standards. Israelis are creative, hard-working, entrepreneurial, argumentative strivers. Life is fast-paced, and the economy reflects this input. Israel has an average gross national product per person above $16,000 – greater than Spain's, less than Ireland's.

With the United States, Israelis have a kind of tempered love relationship, knowing that often they must bend to the wishes of their benefactor, but refusing to on occasion as well. Arab countries claim that it is not Israel but the United States that generally gives in when there are contending issues. Israelis are beholden to the United States for financial aid, for peacemaking efforts, and for support in the international arena. Israel receives far more United States foreign aid per person than any other country. Israelis depend heavily on their co-religionists in the United States for support of nongovernmental projects, and Jewish and Christian tourists from the United States form the backbone of what has been a thriving tourist industry, up until the present Intifadeh.

The majority of Israelis are Western in thought and culture, but an oriental strain is also present, evident especially in popular Israeli music. Israel's Jews may or may not be "religious," for Israelis tend to define themselves first by their cultural heritage and then, if they think it relevant (as most do), by their Jewish faith. They tolerate, not always patiently, their compatriots of the religious right.

By law, buses in Israel must stop running at sundown on Friday night in observance of the Jewish Sabbath and do not begin running again until sundown Saturday. Needing to get from Tel Aviv to Jerusalem on a Friday evening, I find that I am not alone in my frustration. People grumble, make wry jokes, and try to get where they must go, as I do, by waiting until one of a crowded fleet of privately owned minibuses has room for one more passenger.

One out of every four Israeli citizens is a Palestinian, whom Israelis prefer to call an Arab. (In 1945 the term Palestinian is used for everyone who lives within the territory of the British Mandate, Jews and Arabs alike. After the founding of the Israeli state, Arabs begin to use the term "Palestinian" for themselves exclusively. By now the term Palestinian has come to be accepted even in Israel as "the non-Jewish people of the Holy Land.") In 1945 there are 300,000 Jews in Palestine and almost 1,000,000 Arabs. By 1948, the Jewish population within the new state of Israel more than doubles, to 700,000, but only 156,000 Arabs remain. Today the Arab population living within Israel has swollen to 1.3 million, through natural increase.

Below me, visible from Suleiman's Wall, is Jerusalem's Arab Quarter, occupying about one-third of the old walled city of Jerusalem. (The rest of the Old City is divided among the Christian, Jewish, and Armenian quarters.) The winding canopied streets of the Arab Quarter are thronging with tourists on this spring day in 2000, drawn by the array of foods and handwork of a "different culture." Since the beginning of the Intifadeh the Arab merchants in East Jerusalem have been suffering, as do so many others in Israel and the Palestinian Authority, because the tourists are staying away.

Most of Israel's Arab citizens are city dwellers, who cluster in East Jerusalem, in Nazareth, and in other towns in central and western Galilee. They have full democratic rights, including representation in the Knesset and access to all social services. Their children go to Arabic-speaking public schools, and Arabic is Israel's official second language. But Israel's Palestinians tend to perceive themselves as second-class citizens, a barely tolerated minority, non-Jews in a Jewish state, exempted from military service because their loyalty is open to question. (Druze citizens, however, who seem not to identify with Arab Palestinians, do serve in the Israeli military.)

In this period of the Al-Aqsa Intifadeh, the loyalty of Israel's Arab citizens is being severely tried. They are torn between conflicting values. They benefit from Israeli citizenship. They need

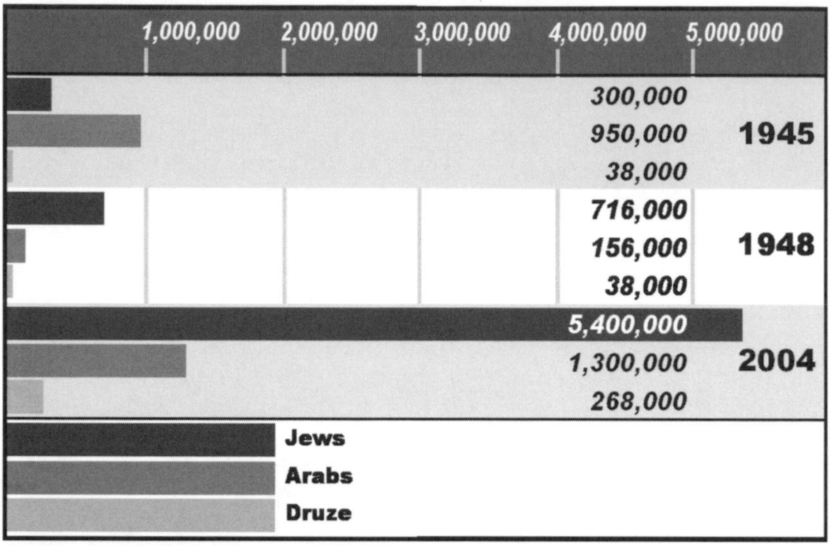

	1,000,000	2,000,000	3,000,000	4,000,000	5,000,000		
				300,000			
				950,000		**1945**	
				38,000			
				716,000			
				156,000		**1948**	
				38,000			
				5,400,000			
				1,300,000		**2004**	
				268,000			

Jews

Arabs

Druze

Source: Israeli Central Bureau of Statistics

Chart 3. Population composition of Palestine in 1945, and Israel in 1948 and 2004.

the jobs that Israel's economy offers, jobs now largely unavailable to the Palestinians in the West Bank and Gaza, where roads into Israel are frequently barricaded. But they bear pent-up resentment for their own situation as well as for that of their fellow-Palestinians in exile. Do they support the Intifadeh, or do they resist or ignore it? Like most Palestinians everywhere, most Israeli Arabs favor a Palestinian state with East Jerusalem as its capital. But if such a state comes into existence, they may choose to become citizens of both countries (as some Israeli citizens hold on to their American passports).

Palestinians

Palestinians are the non-Jewish indigenous people of the Holy Land. For some, their roots go back thousands of years, for others less than a century. The majority of Palestinians are descended from those living in Palestine when Jewish settlers begin arriving in Israel in the late nineteenth century. But as the economy of Palestine begins to improve in the twentieth century, many Arabs enter Palestine seeking employment. As a result, many Palestinians have roots in the Holy Land that are not ancient but relatively recent. As Jewish refugees flood into Palestine in 1947 and 1948, nearly

800,000 refugees are uprooted, lose their homes, and are scattered in diaspora. But despite the turmoil, about two million Palestinians do not lose their homes.

Today there are just under ten million Palestinians in the world (Chart 2). Sixty-two percent are living in diaspora, someplace outside of Palestine. Nearly four million (3.8) are part of families who were never displaced, and they are living today within the West Bank, Gaza, and Israel. Of the six million Palestinians descended from families who lost their homes, one third live today within Israel and the Occupied Territories. Most of the rest live in lands surrounding Palestine, particularly in Jordan, Syria, and Lebanon. Not quite one-fourth of Palestinian refugees (1.35 million) are living in crowded refugee camps as wards of the United Nations, in Gaza, Jordan, Lebanon, the West Bank, and Syria. By far the majority of displaced Palestinians have been able to make some kind of an independent life for themselves where they are living. Nevertheless, front and center in their awareness, always, is Palestine, their once and future home, a homeland of the heart, tugging no less strongly for Palestinians than does Eretz Israel for Jews.

Palestinians are a genetic mixture of all the peoples who have lived in the Holy Land for the past thousands of years. They are of the racial/linguistic family known as Semites, but their blood has strains from Hittites, Persians, Greeks, Romans, Crusaders, and Turks, as well as Arabs. What defines Palestinians and makes them distinct from most Israelis is not their appearance but their Arabic language and the adherence of most to Islam. They are Sunnis, not Shi'ites, and as such are in accord with co-religionists in surrounding Arab countries. They are not fanatic in their observance. They want nothing to do with the *sharia,* a legal code for governing based on strict interpretation of the Quran, and their women wear scarves but not veils. A small percent of people in the West Bank are Druze; but in the Golan Heights Druze make up nearly half of the present population.

About fifty years ago, eight percent of Palestinians were Christian, some with roots going back to the earliest days of Christianity. Most Palestinian Christians today are Orthodox, of Greek, Syrian, Coptic, Armenian, or Russian variation. There are also Syrian Uniate Catholics, the Maronites and the Melkites, who are affiliated with Rome. And there are Palestinians who in the past century have adopted the faith of Protestant and Roman Catholic missionaries, educators, and health-care professionals who have set up churches, schools, and hospitals in Palestine. Christian Palestinians tend to be among the better educated, and when possible, many leave Palestine to seek new opportunities elsewhere. As a result, the Christian population is dwindling. It is now less than one percent of those who live in the West Bank and Gaza, and about thirteen percent of the Palestinians who are Israeli citizens. In other words, among displaced Palestinians (but not among those in Israel), Christians have left the Holy Land in droves. There are twice as many Palestinian Christians living in Dearborn, Michigan, than in Ramallah, and three-fourths of Bethlehem's Christians live away from their homeland. Among other factors, it is becoming increasingly uncomfortable to be a Christian in Palestinian lands, for as resistance hardens, it does so in militant Islamist terms. Christians who take no part in the resistance are often perceived by fellow Palestinians as Israeli sympathizers.

Palestinian Arab families tend to be large, with four or more children. Palestinians value family living and do not begrudge the time it takes to prepare traditional foods. Most Palestinians live in cities and towns. From earliest times, Palestinians have been both rural and urban. In cities, they have been skilled traders and craftsmen, and many are now professionals and highly educated. A decreasing number of Palestinians are farmers. In the countryside, those who follow traditional farming methods are finding that they cannot survive, and like farmers everywhere, they must either cease farming or increase their holdings and modernize. But their position is precarious, for they are not allowed to purchase additional land, and they run the risk of losing their existing land and olive groves to Israeli bulldozers; further, they are denied access to irrigation water. Many quit farming. But when they move to urban areas, they find that chances for employment are bleak.

A few Palestinian farmers wear a garb much like that worn twenty centuries ago. But most Palestinians long ago abandoned this traditional style of clothing in favor of Western dress. Although many Palestinians—including their leader, Yasser Arafat—wear the *kaffiyeh* headdress that marks a nomadic Bedouin tribesman, less than one percent of Palestinian Arabs are nomadic.

In the West Bank, I have seen an Arab in long brown robe and kaffiyeh plowing uneven furrows behind a mule, a scene reminiscent of Biblical times. But I have also seen Arabs in blue jeans using modern equipment for irrigating farms that resemble those of nearby Israeli kibbutzim. (Clearly some Palestinians are able to arrange water rights.) I remember Palestinian construction workers on commercial projects in Jerusalem. They were wheelbarrow-pushers and hod-carriers who probably at that time made the daily trip to work from a Palestinian town in the West Bank, not far outside the city, but now are restrained by roadblocks and interrogation. I remember, too, the well-spoken Palestinian who led me to a dining room table in a Tel Aviv hotel and the Palestinian clerk in Bethlehem who spoke perfect English and assisted me as I made a purchase.

Palestinians in the Holy Land are teachers, students, carpenters, mechanics, shopkeepers, accountants, plumbers, farmers, computer programmers, doctors, librarians, and frustrated and unemployed refugee camp dwellers. They are united only in this: Palestinians must have their own sovereign country, with East Jerusalem as its capital.

People of Surrounding Countries

Like the Palestinians, the people who live in the countries on Israel's border speak Arabic and are overwhelmingly Muslim. Yet, in all of these lands, and particularly in Lebanon, there is also an ancient Christian presence. Most of the people of Lebanon and Syria, and some Jordanians, carry in their blood a blend of all the peoples who in the past traveled or settled along the Fertile Crescent, or occupied the Trans-Jordan plateau country. But most native-born Jordanians feel their roots are far closer to the desert than those of the Lebanese and probably even the Syrians, who themselves have a goodly portion of desert from which to draw inspiration.

The average Jordanian (excluding Palestinians) thinks of himself as a Bedouin, and he can name the desert tribe with which he is linked. However, if he lives in a city or town and engages in urban life, he is a Bedouin only by remote tribal affiliation. One can see Bedouin encampments, with their black coarsely woven goat-hair tents open to leeward, in all the drier parts of the Holy Land, including Israel, but they are especially prevalent in Jordan and the Sinai Peninsula. Once used to a money economy, few Bedouin return to a nomadic way of life, but Bedouin encampments offer housing that is far less expensive than apartments in the cities.

In Jordan, I see many Bedouin tents with pickup trucks parked nearby. In part, the trucks are used to take the children to school. The Bedouin of Jordan and the Sinai Peninsula have learned to profit from services to tourists. Led by a young Bedouin, I descend on camelback from the top of the Moab Plateau, near Mount Nebo, to the shores of the Dead Sea 3,000 feet below. Another time, I take tea in a Bedouin encampment within Wadi Rum at the southern tip of Jordan. Although my host family has a rudimentary complement of animals, they also have three pickup trucks which they use to transport tourists around the spectacular formations of Wadi Rum. In Petra, the "rose-red city of the [Jordanian] desert," Bedouin merchants camped nearby monopolize the trinket trade as well as the camel rides. In the sere landscape of the Sinai, a Bedouin family, who surely can get little sustenance from a land without vegetation, offers me tea and freshly baked bread.

The rapidly expanding capital city of Amman has grown from 60,000 when the British Trans-Jordan Mandate ended in 1946 and the Hashemite Kingdom of Jordan became a sovereign country to its present size of a million and a half. Amman now sprawls in light grey concrete sameness across six of its hills. Most of the two-story buildings in Jordan's cities and towns sprout rebars sticking out from their roof, like unfinished pieces of construction. The roofs are flat, well-suited to expanding upward, and with rebars in place the next floor will go up when the money is at hand.

In a research institute in Amman I exchange ideas with Jordanian scholars, and in the noisy commercial quarter of the city I barter with Arab merchants. I listen to an Orthodox priest in a northern Jordanian city, proud of the heritage he is helping to keep alive. In the port city of Aqaba, where Jordan sends and receives its waterborne freight, I register the pride of a museum-keeper as he shows me his display of Bedouin tribal knives and other paraphernalia.

Along the coast of the Sinai Peninsula I see the results of poor planning and overbuilding as Egyptian developers seek to cash in on an international craze for coral-reef diving that never materializes here but is attracted instead to the Israeli-constructed Egyptian resort city of Sharm el-Sheikh at the southern tip of the peninsula. I sense that their efforts are doomed to become concrete derelicts on the narrow stretch of flat land between the mountains and the Gulf of Aqaba.

Though the people of the countries surrounding Israel are overwhelmingly Arab, Muslim, and supportive of the Palestinian cause, they are entrepreneurs, too, and practical. Most think that association with Israel will pay off, and in an ideal world, commerce always does. Already it has for the Jordanians, whose income from tourism rises measurably with the establishment of diplomatic relations with Israel in 1994. Israelis, now allowed to cross Jordan's borders, are largely responsible for the great increase in tourism in Petra, for example.

Beginning in 1979, the year of the Camp David Accord, Egypt has been at peace with Israel. (For their diplomacy at Camp David *1979* Israel's Menachem Begin and Egypt's Anwar Sadat receive the Nobel Peace Prize. But Egypt's president pays for his diplomacy with his life, snuffed out six years later by a Muslim extremist, in a grim prelude to the 1995 assassination by an Israeli right wing extremist of Israeli Prime Minister Itzhak Rabin, who shares a Nobel Prize with Yasser Arafat the previous year.) Although shortly after the Camp David Accord Israel returns the Sinai Peninsula to Egypt, it does not relinquish the Gaza Strip, to which thousands of Palestinians flee in 1948 only to be frustrated after 1967 when again they end up in Israeli territory. The government of Egypt keeps a tight rein on its Islamist militant faction and probably takes no part in supplying weapons to Palestinian terrorists. Nevertheless, weapons are regularly funneled from Egypt, through clandestine sources, to Rafah, at the southern edge of the Gaza Strip, along the border with Egypt. Israel does not accuse the Egyptian government of complicity, but to close off this conduit Israeli tanks and bulldozers come down hard on Rafah. There are casualties on both sides.

Lebanon and Syria continue to oppose Israel, refusing to acknowledge either its existence or its right to exist. They use the Palestinian refugees still languishing in UN refugee camps, the Israeli invasion of Lebanon in 1982, and the subsequent Israeli complicity in attacks on two Palestinian refugee camps as justification for guerilla *1982* raids in Israel and the support they give to Arafat. Refugee camps in Lebanon and Syria are a breeding ground for resentment and a training ground for Hezbullah recruits. *Hezbullah*, an organization of Islamic militants, is financed largely by Iran but directed by Syria. Iran's support comes because Hezbullah represents the Shi'ite Muslim community in Lebanon, and Iranians overwhelmingly are Shi'ites. Hezbullah, like its counterpart militant Islamic organizations in the Palestinian Authority, provides needed social services for the Shi'ite community, but its members also are committed to the total demise of Israel. They attract frustrated young men in the same way that Hamas and the Islamic Jihad do in Palestine. Indeed, the three organizations are frequently in league.

Palestinian refugees in the UN camps in Lebanon want their former lands back, in addition to the houses and shops they once occupied, and they agitate. Many feel that Yasser Arafat has betrayed them, for the UN Resolution 242 which he is promoting as a "land for peace" basis for settlement in Palestine makes no provision for them. *2000* In the summer of 2000, Israel withdraws its troops from southern Lebanon, troops that originally invaded Lebanon in 1982 to prevent cross-border Hezbullah incursions. For a time, the border has been quiet, but Israel remains wary of its northern neighbors, and with good reason. Syria, which holds Lebanon almost as a fiefdom, claims that it cannot promise to restrain Hezbullah militants. Meanwhile, Hezbullah recruits have been appearing in the ranks of Hamas and the Islamic Jihad.

I have no recent experiences to report from the lands beyond Israel's northern border. In Lebanon in 1958, I crouch behind sandbags at the airport as the country is being torn apart by factionalism. In those days—before Camp David—the only way one can get into Tel Aviv from Cairo, 200 miles distant, is to fly first to Beirut, then to Cyprus, and finally into Israel. Today, it is still not possible to travel between Israel and Lebanon or between Israel and Syria. Not so many years ago, I am ready to spend a month in Syria, flying directly from the United States, when at the last minute the offer is withdrawn; security cannot be guaranteed.

Should peace ever come between Israel and its neighbors, a rich dividend for all parties will be the tourism that could well encompass the entire Holy Land. Meanwhile, both Lebanon and Syria promote tourism, and with good reason. Both countries have countless sites no less valuable than those in Israel to the historian, the archaeologist, and the pilgrim. Tyre and Sidon (Sayda), for example, are in Lebanon, and Antioch—once in Syria—is now just over the border in southeastern Turkey. Damascus, Syria's capital, is one of the earliest centers of civilization. Greek and Roman ruins abound in Syria, and on the horizon in the hilly south are castles built by both Crusaders and Turks. Optimists in the tourist industry, in each of the countries of the region, look forward to a time when borders can be crossed with relative ease.

How each of the countries surrounding Israel become separate entities after the end of the Ottoman Empire is the story told in Chapter 24.

7
A Longing for Peace

*I went to Arafat in order to tell him that in spite of
everything there are still many in Israel who will not let
despair destroy the hope of peace. It is incumbent on all who
believe in the cause of a just peace to work together.*
Shulamit Aloni
*Recipient of the Israel Prize for
Human Rights, January 20, 2002*

Almost all people in the Holy Land and on its borders long
for peace. When informal dialog takes place between
moderate Israelis and Palestinians, all agree that provocation
and retaliation must end.

*In Jordan, in the spring of 2000, I am sharing bread, cheese, and
oranges with my cab driver in a gray-green grove of old and twisted olive
trees. The setting is timeless and placid, and he is optimistic that peace
in the region is just around the corner. "The Egyptians have done it,
and we have done it. Lebanon and Syria will be settled soon," he states
with conviction.*

In dialog, most moderates agree that the Jewish settlements
in the West Bank and Gaza must be abandoned. They agree that
terrorism must be quelled, and that Jewish military presence in the
Occupied Territories must end as well. They agree that it will not
be possible for all Palestinians to return to their old homes, and that
there must be compensation.

But they cannot agree on Jerusalem. In the millennial year, with antagonism running high but before the Al-Aqsa Intifadeh erupts, Pope John Paul II goes to Israel to ask all sides to give and to plead especially for those Palestinians who are stateless and impoverished. But in the years since his visit the situation has only worsened despite strong peace efforts from both the Clinton and Bush administrations, from Arab countries led by Prince Abdullah of Saudi Arabia, and from Israeli and Palestinian non-governmental leaders meeting on their own. This is likely to be the toughest dilemma of our new century, one that now figures into the International War on Terrorism. Israelis and Palestinians desperately want an end to violence, but most feel that justice—and the God of their fathers—is on their side.

Holy Land, Whose Land?

Part II
The Past as Prologue: From Abraham to Arafat

It is in the past that the tensions of the Holy Land today are rooted. History is unavoidable in the Holy Land. Every tell, every pile of ancient columns, every church, indeed every pilgrimage site nudges the traveler to grope for an understanding of the past, to form a working chronology on which to pin one's journey.

What follows is the story of the people and events of this ancient land. The earliest part of the story cannot be called history, for its sources are oral tradition. Hundreds of years separate some events from their written narratives, and the chroniclers do not always agree. Nevertheless, the accounts as they appear in the Hebrew Scriptures (the Old Testament of Christians) underlie the world's three monotheistic faiths: Judaism, Christianity, and Islam. The chronology is rough, and much of it remains in dispute. For dates, I use the widely accepted BCE (Before the Common Era) and CE. Where dates are approximate, the symbol "ca" is appended.

8
The Patriarchs

"The whole land of Canaan,
where you are now an alien,
I will give as an everlasting possession to you
and your descendants after you;
and I will be their God."
Genesis 17:8

"Your name will no longer be Jacob, but Israel."
Genesis 32:28

The archaeological record of settlement in Palestine goes back at least 10,000 years. However, my interest in probing for roots of conflict begins with the story of Abraham, as told in the Book of Genesis.

Abraham

Nearly four millennia ago, Abraham, a man of means and owner of many flocks and herds, is living in the Sumerian city-state of Ur on the Euphrates River in lower Mesopotamia.

With his family, servants, and flocks, along with those of his father and his nephew Lot, Abraham and his party leave Ur *ca.* and travel to the tribal lands of his uncle in Haran, in the region *1850 BCE* known as Padan Aram. Haran is about halfway along the Fertile Crescent between Mesopotamia and the Mediterranean in what is now southeastern Turkey. In Haran, a Sumerian city-state like Ur, Abraham and his family prosper. There his father dies.

75

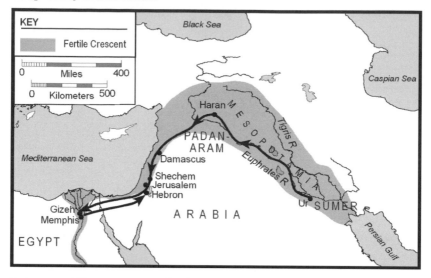

Map 11. The journey of Abraham.

Abraham is often considered to be the world's first Monotheist. Although he comes out of a polytheistic society, he listens when God – the One God – speaks to him in Haran. What God says to Abraham is this: "Go to a land which I will show you, and there I will make you the father of a mighty nation."

On faith, Abraham leaves behind the comfortable life he has known in Haran and becomes a nomad. Traveling with his nephew Lot, their wives, servants and flocks, he begins his journey southwestward along the Fertile Crescent, a route which even at that time is well-traveled. He keeps his flocks north and west of the desert. Eventually, he reaches the hilly land at the eastern end of the Mediterranean Sea. This land has been settled for thousands of years. It has a Bronze Age culture. Early empires from Mesopotamia and Anatolia, and local kings as well, have warred over it. The Hittites have passed through on their way to Egypt, and a few have stayed to claim land.

Abraham stops first at a settlement called Shechem, within the central hill country. This is the site of the present West Bank city of Nablus. Because Abraham stops first at Shechem, but also because Shechem figures prominently in the later history of Abraham's descendents, today both Muslims and Jews consider Nablus as a holy site.

Nablus today is entirely an Arab city, and almost all of its inhabitants are Muslim. It is ringed by Israeli settlements on higher ground. Nablus seethes with opposition to Israeli settlements. Israeli tanks make frequent entries into the city to halt Hamas terrorist activity generated there.

After stopping at Shechem, Abraham proceeds slowly southward, but there is drought in the land. He escapes the threat of famine by going for a time into northern Egypt. Returning from Egypt, Abraham settles in the vicinity of present-day Hebron, near the northern reaches of the Negev Desert. (Lot and his family and flocks take up land near Sodom and Gomorrah, cities at the southern end of the Dead Sea. The present day sites of Lot's settlement have disappeared, destroyed, by tradition, because of the dissolute behavior of their inhabitants). After a long life, Abraham is buried in Hebron, beside his wife Sarah. Later the tomb becomes the burial site also of his son Isaac and his grandson Jacob. Because the patriarchs are buried there, Hebron comes to have great religious significance.

The arid land I see in the vicinity of Hebron is now blooming because of irrigation. For Abraham, it was grazing land and probably received more rainfall than now. Because Abraham settled near Hebron and was buried nearby, Muslims consider the town a sacred site. Most of the town is administered by the Palestinian Authority. Some 400 ultra-Orthodox Israelis, most of them originally from the United States, live in Hebron today, under Israeli protection. In today's Hebron, the atmosphere is often charged.

Ishmael, Isaac, and the Rock of Sacrifice

Three generations of Abraham's descendents can be named by Jews, Christians, and Muslims the world over, because as the first of the Patriarchs, Abraham figures prominently in the foundation of *ca. 1800 BCE* Judaism, Christianity, and Islam. Although Abraham and his wife Sarah are childless and Sarah is long past childbearing age, God tells Abraham that Sarah will have a son who will make him the father of a mighty nation. God will give this nation the land of Canaan – the hill country between the Mediterranean Sea and the Jordan River – as their heritage; in turn, God will require circumcision as a sign of the covenant. It happens as God promises: Sarah gives birth to Isaac.

Meanwhile, Abraham has an older son named Ishmael by an Egyptian servant woman named Hagar. God promises that Ishmael, too, will be the father of a great nation. Out of favor with Sarah, Hagar and Ishmael flee southward into the Negev Desert. Ishmael grows up, takes an Egyptian wife, and by tradition becomes the father of the Arab nation. (Twenty-four centuries later, the Jewish community in Medina passes on to Muhammed another tradition: that Abraham goes to visit Ishmael in Mecca and that together he and his son build the Kaabah, the huge black-draped cubic structure located on a great square in the center of Mecca. Within one corner of this structure is a large black meteorite. In ancient times tribes in the vicinity of Mecca worship the meteorite as the abode of the god Al-Lah. To this day the Kaabah centers Islamic worship in Mecca.)

As he concentrates his hope on Isaac, Abraham's faith is severely tested when God requires that he sacrifice his son. Father and son walk for two days from Hebron to the vicinity of present-day Jerusalem. There on a prominent hill called Mount Moriah Abraham finds a pre-existing Canaanite altar. He trusses Isaac and has a knife in his hand when, at the last moment, an angel stays him. Abraham has proven his faith in God, and Isaac lives. A thousand years later Mount Moriah becomes the site of the great temple built by King Solomon, with the Holy of Holies – the most sacred part of the temple – built directly over what has come to be known as the Rock of Abraham or the Rock of Sacrifice. Muslims revere the same site, where they believe Ishmael, not Isaac, is trussed for sacrifice. Today, the site lies under the spectacular golden Dome of the Rock in Jerusalem on the raised natural platform that Muslims call al-Haram al-Sharif (The Noble Sanctuary). Jerusalem is Islam's third most holy city, after Mecca and Medina.

The Dome of the Rock, which dates from the early eighth century CE, must be one of the world's most beautiful buildings, totally pleasing in symmetry (Photo 23). At the opposite side of the great platform stands the Al-Aqsa Mosque. It is one of the world's largest. During the feast of Id, following Ramadan, the mosque holds at least as many Muslims as the crowds of Jews who once assembled in the courtyard of the Temple that Solomon built on this site. I am gratified to be allowed inside the mosque, required only to remove my shoes. No insistence, even, that I cover my head. I can only assume that Muslim leaders here want people to understand that they, too, have a valid claim on the Holy Land.

Esau and Jacob

Isaac grows up to father two sons, Esau and Jacob. With the connivance of his mother, Jacob, the younger son, cheats Esau out *ca.* of his inheritance. Esau flees to the semi-arid plateau country to the *1750* east of the Jordan River, marries one of the daughters of Ishmael, *BCE* and becomes the father of the Edomites, a people with whom the descendents of Jacob are often in conflict.

The plateau region once called Edom, now a part of Jordan, is cut by deep, dry gashes where it meets the Jordan Valley, but on the upland surface, I see crops growing without irrigation in soil that seems to be easily worked.

Esau prospers in Edom and has flocks of sheep. In time, he forgives Jacob his trickery. Jacob goes to the far-off oasis of Haran to find a wife. He works twenty years for his uncle Laban, is tricked into marrying his cousin Leah, later wins her more attractive sister Rachel, then returns to settle near his father in the northern Negev Desert. God favors Jacob and calls him *Israel*, meaning "to strive with God and prevail." Jacob fathers twelve sons, of whom only the youngest two, Joseph and Benjamin, are by Rachel. Joseph is Jacob's favorite.

9
The Exodus

The Lord said, "I have indeed seen
the misery of my people in Egypt...
So I have come down to rescue them
from the hand of the Egyptians
and to bring them up out of that land into a good and
spacious land, a land flowing with milk and honey..."
Exodus 3:7,8

J acob's twelve sons, the first Israelites, begin the lineage of the
Twelve Tribes of Israel. Their saga is told in the books of Genesis
and Exodus. The brothers are herdsmen. Jealous of Joseph,
whom their father favors, they sell him to Egyptian slavers, and
ca. they give him up for dead. In Egypt, however, Joseph eventually
1700 comes into Pharaoh's service and is placed in charge of grain supplies.
BCE Facing famine in their semi-arid grazing lands and hearing of food
in Egypt, the brothers go to the Nile Valley. Joseph makes himself
known to them and arranges for his brothers to get provisions.

The Israelites in Egypt

Protected by a benign Pharaoh, who may himself have been of
foreign blood, Joseph's brothers and their father, Jacob (Israel), begin
ca. to live with their flocks in the land known as Goshen in the eastern
1700- part of the Nile Delta. Their numerous descendents remain in Egypt
1300 for about four-hundred years, eventually becoming slaves working on
BCE the grandiose construction projects of less-tolerant pharaohs. They

80

Map 12. The Egyptian Empire, ca. 1450 BCE.

pick up the name of *Hebrews* (probably a pejorative term) from a word that means *foreigners,* or *swarthy ones.*

Egyptian Conquests

While the Hebrews are laboring in Egypt, the Egyptians – with iron-age technology learned from their imperial rivals the Hittites – invade and conquer the hill country homeland of the patriarchs, the adjacent coastlands, the hill country to the east of the Jordan River, and probably parts of Syria. Egyptian governors rule *ca. 1450 BCE* in the towns of the region, and Egyptian armies are garrisoned there to hold off invaders. A period of peace and commerce in the region follows, and the Egyptians develop trade links with the wealthy and technically advancing peoples of the eastern Mediterranean islands.

Egyptian rule is challenged by the arrival of the so-called *Sea Peoples*, including the Philistines, who occupy the coastlands. (Historians conjecture that the Sea Peoples may have been the Minoans, whom the Greeks defeat on Crete.) At first, Egypt manages to keep the Philistines at bay, but eventually the invaders become strong enough to defeat the Egyptians. For hundreds of years, the Philistines occupy the coastal plain, and with their knowledge of iron-working and other advanced technology, they pose a threat to other peoples of the region.

Today, the Gaza Strip, the ancient port city of Jaffa, and the commercial center of Tel Aviv are located in the coastal plain once occupied by the Philistines. Tel Aviv is a modern city. It has beautiful beaches and is a good place for travelers to rendezvous. However, it is of only minor interest to the historian or Bible scholar because it was never occupied by the Israelites in ancient times. It throbs with the pace of the New Israel. To the north, in Netanya, a world-class electronics industry is developing, now representing 80 percent of the value of all Israel's exports. On Tel Aviv's beaches, tall hotels house both Israeli sun worshippers and tourists at the beginning and end of their journeys. In relation to both ancient and modern Jerusalem, Tel Aviv and its environs are still like the land of the Philistines: brash, outward-looking, technologically superior, but seemingly without depth of spirit. But now I am ahead of the story.

Moses

In Egypt, where the Hebrews are enslaved, God chooses Moses to be their champion. Born to a Hebrew mother at a time *ca. 1350 BCE* when a Pharaonic edict requires that all newborn Hebrew males be slain, Moses is hidden among reeds near the Nile, then rescued by Pharaoh's daughter. Given an Egyptian name, Moses grows up in Pharaoh's service. He fears retribution for slaying a guard who is beating Hebrew slaves and flees to the desert of Midian, the southern and driest part of what is now Jordan and of Israel's Negev.

In Midian, Moses becomes a shepherd. While he is with his sheep and goats, God speaks to him from a burning bush (by tradition, near Mount Sinai, which would indicate that Moses does a good deal of wandering with his flocks). God commands him to lead the Hebrews out of slavery. Moses returns to Egypt. With the help of divinely imposed plagues, he persuades Pharaoh (probably Ramses II) to "let my people go." He then leads the Israelite tribes away from Pharaoh's army, across the Sea of Reeds—the swampy area to the north of the Red Sea—and into the Sinai Desert. The pursuing soldiers are drowned.

The story of the escape, known as the Exodus, is still written largely and symbolically in the hearts of Jews everywhere. The feast of Passover commemorates the event when the angel of death, sent by God to kill all the first-born sons in Egypt, passes over the dwellings of the Israelites, which have been marked with the *ca. 1300 BCE* blood of a slaughtered lamb. Passover is one of the holy days of the Jewish calendar. It is celebrated wherever Jews congregate but most meaningfully in Jerusalem. (During what Christians now call Holy Week, Jesus and his disciples are in Jerusalem, crowded with visitors at the time of the Passover. On the evening before the actual start of the Passover commemoration, they seek out a room where they can dine together, an occasion which has since become known as the Last Supper.)

No Other God

The Israelites flee southward into the Sinai Peninsula. There on a high peak known variously as Mount Horeb, Mount Sinai, or Jebel Musa (the Mount of Moses), God speaks directly to Moses. He tells Moses to lead the Israelites into the Promised Land, Canaan, where they will multiply and become a great people. Above all, the Israelites are to worship no other god but God. Moses descends the mountain and assembles the Israelites to tell them what he has heard. They must worship only God. But in an age of universal polytheism, the Israelites are not yet monotheists. They believe that other gods exist, and they are all too ready to worship any local god who might do them good. Moses goes a second time to the mountain, and this time he receives the Ten Commandments, inscribed on two stone tablets. Meanwhile, the Israelite tribes encamped at the base of the mountain build and begin to worship a golden calf. When he returns from the mountain, Moses sees the golden calf and becomes so angry that he breaks the stone tablets. The Israelites repent.

Once again, Moses returns to the mountain, where God inscribes new stone tablets. He makes a covenant with Moses and his people. He will give them the Promised Land, leading them in battles against the Canaanites, but they in turn are to remain faithful to him. God gives Moses the complex laws governing religious observances and social amity that the descendents of Jacob (the children of Israel) are henceforth to observe. The tablets and the record of the laws by which the Israelites shall live are placed in a structure called the Ark of the Covenant, which the wanderers carry with them.

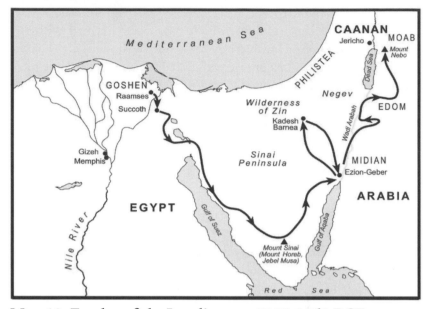

Map 13. Exodus of the Israelites, ca. 1300-1260 BCE.

The commandments that Moses receives on Mount Sinai do not immediately change the Israelites into monotheists. The process takes centuries, during which the Israelites are as ready to adopt the gods of the people among whom they live as they are to remain faithful to the One God. But the covenant that God issues on Mount Sinai, pledging that Israel shall be his people and demanding faithfulness in return, is the lodestar to which the Israelites return time and again. They are repeatedly nudged by prophets who call down God's wrath on those who stray.

Years of Wandering

From a desert oasis called Kadesh Barnea, Moses sends Joshua and Caleb north to spy out the land of Canaan, and they return to tell the people that the land they saw is fertile. But other spies of Moses report that the Canaanites are strong and well armed. The Israelites complain. They are afraid of the Canaanites, who have picked up iron-age technology from the Egyptians and Philistines and with whom they will have to do battle. Indeed, the Canaanites are a far more sophisticated people than the Israelites. The Canaanites are farmers and town dwellers and not nomadic herders. For their doubts and other sins of faithlessness, God decrees that none of the generation that led the people out of Egypt, including Moses, will live to set foot on the Promised Land.

It takes forty years of wandering before the older generation dies off. Their wanderings are first in the Sinai Peninsula, then in the lower reaches of the adjacent Negev Desert, and finally on the *ca.* plateaus of Midian and Edom to the east. There they must fight *1300-* the local peoples, some of them the descendents of Esau. During all *1260* *BCE* this time, God sees that they get sufficient food and water. At last, they reach the better-watered Moab plateau, north of Edom, and engage in the first of many battles with one of the local peoples, the Ammonites, whose chief center is Rabbath Ammon (now the site of Jordan's capital city, Amman). Then they descend from the plateau to camp on the eastern bank of the Jordan River.

The View from Mount Nebo

Moses dies before the Israelites can enter Canaan, but on Mt. Nebo, a hilltop in Moab, to the east of the Dead Sea, he is given a glimpse of the lower Jordan Valley and the future that awaits the people he has led. The land called Moab (together with Edom and Midian to the south) occupies a dissected plateau rising sheer to 3,000 feet above the Jordan Valley and the Dead Sea. A similar dissected plateau rises to the west of the Jordan, crowned by the city of Jerusalem. The Jordan River flows between these two plateaus in a geological trough, a block fault, or rift valley, that actually extends from north of the Sea of Galilee southward to encompass the Dead Sea, the Wadi Arabah, the gulfs of Aqaba and Suez, and the Red Sea. (In Africa, this trough continues into the Great Rift Valley.)

The Jordan River flows southward out of the Sea of Galilee to empty into the Dead Sea, the lowest spot on earth. The portion of the Promised Land that Moses sees is a lush garden on the west bank of *ca.* the Jordan, hot and immensely fertile and dominated by the city of *1260* *BCE* Jericho (which even then occupies a site that is 6,000 years old).

From Amman, I travel thirty miles west to climb the same heights that Moses did. I cannot see Jericho through the haze of pollution, but I can make out the Dead Sea far below. The Franciscan order maintains the site, and a church on the location dates to Byzantine time. On the

Photo 4. Amman, the fast-growing capital of Jordan.

day I am at Mount Nebo, all is being readied for the visit of Pope John Paul II the following day.

Trailing the Israelites

I am intrigued by Amman, a city that has exploded with growth since it was named the new capital of Trans-Jordan, one of the Arab states that emerge at the end of World War II. Then Amman was little more than a village. Now it has a million-and-a-half occupants living in gray-white, flat-roofed limestone buildings of nearly uniform three and four-story height spread out among six hills. The center of Amman occupies an ancient site. Even today the city takes its name from the Ammonites – a nomadic people descended from Lot's youngest daughter – the people against whom the Israelites are pitted, time and again, in the Biblical accounts. I see no evidence of Ammonite occupancy in archaeological digs, but plenty of Roman ruins testify to the former importance of this trade route city. The Greeks name it Philadelphia, but the presence of "Amman" on contemporaneous tomb inscriptions suggests that the name never takes hold.

From Amman, I head south and follow the ancient route of conquerors and traders called the Kings' Highway. The narrow but well-paved asphalt road generally hews to the plateau surface, but twice it must descend from the plateau, winding precipitously down into the wadis that cut into and drain the plateau, before going up again. I begin in the land once known as Moab and head southward through ancient Edom and the stark desert of ancient Midian until I reach the spectacular ruins of Petra.

Petra is worth any effort it takes to reach it. Here, from the second century BCE to the second century CE, the Nabatean trade empire maintains its security and its rock-hewn tombs at the end of a stark and narrow mile-long entranceway known as the Siq. Its unique tombs are a syncretic synthesis of Greek, Roman, and Egyptian architectural features. Most imposing is the great tomb misnamed "The Treasury," suddenly revealed in pink-hued grandeur where the narrow Siq opens onto a wide causeway. I am shocked by the great increase in the numbers of tourists, and hotels to accommodate them, in the six years since I was last in Petra. Jordan has obviously given Petra highest priority in tourism, and it should, for tourism is now the number-one source of income for Jordan.

Many of the tourists in Petra are from Israel, welcome now as the result of the Jordan/Israel peace treaty of 1994. Many others, as I, are following a standard Holy Land tour route that includes not only Israel but also Amman, Mount Nebo, Petra, the port cities of Aqaba (Jordan) and Eilat (Israel) at the head of the Gulf of Aqaba, and Saint Catherine's Monastery at the foot of Mount Sinai in Egypt's Sinai Peninsula. I rush through Aqaba, but I have seen it previously and find it a pleasant and rather quiet resort town as well as a seaport. Eilat is another story. It is Israel's Caribbean playground. Here Israelis of all classes, from wealthy to itinerant, can let their hair down on a boardwalk that resembles Coney Island in its heyday and in nearby five-star luxury hotels where all food is kosher.

Through the Gulf of Aqaba, both Israel and Jordan receive petroleum and other products. The port facilities in both Aqaba and Eilat are well-developed. Aqaba is Jordan's only link with the sea, and both a high-speed desert highway and a railroad head north from there to Amman. Possessed of several Mediterranean ports, Israel is not totally dependent on Eilat, but Eilat facilitates its trade with Asia. In 1956, when Egypt blockaded the Straits of Tiran, at the south end of the Gulf of Aqaba, the Israelis were desperate, for they counted on this sea route to get petroleum. The 1956 war between Israel and Egypt resulted in Egypt's temporary loss of the Sinai Peninsula.

The Gulf of Aqaba has some of the world's most beautiful coral beds, and scuba diving attracts visitors to both Aqaba and Eilat. Diving may be even better from the shores of the Sinai Peninsula, but I wouldn't have known it from the sad condition of the half-built hotels that line the

Photo 5. The ancient rock-hewn tombs of Petra.

narrow coastal plain of the peninsula. Egypt's most popular resort now is the one the Israelis developed at the southern tip of the Sinai, at Sharm el-Sheikh.

There can be no desolation so absolute as that which confronts the traveler in the Sinai. Peaks are sharply etched, devoid of vegetation, defiant. But the road is smooth, and at length I reach the base of Mount Sinai, the highest peak in a roughly dissected, rocky, and extremely arid region. On a nearby and slightly lower peak is Saint Catherine's Monastery, probably the oldest continuously occupied monastery on earth, guarding the traditional site where Moses receives the Ten Commandments. Portions of the monastery walls expose stone and mortar construction, preserved in the desert dryness, that dates back more than 1,500 years. In one vault, an eerie seated mummy, clothed in ecclesiastical robes, preserves the body of a revered monk from long ago. Nearby is a cache of monks' skulls that has been accumulating for many centuries. The monastery's present complement of black-robed, bearded Orthodox monks is less than two dozen, and these few have to cope with the swarms of tourists who now come during the three hours, twice a week, that entrance to the monastery is allowed. Because of the crowds, I am prevented from entering the library filled with ancient manuscripts, where the oldest known copy of the Bible—the Codex Sinaiticus, dating to the fourth century CE—was discovered a century ago. Portions of this priceless document are now in museums in St. Petersburg

Photo 6. The Gulf of Aqaba from the resort city of Eilat.

and Leipzig; nevertheless, I was looking forward to simply experiencing the monastery's ancient library. The footpath from the road to the monastery leads past a wall, over which I can see a monk watering a garden. There is nothing else green in all of the Sinai, it seems, but here at Saint Catherine's the monks are able to grow figs and grapes. The almond trees are in bloom.

Reentering Israel, I head north along the Wadi Arabah, the exceedingly dry rift valley that descends gradually northward from the Gulf of Aqaba to the shores of the Dead Sea, 1,300 feet below sea level. On either side of the Wadi is a harsh, rugged land, sculpted by wind and deeply eroded. Springs sustain a few bushes in the transverse wadis, but there is no surface water. South of the Dead Sea, I see road signs leading toward desert areas called Paran and Zin, wilderness areas named in Exodus where the Israelites camp. Near the southern end of the now-shrinking Dead Sea, I am shown the supposed site of the destroyed cities of Sodom and Gomorrah, where Lot's wife, looking backward on the flaming cities, turns into a pillar of salt.

There is reason to believe that the traditions associated with Genesis and Exodus take place at a time when the whole desert and semi-arid region receives more rainfall than now. This could explain the traditional site of the destroyed pleasure-loving ancient cities near the southern end of the Dead Sea. The site is now exposed as mineralized desert. It could also help to explain how tribal peoples numbering in the tens of thousands could be sustained during their desert wanderings, manna notwithstanding. Today, the white

Photo 7. Saint Catherine's Monastery, near Mt. Sinai.

droppings of insects living on a desert bush are collected by nomadic peoples for food, and the collected droppings are called "manna." At the very least, there must have been springs in the days of the Exodus, for even now I see occasional flashes of green in wadi cuts.

As the Dead Sea shrinks, possibly from climate change but certainly because of the withdrawal of irrigation water from the Jordan River, both the Jordanians and the Israelis are exploiting the rich mineral salts that are being exposed. On each side, a thriving industrial complex turns out not only agricultural chemicals but also bath salts, facial masks, and cosmetic products that are sold all over the world. The Dead Sea has also spawned a spa industry, drawing people who come to bathe in the mineral-rich and exceptionally buoyant waters. One look at the mud-covered bathers emerging from the water convinces me to forgo the experience.

The Torah

The story of the Patriarchs and the epic of the Exodus are passed on by the Hebrews from one generation to the next mostly as oral tradition, for only gradually do the Hebrews produce scribes. The earliest written fragments of the Exodus possibly date from the tenth century BCE, but not until the latter part of the sixth century are various versions of the epic compiled by anonymous priestly scribes, whose interest in part is in validating the role of the priests. Scholars can detect at least four sources interwoven into the record that finally emerges. Two of these probably date from the tenth or ninth centuries, and two from the seventh and sixth centuries. The writings are inscribed as the Books of Genesis, Exodus, Leviticus, Numbers, and Deuteronomy. These five books form the Torah—the first five books of the Hebrew Bible—and likewise the first books of the Christian Old Testament, the Pentateuch. The stories, repeated around campfires and in caravanserais, are probably a source from which—more than a thousand years later—Muhammed, an overland trader from Arabia, acquires many of the ideas that eventually are written in the Quran. Most importantly, they are the world's first codification of monotheism, the overriding concept shared alike by all groups who come as pilgrims to the Holy Land.

10
The Promised Land

*And now, Israel, take notice of the laws and customs that I
teach you today, and observe them, that you may...
enter and take possession of the land that Yahweh,
the God of your fathers, is giving you.*
Deuteronomy 4:1

The Israelite epic continues in the Promised Land, the land of Canaan. Canaan, by Moses' designation in the Book of Numbers, includes all the land that is now thought of as the Holy Land: from the Mediterranean Sea to and beyond the Jordan River, and from the slopes of Mount Hermon and the Golan Heights in the northeast to the Dead Sea in the south. The people of Canaan are a mixture of all who have passed along the Fertile Crescent in thousands of years past and found the land suitable for their crops or flocks. They are polytheists. They worship the gods brought from Mesopotamia, and to these some have added the gods of the Hittites and the Egyptians. They live within a number of small contending kingdoms, whose rulers maintain armies. These are the people, the territories, and the rulers whom the nomadic Israelite tribes must subdue.

ca. 1260 BCE

Battling the Canaanites

Led by Joshua, warriors among the tribes cross the Jordan River near the northern end of the Dead Sea and attack Jericho. Eventually Jericho falls, and for the next 200 years the twelve tribes of Israel fight

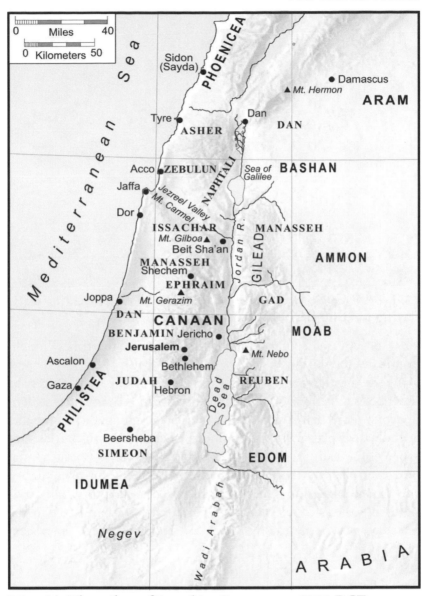

Map 14. The tribes of Israel in Canaan, ca. 1100 BCE.

to claim the portions of the land of Canaan that have been allotted to each. God has promised the Israelites that they shall rule over all the land "from Dan [in the far northeast] to Beersheba [in the Negev]." Three of the tribes (eventually four, when Dan migrates north) remain east of the Jordan River. Six are apportioned the northern and central part of Canaan (but after Dan leaves, five remain); and

ca. 1260- 1060 BCE

Photo 8. Excavations on the tell near Beit Sha'an, revealing walls dating to 1000 BCE; Mt. Gilboa in the distance.

three occupy the southern hills. The largest of the tribes, Judah, dominates the south.

The battles between the Israelites and the Canaanites, as described in the Book of Joshua, are bloody, and the Israelites seldom give quarter. What is depicted as a relentless conquest is probably a gradual displacement, sometimes punctuated with battles, but more often leading to a cultural blending. The southern coastal area controlled by the Philistines does not yield, nor does that of the Phoenicians on the coast north of Philistine territory. The lands bordering the Mediterranean Sea remain a festering threat to the Israelites, who settle mostly in the hill country east of the coastal plain.

Tribal Contention

Tribal judges preside over the various Hebrew settlements, and prophets attempt, often in vain, to keep the people loyal to their God *ca.* and to Mosaic law. But surrounded by Canaanites, and probably *1200-* intermarrying with them, many of the Israelites forget their heritage. *1050* In addition, the Israelite tribes are contentious. The northern tribes *BCE* refuse to cooperate with Judah, or even with each other. Not until the end of the eleventh century are the Israelite tribes sufficiently unified to face an enemy in concert.

Saul

Saul makes the first efforts toward unification, but he violates the rules of holy war by taking prisoners and booty. For this, the prophet Samuel tells him that God will spurn him. Saul leads the Israelites in *ca.* a fight against the Philistines for control of the strategic Jezreel Valley, *1050-* the routeway to the Mediterranean. The Philistines overwhelm his *1010* *BCE* troops, slay his sons in front of his eyes, then pierce him with arrows. Saul falls on his own sword. This occurs on Mount Gilboa, near the ancient (and modern) city of Beit Sha'an.

Deep in the diggings of the Beit Sha'an tell, I see the remnants of what probably is a Philistine wall, to which the victors fasten the bodies of Saul and his sons. From the tell, I can see Mount Gilboa rising above the valley to the northwest, a hilltop that any army would most assuredly need to control. I will come back to Beit Sha'an later in this narrative.

11
Kingdoms and Power

Wherever David went, Yahweh gave him victory. David ruled over all Israel, administering law and justice to all his people.
2 Samuel 8:14,15

As Saul is in the north trying to unify the Israelites, the Philistines go on the attack. They approach the southern hill country of Judea and threaten to overwhelm the Israelites there. The Israelites have reason to be afraid, for the Philistines are well-armed with forged weapons and hammered shields. David, the shepherd boy anointed by the prophet Samuel to be Saul's successor, confronts the giant Philistine warrior Goliath and slays him by using only a slingshot. The Philistines withdraw—for by agreement the match would determine the battle—and David's reputation is established.

ca. 1030 BCE

David

After Saul's death, David takes on the mantle of leadership. He wins victories both to the west against the Philistines on the coastal plain and to the east against the Ammonites and others on the plateau of Moab. He sends the Hittite soldier Uriah, husband of Bathsheba, whom he covets, to certain death in an assault on the walls of Rabbath Ammon. In Canaan, he defends and makes secure the territories of the Hebrew tribes. Under David, the Israelites are now unified for the first time since they enter Canaan.

ca. 1010- 970 BCE

For the capital of his hard-won kingdom, David chooses the ancient site of Jerusalem, a site that in previous generations has

96

served as the leading city of the Jebusites, one of the Canaanite tribes. Surrounded by forested slopes, David's chosen site lies on the salubrious, well-watered plateau that rises above the hot, humid, and fertile Jordan Valley. He builds a wall to enclose and protect his city. On the stones of a Jebusite foundation, David builds his palace. There he brings the Ark of the Covenant, containing the laws given by God to Moses in the Sinai.

In Jerusalem, I am shown the site of David's palace, which lies at the foot of Mount Zion, to the southwest of the Temple Mount. Archaeologists have established a layer of stones built on a bronze-age foundation that may be the base level of David's palace lying on a Jebusite foundation.

Solomon

Solomon, David's son and successor, brings power and wealth to the united kingdom. His territory encompasses all the land from north of Damascus to the Gulf of Aqaba, and from the Mediterranean Sea to the plateau of Moab and beyond, possibly to Mesopotamia. Wealthy from trade and the booty of conquest, Solomon builds a spectacular temple. He chooses as his site the high and flattened rise the Israelites know as Mount Moriah, the Mount of Sacrifice. Ever since Solomon builds his temple there, the site has been known to Jews (and later to Christians) as the Temple Mount. Solomon buys cedar from the mountains of Lebanon, secured through Phoenician-controlled Tyre, and he employs Phoenician craftsmen to carve it. Solomon's Temple follows prescribed measurements given by God to Moses in the Sinai. He builds the Holy of Holies at the highest point of the Temple Mount, over the traditional site of the Rock of Sacrifice, and there he enshrines the Ark of the Covenant. Solomon builds a protective wall to encompass his enlarged city. Tradition has it that Solomon is visited by the Queen of Sheba (probably present-day Yemen in southwestern Arabia or possibly Ethiopia). *ca. 970-930 BCE*

Divided Kingdoms

The unification of the Israelites ends with Solomon's death. To build his empire and his Temple, Solomon has required harsh labor

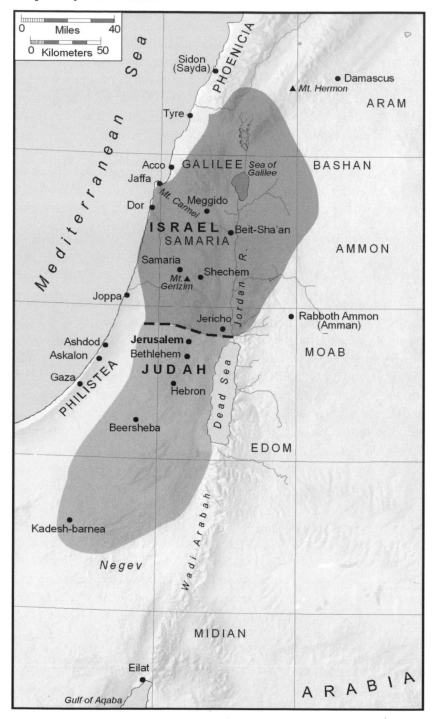

Map 15. The Northern and Southern kingdoms, ca. 800 BCE.

and heavy taxes from the people of his kingdom. When his son and *ca.* successor promises even harsher measures, the ten northern tribes *927-* revolt. There are now two kingdoms, one in the north and one in *721 BCE* the south.*

Not until the second century BCE will the Jews of Israel again be unified under one king, and then only for a hundred years. The southern kingdom known as Judah, from the name of its largest tribe, is the smaller and less fertile of the two. However, it contains Jerusalem, the focus of Hebrew consciousness. On the east, it reaches to the Jordan River (and sometimes beyond). On the south, it goes into the northern Negev Desert. On the west, where its hilly slopes descend, it is bordered by the Philistine-held coastal plain. The northern kingdom, called Israel, has a moist and verdant northern area where the waters coming off Mount Hermon pour out in springs that mingle and flow into the Sea of Galilee. It also has most of the fertile Jordan River lowlands, and a central hill and valley region that reaches to the sea in the long ridge known as Mount Carmel. The boundary between the two kingdoms runs just south of the dry and sparsely populated central hill country, later known as Samaria.

For the next two centuries, a series of kings rule in the two kingdoms. Often the kingdoms are at war with bordering peoples, and sometimes with each other. Kings and people alike are often profligate and are as likely as not to take up with the gods of the peoples against whom they do battle and with whom they sometimes intermarry. Prophets move among the kingdoms, foretelling their doom and the destruction of Solomon's Temple. This is the period

---

*How do the Twelve Tribes, and later the Ten Lost Tribes, come to be numbered? Jacob has twelve sons, whose descendents, formed into separate tribes, return from Egypt to settle in Canaan. The descendents of Levi are to be priests and thus are not to be allotted land. The descendents of the sons of Joseph—Ephraim and Manasseh—are given status as separate tribes eligible for separate territorial allotments. Of the twelve tribes who gain territory in Canaan, nine are in the north and three—Judah, Benjamin, and Simeon—are in the south. Simeon's tribe receives no land of its own but is given the desert portion of Judah's allotment. When the tribes, united under David and Solomon, split to form two kingdoms after the death of Solomon (ca 927 BCE), Judah and Benjamin are the two tribes named as comprising the southern kingdom, hereafter named Judah. By this time, Simeon as a tribal entity has disappeared. In 721 BCE, the Assyrians conquer and disperse the nine northern tribes. Together with the tribe of Simeon, they become known in history as the Ten Lost Tribes.

of the prophets Amos, Hosea, Elijah and Elisha, Isaiah, Jeremiah, Micah, and Nathan. On Mount Carmel, the forested ridge that extends from the hills of Samaria westward to the Mediterranean, Elijah demonstrates that the One God has power and Baal, the god of the Canaanites, is powerless. But still the Israelites are faithless more often than faithful.

12
In the Wake of Empires

*In the nineteenth year of Nebuchadnezzar king of Babylon,
Nebuzaradan…an officer of the king
…entered Jerusalem. He burned down the Temple of
Yahweh, the royal palace and all the houses in Jerusalem…
[He] deported the…population [except for] some of
the humbler country peoples…"*
2 Kings 25:9-12

hat about the Canaanites, the indigenous people who lose the battles fought for the Promised Land? The Canaanites, who leave no written record, are partially wiped out by the advancing Israelite tribes. Cultural intermixing is attested to by the prophets' continual tirades against the Israelites for taking up with the gods of the Canaanites. The archaeological record suggests that some of the defeated Canaanites flee to the coastal plain, intermarry with the Philistines, and in 721 BCE are taken captive by *721 BCE* the Assyrians. After this, the Canaanites, along with the Philistines, disappear from the stage of history. The Phoenicians on the coast likewise yield to the Assyrians, but by this time the focus of Phoenician power has shifted westward to Carthage, Sicily, and Spain.

The Lost Tribes and the Samaritans

The conquest of the Assyrians dooms the northern tribes that form the kingdom of Israel. It is their misfortune to occupy coveted lands on *ca. 721-597 BCE* the trade route between Egypt and Mesopotamia. The Assyrian invaders torch their cities and carry off many of their people into slavery, dispersing

101

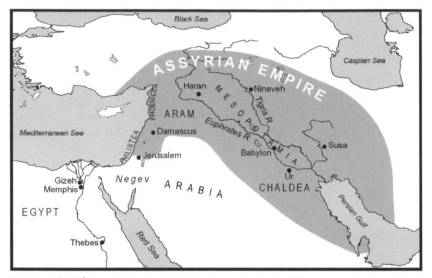

Map 16. The Assyrian Empire, ca. 700 BCE.

them eastward among the far-flung settlements of the Assyrian Empire. Those who survive in their lands of exile eventually blend in to their new surroundings, and history hears no more of the so-called *Lost Tribes*. In their homelands, the Assyrians replace the conquered Israelites with peoples conquered elsewhere. The newcomers bring their own gods, but they also make an effort to worship the God of the Israelites who are left behind and with whom they intermarry. From the new blend of peoples and religions, a separate group evolves in the hilly lands of central Palestine, a group called the Samaritans. The Judeans never accept the Samaritans as legitimate. They dispute their understanding of Mosaic law, and they denigrate the separate Temple the Samaritans build on Mount Gerizim near ancient Shechem. (Today the land of the Samaritans comprises the bulk of the West Bank, with jurisdiction divided between Israel and the Palestinian Authority.)

The Babylonian Captivity

Judah, less strategically located than Israel, manages to strike a bargain with Assyria and for the next hundred and fifty years becomes a vassal state. But by the beginning of the sixth century, the Chaldeans, whose chief city is Babylon in Mesopotamia, have conquered the Assyrians, and in 597 they conquer Jerusalem. They deport thousands of Judeans to Babylon, on the banks of the Euphrates River. They are

597-586 BCE

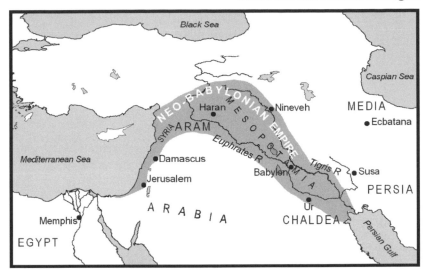

Map 17. The Neo-Babylonian (Chaldean) Empire, ca. 580 BCE.

selective, however. They take only the professionals, priests, craftsmen, and the wealthy.

In 586 the Chaldeans return to Jerusalem, raze the city, and destroy Solomon's Temple, as the Prophets had predicted. They carry off all the remaining residents of Jerusalem to captivity, leaving only country folk to till the soil. The Book of Jeremiah, written in Jerusalem at this time, chronicles the misery of those left behind, with Temple destroyed and countryside a wasteland.

To escape exile, some of the Judeans flee into Egypt, both to upper Egypt and to the area that later becomes Alexandria. The people of Judah are now split into three groups: those in Babylonian exile, who are literate and leave a record; those who flee to Egypt and probably never return; and those left behind in Judea, the farmers and herdsmen who must face famine and desolation. It is thought that Jeremiah dies in Egypt.

In Babylon the exiles weep. They realize now how precious is their heritage. Unlike the scattered northern exiles, the Judeans in the Babylonian Captivity stay together and draw strength from each other. Exile strengthens them in their worship of God. Over and over again, they retell the legends of their past, and the priests and scribes labor to pull together a written record. Although the earliest writer of Psalms – devotional poems meant to be sung – is David, it is clear that some of the Psalms are set four hundred years later in the period of exile. Most scholars now think that the Psalms known as the exilic and post-exilic Psalms are actually poetic evocations written as late as the third century BCE. The Books of Daniel and Esther are likewise set in the period of exile but are probably not composed until the mid-second century. For Jews, the exile is a watershed experience.

The Persian Empire

The Babylonian Captivity lasts some fifty years. The Persians defeat the Chaldeans, and the next year the enlightened Persian ruler, *ca. 539-330 BCE* Cyrus – in awe of the powerful god of the Judeans whose believers display a tenacious hold on their faith even in captivity – wishes himself to gain favor with this god. He commands the Jews not only to return to Judah but also to rebuild their temple in Jerusalem.

Not all of the exiles wish to return, however. The defeated Chaldean Empire extends eastward to the Indus and north to encompass the territory gained from the Assyrians. The Persians not only take over all this territory but also proceed to enlarge it, building the most powerful and best-administered Empire the world has yet known. Many of the Jews in exile, seeing opportunity, scatter throughout this vast Empire, living in cities and towns and becoming merchants and administrators. They fare well. But they do not forget their heritage or lose their identity. After 1948, many Jews in Iran and almost the entire Jewish community in Iraq depart for Israel (Chart 4), and the once thriving Jewish communities that could be traced to the period of the Babylon Captivity have now disappeared. Even today throughout the vast area of Asia where the Persian Empire once held sway there are still a waning number of people who may no longer practice Judaism but are aware of their Jewish heritage.

In Beit Sha'an, I talk with a cab driver who came to Israel as a boy when his family left Baghdad. He knows Arabic as fluently as Hebrew. On the Silk Road in China, I learn of Jewish traders who for a thousand years and more were a link between China and the cities of the Middle East. In China I learn also of the ancient capital city of Kaifeng, where Jews established a thriving merchant community, traces of which lasted until the coming of the Mao regime.

Most of the Jewish community in Egypt, like that in Babylon, does not return, forming part of a growing Jewish presence both in

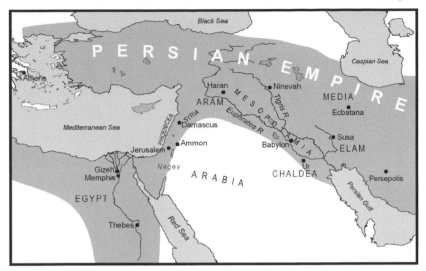

Map 18. The Persian Empire, ca. 450 BCE.

upper Egypt and the cities of the Delta. Later, this community plays a prominent role in Alexandria, the city founded by Alexander the Great.

My visit to Israel coincides with the two-day Feast of Purim, celebrated by Jews all over the world in memory of the Jewish Queen Esther, whose story is told in the Book of Esther, written in the second century. As the favorite of a Persian ruler in Susa (the new capital of the Empire), Esther is able to save her people from the cunning and wicked Persian minister Haman. From this story, we realize that although the Jews settle in diverse communities throughout the Babylonian/Persian realm, they remain a separate people. In Israel, the celebration of Purim resembles a combination of Christmas (the giving of presents) and Mardi Gras (masked costumed revelers dancing in the streets and lavish private parties). Purim is especially fun for Israeli children, who get to dress in costume. I remember an ultra-Orthodox father in a long black coat smiling indulgently at his two costumed children as they wait to join in the dancing.

Return of the Exiles

Ordered to return home by Cyrus, a portion of the exiles begins to filter back in 538. They settle in Jerusalem or elsewhere in Judea, *538 BCE*

105

Photo 9. Celebrating the Purim Festival in Jerusalem.

and some make new homes in the northern territory that later comes to be known as Galilee. But they want little to do with the dry central hill country of the Samaritans, for they consider the Samaritans tainted.

The period of captivity has a linguistic effect: In Babylon and Persia the Israelites learn to speak and write Aramaic, the trade language used within the Persian Empire. They bring back Aramaic as a common tongue, and gradually Hebrew becomes only a liturgical language. Aramaic, like Hebrew, is a Semitic language but with significant differences from Hebrew, so that the two languages are not mutually understood.

Temple and Torah

In Jerusalem, now part of the Persian Empire, the returned Judeans rebuild the Temple. Although short of both manpower and funds, they erect a temple far more modest than the one that the Babylonians destroyed. The task of building the Second Temple is finished by the year 515. To help the returned exiles remember their heritage and to reinforce the role of the priesthood, Jewish priests and scribes codify the partly oral, partly written traditions in the Torah, the first five books of the Jewish Scriptures (Genesis, Exodus, Leviticus, Numbers,

515 BCE

Deuteronomy). Ever since, this written record has enabled Jews to retain their identity, regardless of where displacements have set them down.

Is it possible that the people of the Ten Lost Tribes would have retained their identity had they also had access to a written record? Surely it has been the threat of assimilation that has given an urgency to the work of Jewish scholars through the centuries and has spurred Jewish families to be faithful in their observance of Jewish rites and traditions.

In addition to the Torah, the compilations of the sixth, fifth, and fourth century BCE scribes include the poetry of David and other psalmists, the wise sayings ascribed to Solomon, the teachings of the prophets, and the record of activities before and after the Babylonian Captivity. As a group, these writings are assembled as the Hebrew Bible. Much later, when early Christian scholars consider the authenticity of the books that become the Christian Bible, the writings of the Hebrew Bible are accepted as the Old Testament.

Jews and Christians alike have spent millions of hours and billions of words trying to understand, piece together, ascribe, and decode the writings of the Old Testament. Among practicing Jews there can be no more honored profession than that of the Torah scholar.

In Jerusalem, unlike in Tel Aviv, I see hundreds of men and boys with sallow faces, side curls, black hats, and black overcoats, who are members of the ultra-Orthodox segment of Jewish society known as the Haredim. The men devote their entire adult life to the study of Scripture and Scripture commentaries. Their observance of Deuteronomic law is strict to the letter. They are the most numerous among those praying at the Western Wall just inside Jerusalem's Old City. Following ancient custom of memorizing or praying with the whole body, they sway back and forth as they read their prayers, bewailing the fate of their twice-destroyed Temple. They refuse army service but do alternative service. They are an extremely conservative political minority, and in the Knesset, Israel's parliament, they influence the far-right groups that hold the swing vote, which means no political party can rule without their consent. It is the Haredi vote that has succeeded in halting all bus traffic throughout Israel between sundown Friday and sundown Saturday. Most Israelis, who tend to be either less-religious or totally secular, would like to see the Haredim disappear. But they will not, and they are growing relatively more numerous because their birthrate is high.

Photo 10. Haredim praying at the Western Wall.

I befriend an Israeli teacher named Esther. She is distraught, having just come from a meeting with her 18-year-old daughter. The daughter has committed herself to ultra-Orthodox teachings, is studying in an ultra-Orthodox school for females, and is doing alternative military service by working in a school for autistic children. Someday she fully expects to be the wife of a Haredi scholar. My friend knows what that will mean: Her daughter will have as many children as God provides; meanwhile, she will have to work to support the family while her husband carries on his scholar's studies. She knows that the government provides partial support for Haredi families, but she knows too that many Israelis see the Haredim as parasites because of this. Her daughter will be forever marginalized, forever harried. (I am reminded of "Fiddler on the Roof" set in czarist Russia in an ultra-Orthodox village.) Esther is an observant Jew; her husband wears a skullcap, known as a yarmulke. When I am in their car driving between Beit Sha'an and Jerusalem, he offers a prayer aloud for our safe journey. But neither of them is in sympathy with the Haredim.

Israel under Persian Rule

The two centuries of Persian rule in Palestine are largely benign, and the Jews prosper. But they live among polytheistic peoples, and some intermarry with them, diluting faith and tradition. The Persian rulers take great interest in the religions of their subjects. In the middle of the fifth century the Persian king details two of the Judeans in his service, *ca* Ezra and Nehemiah, to go to Jerusalem, and to spur the Judeans there *440 BCE* to strengthen the walls of their city. They do this successfully, but Ezra finds other flaws that need strengthening, especially laxity in religious observance. He rails against the Judeans who have intermarried with non-believers, forbids further intermarriage, and tugs the community toward strict observance of the Torah. The accounts of his efforts (in the Books of Ezra and Nehemiah) make it clear that the essential features of Judaism, born of reflections during the Babylonian Captivity and the subsequent compilations of the scribes, date from this post-exilic period. In general, this is a period of strong personal piety and strict corporate worship. The Jewish community has the Torah, and Judaism has come of age. The Jews engage in trade and crafts in addition to farming. Using Aramaic, they put aside as archaic the Hebrew tongue in which the scribes are writing. By the fourth century BCE, the Torah is available in Aramaic translation.

During the Babylonian Captivity the term *Judeans* (from which the term *Jews* evolves) is used to designate the captives from conquered Judea. Eventually, on their return, the term is applied by the new Persian rulers to all of the Israelites who live in Judea, Samaria, or Galilee. As for the Judeans themselves, they soon cast off the designation *Hebrews* or *Israelites*, and tend instead to refer to themselves by the region in which they settle, as Judeans or Galileans (few of the returning exiles settle in Samaria).

13
Greeks and Romans

*I do not separate people, as do the narrow-minded, into
Greeks and barbarians.
I am not interested in the origin
or race of citizens.
I only distinguish them
on the basis of their virtue.*
Alexander the Great

*On the west side of the Dead Sea,
but out of range of the noxious exhalations of the coast,
is the solitary tribe of the Essenes.*
Pliny the Elder
Natural History

The Persian Empire comes to an end in the fourth century when Alexander the Macedonian defeats the Persians and establishes a new world order – that of Greek, or Hellenic, culture. In 332, Alexander's armies march *332-* through Palestine on their way to Egypt, putting an end to *323* Persian rule there. He returns through Palestine, stopping *BCE* neither to destroy or pillage, because he is in a hurry to defeat the Persians on their home territory. This he does, then makes his way eastward as far as the Indus River, leaving behind him a string of cities named in his honor and legends of his prowess that surface in far places of central Asia to this day. Alexander returns to Persia and contracts a deadly fever. He is only thirty three when he dies.

110

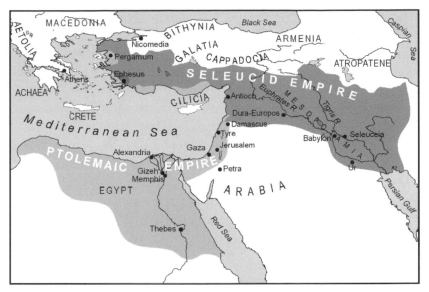

**Map 19. The successors of Alexander the Great, the Ptolemaic
and Seleucid Empires, ca. 250 BCE.**

The Legacy of Alexander

Upon Alexander's death in Mesopotamia in 323, his vast
Empire – including the Jewish homeland – is divided among his
generals. In this way, the Jews come under Greek rule, first of the
Ptolemys from Egypt and later of the Seleucids from Syria. Colonies
of Greek settlements appear, and many Jews living among them adopt
Greek names and Greek ways. The Greeks settle returned soldiers
in their colonies, and the soldiers crave Greek products and Greek
entertainment.

A number of Greek trading towns occupy the trade routes from
Damascus southward toward the Nabatean capital at Petra and from
the Jordan Valley westward to the sea. Most of these Greek towns
are east of the Jordan River. The most prominent among them is
Philadelphia, now Amman, named for a Ptolemaic ruler. Under the
Greeks, Beit Sha'an, the city guarding the Jezreel Valley, comes to be
known as Scythopolis, after the Scythian mercenaries who have settled
there. This is the beginning of the semi-self-governing league of cities
that is later to be known collectively as the Decapolis. The Decapolis
cities are Greek; most of the Jews who live there are hellenized.
They provide the skilled labor, such as carpentry, weaving, and glass

111

making, to build and furnish the Greek cities. Not a Decapolis city, but notable for its sophistication, is the Hellenic Jewish city north of Nazareth known as Sepphoris. Elsewhere in Judea and Galilee, the less-educated Jews resist Greek culture and remain as pastoralists and farmers.

Most educated Jews are literate in Greek in addition to Aramaic and a smattering of liturgical Hebrew. As Jews become hellenized, some also become secularized. To counter this, priests and scholars work to preserve the forms of traditional Hebrew worship. At the far end of the spectrum, reform groups arise, and their members live apart from the Jews of the cities or the Temple in reaction to what they feel is a departure from Mosaic Law. In the caves of the northern Negev Desert, their scribes record their activities on vellum and transcribe copies of the Torah.

The Essenes and the Dead Sea Scrolls

ca.
150
BCE
Sometime in the second century BCE, a group of Jewish puritans called the Essenes, who have withdrawn from society to observe strictly the laws of the Torah, decides to secure their scrolls in large clay jars deep within the cave they use for meetings. More than two thousand years later, in the caves of Qumran, an illiterate Bedouin boy finds scrolls of parchment in clay jars. The year is 1948. He takes them to his father, who fortunately decides to sell them instead of using them to start a fire. In this way, scholars eventually acquire the first of a trove of Dead Sea Scrolls that are subsequently found in a number of caves near Qumran, fronting the northwestern shore of the Dead Sea.

In forty years of carefully piecing together fragments of the Dead Sea Scrolls, scholars have learned much about Judaism and the life of Jewish people a century or so before the birth of Christ.

I spend some time in the impressive Museum of the Scrolls in Jerusalem learning about the Essenes and seeing actual fragments of the scrolls. Understandably, the most precious scroll, an almost intact transcription of the Book of Isaiah, can be viewed only as a copy. Both Jewish and Christian scholars continue their search for ancient manuscripts, for the canon of both the Hebrew Scriptures and the Old and New Testaments is based only on copies of copies, and on translated versions at that. Thus, the Dead Sea Scrolls are a world treasure. One only wonders how many manuscripts of the past have been used to start fires.

The Maccabees

By the second century BCE, the Ptolemys have been superseded in Palestine by the Seleucids, who rule from Syria to the north. A harsh Seleucid ruler desecrates the Temple and tries to force the *167-* Jews to abandon their form of worship. The Jews revolt in 167. They *63* are led by the five sons of the High Priest, from a family known *BCE* as the Hasmoneans. The brothers, fierce and disciplined in their revolt, become known as the Maccabees (meaning *hammers*). The Maccabeean revolt and the century of strife-torn self-rule that follows produce one great ruler, Judas Maccabeus, and a series of ineffectual ones, all Jewish priests with Greek names. This period is known as the Hasmonean Kingdom. In this period, numbers of Jews move into the fertile northern region known as Galilee.

Once belonging to the Canaanites, then wrested away by the Hebrews, Galilee falls to the Assyrians in the eighth century BCE, subsequently to the Persians, and is first ravaged then neglected under the Seleucid Greeks. By the beginning of the first century BCE, Galilee, under Hasmonean protection, again has a strongly Jewish population. Later, the region of Galilee figures prominently both in the Christian Gospels as the site of Jesus' ministry and as a refuge for Jews who are banished by the Romans from Jerusalem after 70 CE.

The Septuagint and the Apocrypha

The record of the Jews in the years after the return from captivity in Babylon is sketchy. It is told, in part, in writings known collectively as The Apocrypha. The Apocryphal books first appear *ca.* in the Septuagint, the Greek translation from the Hebrew ordered by *200-* Ptolemy and supposedly completed in Alexandria by seventy Jewish *50* scholars. A date of around 200 BCE can be given for the Septuagint, *BCE* with many subsequent additions and revisions during the following century and a half. The Books of Maccabees, which tell the story of the Jewish revolt from Seleucid rule and the subsequent century of Jewish rule, are a part of the Apocrypha, but they are obviously written

113

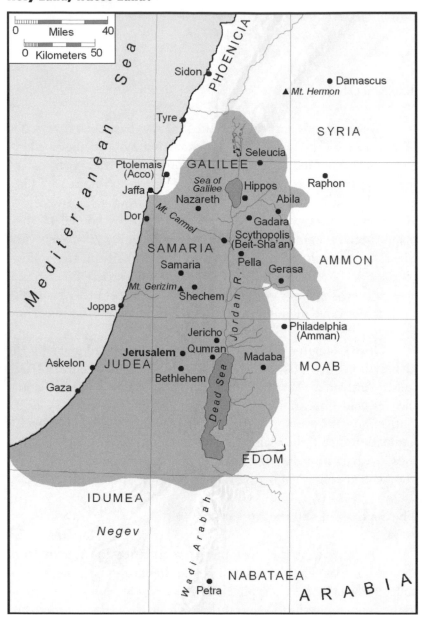

Map 20. The Hasmonean Kingdom, ca. 100 BCE.

much later than the original commissioned Septuagint translation. Jewish scholars are united concerning the Apocryphal writings. They accept them as valuable historical documents but without canonical status. Most of the Apocrypha appears in the Catholic Biblical canon, but Protestants (other than Anglicans) generally reject its canonical status on grounds that the Apocryphal books are not a part of the original Hebrew Scriptures. Part of the Old Testament canon or not, the Apocryphal writings are valuable for what they tell of the 400-year period before Roman rule begins. They reflect the struggle of the Jewish people to maintain their faith and way of life under foreign rule and in the face of alien Persian and Hellenic cultures.

The Beginning of Roman Rule: Herod the Great

The legions of the Roman general Pompey have no trouble conquering the Hasmoneans, whose political uses of strict Torah observances (for example, circumcision ordered for all males under their jurisdiction) have alienated not only the Greeks of Palestine but many Jews also. In 63 BCE Pompey declares Palestine a Roman province and attaches it loosely to Syria, the remnant of the Seleucid Empire, which Rome has already conquered. *15 BCE*

The story goes that when Pompey reaches Jerusalem's Temple Mount, with great curiosity he bursts through the Inner Sanctum into the Holy of Holies. He finds nothing, no statues, no images. How can he hope to understand the Judeans, who worship a god they cannot see? He decides to let the Judeans handle their own religious affairs.

Pompey is willing to be flexible, so long as Rome's primacy is maintained. For example, he gives the Decapolis trade cities limited autonomy, including the right to coin money. He lets the Jews maintain the fiction that their kingdom still lives. Herod, a prosperous Jew from the northern Negev province of Idumea (a Greek name derived from the ancient Edom), ingratiates himself with Rome, and Pompey taps him for the monarchy. Herod has little reverence for Hebrew tradition; his family's conversion by the Hasmoneans had been forced. Ruling with absolute authority, King Herod sets about to impress the Romans. With the tribute he exacts from the Jews under his authority, he embarks on a huge building spree: he builds the Roman capital and port of Caesarea, provides it with an aqueduct, builds a network of roads, theaters, baths. The Romans are indeed impressed, and they reward him with the title Herod the Great.

Herod turns his attention to the Temple, a sorry affair by Roman standards. By the year 15 BCE Herod completes the enlargement and refurbishment of the Temple, which is now grander than it has ever been at any time in its past. He levels thirty-five acres for the platform of the temple, and buttresses the platform with strong stone foundations. The plan of the temple dates back to Solomon, and the Holy of Holies as always is over the presumed Rock of Sacrifice. There is a large exterior Court of the Gentiles (for non-Jews who wish to do business on temple grounds). Only Jewish males are allowed within the inner court of the Temple proper. Only priests can approach the inner sanctum, where sacrifices are made. And only the High Priest can enter the Holy of Holies. The religious hierarchy keeps order in its sphere, as King Herod does in his. Rome is reasonably satisfied. At any hint of disorder, there is the certainty of Roman punishment.

ca.
6-4
BCE
Herod dies in 6 or 4 BCE (the record is contradictory); thereafter, the Romans rule Samaria and Judea directly, leaving Herod's line to rule for the next several decades in Galilee and the Trans-Jordan province of Perea. (Perea includes the Jordan Valley and adjacent eastern slopes from about Pella southward to the Dead Sea.) It is under the rule of Herod's son, Herod Antipas, that most of the events of Jesus' life take place. Rome appoints a series of legates to rule over the remainder of Palestine, including the seacoast, the hills of Samaria, and most especially Judea with its city of Jerusalem. In the Decapolis cities and the Hellenized Jewish cities Roman rule is welcome; Roman administrators are well-educated: they speak Greek as well as Latin, enjoy Greek entertainment, and treat their provinces fairly rather than capriciously, as had been the case under Herod.

By 25 CE the name of the Roman legate is Pontius Pilate, who governs from his capital at Caesarea, coming to Jerusalem only at seasons when the Judeans gather for their religious festivals. Rome expects its legates to keep order. And when the city is crowded, and emotions run high, there is always the prospect of trouble.

14
Sources and Evidence

*...I am Cyrus, King of the world. When I entered
Babylon...I did not allow anyone to terrorize the land...I
kept in view the needs of the people and all its sanctuaries
to promote their well-being...
I put an end to their misfortune.*
Cuneiform inscription
*Clay cylinder discovered in 1879,
now in The British Museum*

After 63 BCE, the history of Palestine becomes a little less conjecture and a little more corroborated by written accounts, and somewhat easier to trace through coins and other archaeological finds. However, for the years before Rome, there are certain known dates around which Biblical accounts, based almost entirely on oral tradition, can be pinned.

Corroboration and Discrepancies

We know with precision the dates of Egyptian dynasties and the periods of rule by the Assyrian, Chaldean, and Persian Empires, the Ptolemys, the Seleucids, and the Hasmoneans. Although the Bible (the Hebrew Bible and the New Testament) records events that occur in time and place, it is not primarily a work of history, but rather an account of the relationship of humans to God under historic circumstances. Imprecision and contradiction become apparent when its various writers are compared, or when named rulers or dates fail to concur with known history. Archaeologists

117

hoping to find corroborative evidence for the Biblical narrative have been digging in Palestine for two hundred years, and they are slowly piecing together the past. There is a good deal of corroboration when it comes to place names but precious little regarding persons.

However, there are also frustrating discrepancies between the Biblical accounts and the archaeological record. Careful digging in the 10,000-year-old site of Jericho, for example, has thus far yielded no evidence of the battle fought by Joshua when the Israelites first entered the Promised Land. There is likewise no clear-cut archaeological evidence of the kingdoms of David and Solomon.

The dig that could yield evidence can never be done, for the site of Solomon's Temple is now occupied by Islam's sacred Dome of the Rock. In recent years, Palestinians in charge of the Haram al-Sharif have been removing material from under the Dome and depositing it in a quarry outside the city. Israelis suspect that the diggers are deliberately trying to destroy any evidence that might eventually give Jews a legitimate historical claim to Jerusalem. Israelis have attempted to tunnel under the Dome, but they have been stopped by Palestinians, who claim that their efforts not only trespass but also physically undermine the stability of the Dome.

Evidence of the Roman period of rule is widespread in the Holy Land, but most Roman ruins date from the high period of Roman construction after 100 CE, not from the time of Christ. Thus, they give no definitive record of the appearance of the Holy Land at the time of the Gospel accounts. Even Jerusalem is almost totally rebuilt early in the second century.

It is not likely that the politically unimportant people who accompany Jesus would have left inscriptions. And Torah prohibition against engraved images means that there are no Jewish gravestones or monuments from this early period from which archaeologists could assemble a historic record. However, on a stone plaque unearthed in Caesarea, the port city that Herod builds for the Romans as their capital and names after the emperor, I see a commemorative stone plaque on which is clearly inscribed in Latin the name of the Roman legate Pilatus.

That Jesus actually lived and taught in Palestine has strong place-name corroboration and is also mentioned in the accounts of the

Jewish/Roman historian Josephus, who writes in the seventh decade of the first century. I will speak more of Josephus in a later chapter.

The Gospel Record

The first four books of the New Testament, known as the Gospels, are the chief source for what we know of the life of Jesus. From the Gospels, we learn that a Jewish Galilean named Jesus is born in Bethlehem, grows up in Nazareth, teaches chiefly in Galilee in a ministry lasting only three years, gathers followers who believe him to be the Messiah (Redeemer) promised in the Jewish Scriptures, travels on occasion to Jerusalem to attend festivals, falls afoul of the religious leaders there, is condemned to a criminal's death, rises again, and ascends into heaven. The Gospels are called Matthew, Mark, Luke, and John, but none of the Gospels names its author. These names come to us via tradition and inference.

There is little doubt that all of the Gospel writers are Jewish, but they write in Greek. The name Christ, or *Christos,* is the Greek word for Messiah, and soon the Messianists are beginning to be called *Christians,* at first a derogatory term. By the time the gospels appear, word of Jesus' teachings has spread far beyond the Jewish community in Judea to Jews and others in the wider world, especially of the eastern (Greek-speaking) Roman empire. By tradition, Matthew and John are Jesus' disciples, and Mark and Luke are the same as the Mark and Luke named in the Book of Acts (properly, Acts of the Apostles), which has been placed after the Gospels in the New Testament canon and records the happenings within the new Christian community in the months and years following Jesus' departure. But of the Gospel writers, collectively known as the Four Evangelists, only John gives internal evidence that he has first-person knowledge of Jesus. All the Gospel authors write some decades after the Ascension, at a time when it is becoming apparent that the events of the life of Christ must be set down in a systematic fashion, among other reasons to avoid controversy occasioned by contradictory hearsay. Internal evidence indicates that they have access to collections of Jesus' sayings that have been written down from oral tradition, but these primary sources are now lost.

Matthew gives the longest, most complete account of Jesus' life and teachings. He takes pains to present Jesus as God's fulfillment of

Hebrew Bible prophecies, as the promised Messiah or Savior. Probably he writes while living in a Jewish community (some scholars suggest Antioch) outside Palestine. As a Jew, Matthew would have spoken Aramaic, but he writes in labored Greek. He has access to the Gospel of Mark, as well as to a source that is inferred but has disappeared. The Gospel of Matthew is written sometime between 80 and 90 CE.

Mark, by tradition (uncorroborated by modern scholarship), is the son of a woman from Jerusalem named Mary, at whose house the earliest Christians meet. Thus, he may have been an early believer but not one of the twelve disciples. If so, he may well have taken his account from first-person sources. Tradition places him among the Seventy whom Jesus commissions to spread his gospel. There is a John Mark who accompanies Paul on many of his travels and is with Peter in Rome. But Mark is a common name in the Roman Empire, and the two Marks may be separate individuals. Mark writes his Gospel in Greek from somewhere outside Palestine (his knowledge of Palestinian geography is faulty) to an audience that is probably not Jewish. His Greek is neither polished nor literary, but straightforward. It is not his mother tongue. Most scholars think that the Gospel of Mark was the first to be written, probably around 64 CE.

Little is known about the author of the Gospel of Luke. There is a tradition that Luke is a physician, but scholars now dispute this. It is clear that the author of Luke is an educated man and writes fluently in Greek. He knows the Septuagint. He also knows the Gospel of Mark, which he uses as a source. He probably uses other written sources now lost, for his Gospel contains a good deal of material not found in either Matthew or Mark. Like Mark, he too may have spoken with first-person witnesses. Luke the Evangelist is undoubtedly the author of the Acts of the Apostles. But the author of the Gospel of Luke and the Acts of the Apostles may or may not have been the Luke who was with Paul during his two years of imprisonment in Caesarea, from 58 to 60 CE. His narrative of the Book of Acts ends with Paul's imprisonment in Rome. Most scholars date the Gospel of Luke and the Book of Acts sometime between 80 and 85 CE and agree that they are a single two-part narrative. Because of their sources and their similarities, the Gospels of Matthew, Mark, and Luke are known as the Synoptic Gospels.

The Gospel of John is quite different from the other three. It gives the fullest account of Jesus' trial, crucifixion, and resurrection, but it lacks the familiar parables of the other three Gospels. John writes as a Jew to Jewish Christian communities. It is not certain that John is familiar with the other three Gospels, and he may have used an entirely different source. The Gospel of John cannot be dated with precision, but tradition places it near the beginning of the second century. Probably the version that has come down to us is completed at that time, although the self-described "beloved disciple," who is with Christ during his ministry, may have narrated or recorded his account much earlier. John the beloved disciple is an untutored fisherman and probably speaks Greek as well as Aramaic, but he is not a man of letters. John the Evangelist writes in fluent Greek. For this reason, many scholars think that late in the first century an unnamed scribe edits the version of the Gospel of John that becomes part of the New Testament canon. The writer of the Gospel of John is probably also the author of the three letters (1 John, 2 John, and 3 John) that are part of the New Testament canon, but he is not the writer of the Book of Revelation. There are two contradicting traditions concerning John's later years. By one tradition, he is an early martyr. By the other, he becomes the leader of a Christian community in Ephesus in Asia Minor where he brings Mary, the mother of Jesus. By this tradition, both John and Mary die of old age.

The house where Mary supposedly lives is preserved to this day on the outskirts of Ephesus. It is one of the places I visit when in Turkey some years ago. I view the site with a great deal of skepticism, for it is substantial and does not appear to be of sufficient age to be authentic. But I do not at the time (and do not now) doubt the possibility that in their latter years John and Mary could have lived in Ephesus.

15
Jesus Christ

*Now there was about this time Jesus, a wise man, if it be lawful to call him a man; for he was a doer of wonderful works...He drew over to him both many of the Jews and many of the Gentiles. He was [the] Christ...
And the tribe of Christians, so named from him, are not extinct at this day.*
Flavius Josephus
Antiquities of the Jews, Book 18, Chapter 3

The people that walked in darkness have seen a great light; on those who live in a land of deep shadow a light has shown...For there is a child born for us, a son given to us, and dominion is laid on his shoulders.
Isaiah 9:1,6

The Four Evangelists are familiar with the Hebrew Scriptures, and they assume their readers are also. They make frequent reference to the Prophets of old, particularly Isaiah, who in the eighth century BCE foretells the coming of a messiah, a savior for the Jewish people. Isaiah's prophesies resonate in Roman Palestine no less than under the rule of the Assyrians and subsequent conquerors. The Jews look for a messiah who will lift their yoke.

Matthew, Mark, Luke, and John present Jesus Christ (*Jesus* is the Greek form of *Joshua*, a Hebrew name meaning *savior*) as the fulfillment of Old Testament prophecy, but not as the militant savior in the tradition of King David for which the Jewish community has longed. Jesus is presented as the Son of God, as preacher and healer, as redeemer through the ultimate sacrifice, as one resurrected from death to life, and as ascended Lord who bids his followers to spread the Good News. During Jesus' brief three-year public ministry, some of the Jews who meet him or learn of him come to believe that he is indeed the Messiah. Others reject him as an imposter and insist that their messiah has yet to come. From the nucleus of Jewish believers, termed Messianists, the movement later to be called Christianity is born.

In the Gospel accounts, details of time and place are often of less importance than events and their significance. Nevertheless, from comparing the four Gospels, it is possible to piece together a chronology and tie it to places where events occurred.

Birth

In the Gospel account, fulfillment of prophecy begins with the visit of the angel Gabriel to Mary, a virgin engaged to Joseph, a carpenter. Mary learns that she will conceive and bear a son who will save his people. Both she and Joseph can trace their lineage to King David, and the prophets have said that a Messiah will come from the house of David.

In Nazareth, I visit the Church of the Annunciation, purporting to be on the site where Mary learns from the angel Gabriel that she is to become the mother of Jesus. The Church, a site overseen by Franciscans, contains recently installed modern murals from all over the world depicting the Annunciation.

According to the Gospel of Luke, Jesus of Nazareth is born while Herod is still king, so the actual date of his birth may be anytime between 7 and 4. Mary and Joseph travel to Bethlehem in Judea *ca.* (Joseph's birthplace) to be counted in the imperial census ordered *7-4* by Caesar Augustus. The town is crowded, and the only quarters the *BCE* couple can find are in a stable, probably located within a cave. There Jesus is born.

My visit to Bethlehem (Photo 2) is one day after the Pope's visit, and Bethlehem is teeming with young people from all over the world—especially young Roman Catholics—who have come to hear a Mass the Pope will give on the Mount of the Beatitudes in Galilee the following day. Today is their day to see Bethlehem. The lines to the Church of the Nativity are long and slow moving, and the young pilgrims while away the time by singing folk songs in scores of languages and joining in folk dances. Eventually, I abandon the attempt to get into the Church of the Nativity, which is overseen by Orthodox groups, and go instead to an adjacent and fairly recently constructed Franciscan church, where the Roman rite is broadcast around the world every year on Christmas Eve. Below this church are grottos, and here I can get an idea of the stable quarters that the Holy Family occupied. Stables, I learn, were often situated in caves; hence, the site is probably much closer to the original in feel than the embellished site at the nearby Church of the Nativity.

Learning that a young child, to whom wise men "from the East" come to pay tribute, may someday be a threat to his rule, Herod orders the execution of all males in his kingdom under the age of two. Forewarned in a dream, Joseph takes his family into Egypt, where they live for an indeterminate period, certainly until after Herod dies.

Early Years

Jesus grows up in his family's home in Nazareth, in the northern province of Galilee. Probably his family's roots in Galilee are not deep, for Joseph was born far to the south in Bethlehem. Both Mary and Joseph are Judeans, now resettled in the north.

Luke records that when Jesus is twelve, he journeys with his family to the Temple in Jerusalem, engages in discourse with scholars in the Temple, and gives his parents anxious moments when they find *ca. 5-8 CE* he is not among the group of people returning to Nazareth. They return to the Temple and find him there. From then until about the age of thirty, nothing is known of Jesus' early life. Tradition assumes Jesus learns the carpenter's trade from his father Joseph. Nazareth, a small town, is only four miles away from the thriving city of Sepphoris, where (as revealed by recent archaeology) many well-to-do Greek-speaking Jews live. A carpenter of Nazareth could have found much in Sepphoris to keep him busy. If indeed his work takes him to Sepphoris, Jesus would undoubtedly come to know Greek as well as his native Aramaic. The Hebrew he knows is from his study of Scripture.

Baptism, Ministry, and Travels

At about age thirty, Jesus begins the teaching and travels that *ca.* are chronicled in the four Gospels. One of the first events recorded is *24-27, 25-28,* his selection as a reader in the synagogue in Nazareth, an honor that *or* could only have been bestowed on someone who is deemed worthy *26-29* and who reads Hebrew flawlessly. *CE*

Walking through a busy Arab bazaar in Nazareth, I arrive at a small Christian church that sits on the site of an ancient synagogue and has been restored to be as faithful as possible to original construction. Like so many places I visit, the event might have occurred there.

At the beginning of his ministry, Jesus is baptized by John the Baptist, his contemporary and the son of his mother's cousin, who may have been a member of the Essenes sect and who has been traveling the country preaching and prophesying. The baptism takes place at the southern end of the Jordan River, near where it empties into the Dead Sea. At this time, the Jordan River holds far more water than at present, for most of its flow is now tapped for irrigation, and little reaches the Dead Sea.

Whether the baptism site is on the east bank or the west bank of the river is now under contention. The west bank has long been a cherished pilgrimage site, where busloads of believers, especially from North America, come to renew their baptismal vows as they immerse themselves in Jordan River waters. The site is usually crowded. My bus drives nearby but does not stop at the site, and I am not disappointed.

Recently, Jordan has found what it considers to be indisputable evidence that the baptism of Jesus takes place on the eastern (or Jordanian) bank of the river. Indeed the account in the Gospel of John speaks of a site "beyond the Jordan," which implies the east bank. Jordan times the site dedication to coincide with the Pope's visit to Jordan. Preparation of accommodations at the new site has been the number-one use for limited Jordanian tourist funds in the year before my most recent trip to the Holy Land. It appears as if Jordan and Israel are in for a protracted skirmish over which is the real site. The stakes in tourism are not to be belittled. The course of the river has probably

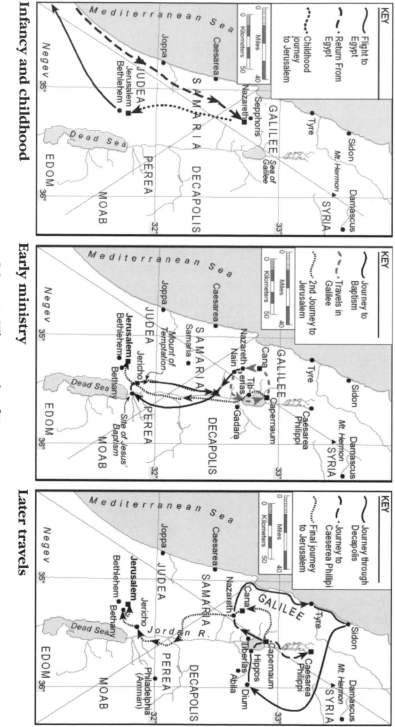

Map 21. The travels of Jesus.

shifted several times in the past two thousand years, so both claims, or neither, may have validity.

Following his baptism, Jesus stays for forty days in what Matthew and Luke call "the wilderness." The Gospel writers do not locate the wilderness, and probably do not need to, for the experience that Jesus has there – resisting repeated temptations by the devil and being strengthened thereby – need not be site-specific.

Nevertheless, when I read this account, I recall the Judean Desert, the dry and sharply dissected region that lies between the Jordan Valley and the western plateau. The Judean Desert is in a rain shadow, cut off from the moisture-bearing winds that blow inland from the Mediterranean Sea. As I go by bus north from Jerusalem to Beit Sha'an, I am struck by the contrast between the semi-arid but wooded plateau where Jerusalem sits and the desolate appearance of much of the Judean Desert. By contrast, the Jordan Valley, which can only be reached via the desert descent, is lush and green from irrigation. The Jordan Valley, most of it within the West Bank, is now heavily settled by both Jewish and Palestinian farmers. The Jewish settlers live and work on prosperous kibbutzim. Some of the Palestinian farms are large, modern and seemingly prosperous, while others are small and traditional. I try to picture the Jordan Valley as it must have been when Jesus was tempted in the wilderness or when he walked there on journeys between Galilee and Jerusalem. The furrows in the fields must have been like the irregular ones I see on small traditional plots, and the farmers urging their donkeys would have been garbed similarly to those I see walking behind their animals.

After this period of preparation, Jesus goes north again into the Galilee region and is invited to a wedding feast given by his mother's friend. The event occurs in Cana, a village to the north of Nazareth. There he performs his first miracle, turning water into wine.

Cana is a challenge to the pilgrim. There are three churches there, of three different persuasions, each claiming to occupy the site of the miracle. I am taken into a church maintained by the Roman Catholic Franciscans. Aesthetically, the church is pleasing. But the dilemma persists, and in the end precise location makes no difference.

127

Jesus adopts as his home base the fishing village of Capernaum, on the north shore of the Sea of Galilee, to which he returns from each of his journeys. There he recruits his disciples, several of whom are fishermen. During the course of his ministry, Jesus performs miracles connected with the Sea of Galilee: He walks on water, he multiplies the catch, he calms raging winds, and he turns two fish into enough to feed 5,000 people. He crosses the sea to the "land of the Gadarenes" on the southeast, where he heals a man raging with madness. And he enters Galilee by way of the Decapolis, which means he must return to Capernaum by sea. Matthew, Mark, and John call this body of water the Sea of Galilee, Luke calls it the Lake of Gennesaret, and during Jesus' time the Romans call it the Lake of Tiberias. The name on Israeli maps is Lake Kinneret.

From the shores of Tiberias, once the Roman administrative city on the west shore of the lake and now an Israeli resort town, I board an oversized boat that purports to model an ancient fishing vessel. Later, in a kibbutz on the western shore of the Sea of Galilee, I see a small boat recently recovered from deep mud along the shore. According to carbon dating imaging, it has been underwater for about 2,000 years. The site is now a national park, and the boat, having been carefully treated by impregnation with a preservative, is handsomely displayed. As I see this small boat, I am inclined to think it is more like the one in which Peter and Andrew fished and Jesus took sail for the opposite shore.

The larger boat that I am in pulls away from the shore for a two-hour quiet time of reflection. From the center of the Sea of Galilee, I can see the hills that nearly surround it, quite low and gentle to the north and higher to the east than to the west. To the north, I can see the hillsides where Jesus preached to the "multitudes," where he told parables, and where the Lord's Prayer was first spoken. To the south is the outlet of the lake into the Jordan River. A guide points southeastward, in the direction of the ancient Decapolis sites of Gadara and Hippos, both of which I hope to see later at close range. Gadara is in Jordan. Hippos is adjacent to the Golan Heights, territory claimed by Syria but controlled by Israel. The Golan territory that borders on the northeast shore of the Sea of Galilee remains the sticking point in the negotiations between Israel and Syria over the return of the Golan.

When I reach the northern shore, I find the site of ancient Capernaum covered with churches, and it is here that I am shown the

Photo 11. The northern shore of the Sea of Galilee.

foundations of a house that tradition says is the house of the brothers Peter and Andrew, Jesus' first disciples. A church with foundations dating to the second century is adjacent to the site. The Mount of the Beatitudes is nearby. It is not a mount but a gently sloping hillside. I am disappointed because it is not possible to sit on its grassy slopes as listeners once did. Today, barbed wire fences off these slopes. All sitting must now be done in churches or in adjacent courtyards. Nevertheless, the significance of the Beatitudes and the Lord's Prayer remains, even if heard from a bench instead of a hillside.

A week after my visit to the Mount of the Beatitudes, the barbed wire must have been removed temporarily, for the grassy slopes hold thousands of young pilgrims, those whom I see in Bethlehem and many thousands more, who gather at this site to hear the Pope say Mass. Nearly eighty years old and infirm, the Pope does not spare himself as he travels this week on his personal pilgrimage to sites in the Holy Land. Protecting the Pope yet allowing him access to all the places he wishes to visit presents the Israelis with the greatest crowd control and security challenge they have ever faced. I am impressed with how smoothly all seems to be going.

During his ministry, Jesus makes the 80-mile journey to Jerusalem several times to attend festivals at the Temple, probably traveling one way through the semi-arid hill country of Samaria and the other along the Jordan Valley. To reach Jerusalem from the Jordan Valley, he must go through Jericho, then turn westward, reaching the plateau on the road that climbs the dry and dusty Judean Desert slopes. In Bethany, on the outskirts of Jerusalem, he is befriended by Mary and Martha and their brother Lazarus, with whom he often stays. Mary washes the dust from his feet. Martha bustles about preparing the meal. On one occasion, the Gospel narrates that Jesus raises Lazarus to life after he has been dead four days.

I visit Bethany, now an Arab town within the Palestinian Authority. The traditional site of the tomb of Lazarus is barely accessible, down a steep flight of stone steps leading to a tiny room that may or may not be a tomb. At the entrance, merchants are out in force, selling postcards and Holy Land souvenirs.

At the beginning of the third year of his ministry, Jesus journeys to the ancient but still active Mediterranean ports of Tyre and Sidon, gateways to Lebanon. On his return, he makes a side trip through the Decapolis region, east of the Jordan. The Gospels do not give a reason for this itinerary, but we can map it. The road to the Mediterranean leads through Magdala and Nazareth, westward along the north face of the Mt. Carmel ridge to the site of present-day Haifa (then Ptolemais), and then north along the coast to the ancient Phoenician ports of Tyre and Sidon, which are under Roman jurisdiction. It doesn't make sense for Jesus to take the long way home "by way of the Decapolis" unless he has a mission there. But nothing more is said.

Later in the trip, I manage to visit both of the Decapolis sites where his return might have been facilitated. Most authorities take for granted that he passes through the larger and more famous site, Gadara, and enters the lake from this place. But the deep Yarmouk Valley, tributary to the Jordan, cuts between Gadara and the lake, making access exceedingly difficult. The Gospels speak of an earlier visit that Jesus makes to the "land of the Gadarenes," but I conclude that this earlier visit is not to Gadara itself but to that part of the region of Gadara that is tangent to the lake. I engage a taxi driver to take me to the undeveloped archaeological site of Hippos (Photo 3), high above the east shore of the lake, and I conclude that it is through

Hippos and not Gadara that Jesus probably returns. At the foot of the fairly steep but direct slope from Hippos, a boat could moor, taking Jesus back to Capernaum. This, of course, is conjecture, but I feel fortunate to have seen the ruins of Hippos, which is subsequently being developed as an official archaeological site (Photo 17).

At another time, Jesus and his disciples travel north to the Roman resort city of Caesarea Philippi, whose present-day name of Banias is an Arab adaptation of the Greek "Panias". The Greeks had dedicated this site to the nature god Pan. It is in Caesarea Philippi that Peter first acknowledges the divinity of Jesus, "son of the living God."

Because I sense how precious water is in much of Israel, it is gratifying to find it here in abundance, as well as in the entire Hula lake district, a marshy region that collects the waters flowing off Mount Hermon and sends them southward to the Sea of Galilee. The entire area north of the Sea of Galilee is verdant and fertile, and heavily cultivated. (Later I learn that many of the workmen in this agricultural area are paid laborers from countries other than Israel.) To the north and east is Syria, and to the immediate east is the Golan Heights. In Banias school children are on holiday, and I see a group of attractive teenage girls, very dark, who giggle as they pass. They grant my request to take their picture, and when I remark that they seem happy, one replies, "We have to be; we have no place else to go." My guide tells me that they are Ethiopian Jews, who are proving to be the most difficult to acculturate of all the in-gathered peoples. (I can't help but speculate whether one part of their difficulty may be the latent skin-color fixation that seems to lie at the heart of discrimination all over the world.) West of Banias, I stop at a kibbutz equipped with guesthouses, a lovely place with flowing water and wildflowers and plenty of grassy areas. Here, in a spring at the edge of the kibbutz, I witness a baptism in a very private ceremony performed not in the Jordan River but on the grassy banks of one of its many sources.

Jerusalem

On his final journey – coinciding with the days before the feast of the Passover – Jesus, together with his disciples and a host of followers, makes his way from Capernaum to Jerusalem. They travel southward down the east side of the Jordan River Valley, linger in Perea, cross to Jericho, then climb the dry Judean hills to reach Bethany. Dusty from the last phase of the trip, Jesus and his disciples rest in Bethany and probably are tended by his friends Mary and Martha. He asks his disciples to secure a donkey for him. Riding the donkey, he then goes on to the Mount of Olives (a hill, not a mountain, overlooking Jerusalem), descends the steep path to the bottom of the hill, crosses the Kidron Valley, and enters the city through one of its gates.

I descend the Mount of Olives by the same route, moving from the brilliantly domed Russian Orthodox church at the top to the Garden of Gethsemane at the bottom. As I descend the hill, I realize that its middle slope is now a vast necropolis of closely packed tombstones, an ancient and modern burial place of Jews from all over the world, who chose to be buried in view of the Temple Mount and overlooking Jerusalem. Had I continued on foot, I would have followed Jesus' route as he entered the city. But I take an easier way, by bus and then foot, to reach the Temple Mount.

Jerusalem is crowded at this Passover season. Jews have come *Pass-* from near and far to celebrate. By this time Jesus is well known, and *over* crowds accompany his journey through the city to the Temple Mount. *Week-* They carry palm branches and shout, *"Hosanna!,"* following Hebrew *day 1* processional tradition that by this time is more than five hundred years old. My Israeli guide translates Hosanna as a Hebrew word meaning *Lord Save Us.* The crowd does not say, "Lord Save Us from Roman Tyranny," but they can imply it. People in the crowd, chafing under Roman rule, are looking to Jesus, the Messiah, to lead them in revolt. During the coming days, they learn (to the disappointment of most) that Jesus is indeed leading the way, but to a different and apolitical goal.

Jesus spends the first days of Passover week preaching and *Pass-* teaching in the Temple. He foretells the coming destruction of the *over* Temple, a prediction not likely to endear him either to the priests *Week-* or the gathered crowd. *days 2-4*

The Temple Mount, now the Islamic holy place called the Haram al-Sharif, today bears almost no resemblance to its appearance during the time of Christ. Later, I see a scale model of Herod's reconstruction of the

132

Temple, and I form a pretty good idea of the layout: an outer courtyard where merchants sell animals for sacrifice, and trinkets as well, an inner courtyard where worshippers gather, and a restricted High Altar area (now enclosed within the Dome of the Rock).

In the outer courtyard, Jesus rails against the money changers. At night, he and his disciples return to the Mount of Olives, where they probably sleep in temporary quarters set at the base of the hill to accommodate the Passover visitors.

Trial, Death, Resurrection, and Ascension

On the fifth day of this Passover week, Jesus sends his disciples to secure a room where they can eat together. At supper the disciples learn from Jesus that one of them will betray him, and Judas leaves the gathering to meet with conspirators from the Temple. In company with the remaining eleven, Jesus then institutes the ritual, using bread and wine, which Christians everywhere observe as Holy Communion or the Eucharist. *Passover Week day 5*

The exact site where "the Last Supper" takes place has several claimants. I visit one Norman-style site, probably built by Crusaders, that is impressive but hardly evocative of first-century Jerusalem.

Then Jesus crosses the Kidron Valley to the Garden of Gethsemane at the foot of the Mount of Olives. Gethsemane means oil press, and most certainly in Jesus' time, the production from the trees on the Mount of Olives is carried down slope to be pressed into oil. But the season for harvesting olives is in autumn, and visitors to the Temple on this week can find shelter here, as Jesus and his disciples probably do.

Now, however, there is no olive press, but only very old olive trees in a tranquil setting. Next to the garden is one of the most beautiful churches I've seen in the Holy Land, capped with multiple small domes. It is a recent Franciscan undertaking, with frescos contributed by artists from all over the world.

In the quiet garden Jesus prays, but his disciples cannot resist sleep. At length, Jesus is taken by a detail of priests and soldiers who escort

Photo 12. Ancient olive trees in the garden of Gethsemane.

him first to the house of Annas, formerly the high priest, and then to that of his son-in-law, Caiaphas, who now holds the office. Caiaphas considers Jesus a heretic and a troublemaker, but he wants the Romans to deal with him because the religious courts do not mete out death sentences to dissenters.

The monks in an Armenian monastery claim to have uncovered the site of the house of Caiaphas, and a grizzled attendant beckons me past the monastery gate to see it. He speaks no English, but puts forth one word, "Caiaphas." We go down several layers, climbing over debris, until we reach digs that could certainly have been the house of a dignitary from the ancient past. I'm ready to accept the claim, and I thank him, only to learn later that two other sites also make claim to the house of Caiaphas. The Armenians have been in Jerusalem almost from the beginning of Christian pilgrimage, and Armenian Christianity is among the oldest. But through the centuries, the Ottoman Turks, the Georgians, and the Russians, let alone the Greeks and other Orthodox groups in Jerusalem, have made things so difficult for the Armenians that they have built their own fortress within a fortress. To reach the Armenian section, I have to climb a steep hill, and by luck I stumble upon the open gate and the friendly attendant.

Ordinarily, one would not need to use such a difficult entrance into the Old City, but I manage to visit Jerusalem on the Sunday that the Pope has chosen to say Mass at the Church of the Holy Sepulcher. The Pope wishes to reflect and pray in this most holy site in Christendom, and thanks to the strict crowd control of the Israeli army and the Jerusalem police, he gets his wish.

Without access to television or English-language newspapers, I am blithely unaware of the press of crowds that awaits me. For security, all gates are blocked. A soldier tells me that if I climb the hill into the Armenian section I can get through the walls. He is right. Proceeding into the Old City, I do not see the Pope, who is heavily escorted through a gate that is secure. But I see a group of invited and colorfully garbed clerics, representing all branches of Christendom, marching in slow cadence through the city streets on the way to the Church of the Holy Sepulcher. Because it is Sunday, I attend services in the oldest protestant church in Jerusalem, an Anglican church only two blocks away, served by a priest with the name of Neil Cohen. His English Jewish heritage is obvious, and his church has sent him here to minister to Christian Jews. His congregation is eclectic; a Chinese woman who is living in Jerusalem to study Hebrew guides me there.

From the religious courts, Jesus is remanded to Pontius Pilate, *Passover week day 6* who rules ordinarily from the port city of Caesarea but is on an official visit to Jerusalem. Pilate probably anticipates trouble from the crowds gathered for the Passover season. He stays in the Antonia Fortress, adjacent to and overlooking the Temple Mount. Pilate questions Jesus, finds no fault in him, and is pleased to learn that he is a Galilean. That puts him in the jurisdiction of Herod Antipas, the ruler of Galilee and the trans-Jordan province of Perea, the same Herod who earlier executes John the Baptist. Herod also is in Jerusalem for the Passover. Pilate sends Jesus to Herod, and Herod is delighted. He has heard about Jesus but never met him; perhaps he can get Jesus to perform a miracle. But Jesus remains totally silent in Herod's presence. His soldiers taunt him, then send him back to Pilate. Pilate confronts the Temple leaders and the crowd they have assembled. He tells them that both he and Herod have examined Jesus, and there is no basis to charge him with treason or insurrection. But the crowd, small enough in number to fit in Pilate's courtyard, and probably hand-picked by temple authorities, is insistent, calling on Pilate to crucify Jesus. To mollify the crowd, Pilate orders Jesus scourged, and his soldiers mock him with a crown of thorns.

The Antonia Fortress has long since disappeared, but in the bowels of its former site, I am shown marks etched in stone where Roman soldiers

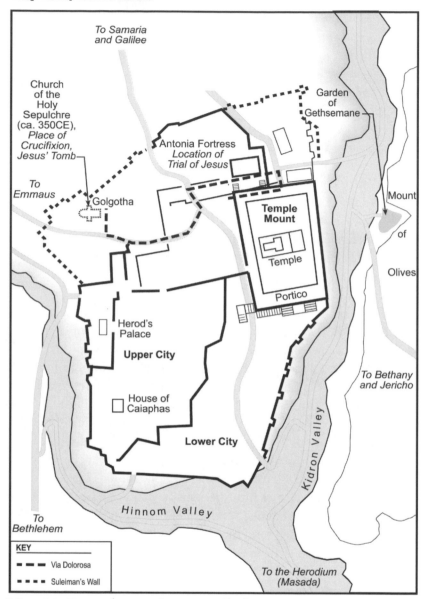

Map 22. Jerusalem at the time of Christ.

*once amused themselves with a last-man-out game, with chits or tokens
representing prisoners. The prisoner represented by the losing chit is
scourged and mocked. Although Jerusalem as a whole has changed from
the way it looked in Jesus' time, and the Antonia Fortress has disappeared,
there is good reason to believe that the foundations and basement of the
fortress remain.*

From a balcony, Pilate shows the scourged Jesus to the crowd (*Ecce Homo!*), hoping to avoid the decision he is reluctant to make. When he realizes he has no alternative, considering the mood of the crowd, he washes his hands symbolically to relieve himself of guilt, then condemns the prisoner to be crucified.

From the courtyard of the Antonia Fortress, Jesus starts his last journey, carrying his cross, along a route now labeled the Via Dolorosa. Most pilgrims wish to pause reflectively at each of the stops, or Stations of the Cross, representing events that take place on the horrific journey. Some of the events are chronicled in the Gospels but others are backed only by tradition.

With the press of people who come to the Holy Land this week because the Pope is here, as well as others who, like I, schedule the trip well in advance without knowing of the papal visit, the Via Dolorosa is hardly a reflective experience.

For Jesus, the painful, humiliating procession ends in an abandoned stone quarry called Golgotha, the place outside the city walls where criminals are crucified. There Jesus endures the agonizing death that is the Roman method of execution. A wealthy Jew, Joseph of Arimathaea, offers his nearby tomb as a burial place, and this is where the body of Jesus is laid. A heavy stone is rolled across the entrance to the tomb, and soldiers are put on guard.

The next day is the Sabbath, when no activity can take place. But early on the morning of the third day after burial, women who come *Easter* to anoint the body of Jesus–Mary of Magdala, Mary the mother of James, and others–find the stone rolled away and the tomb empty. Angels appear to them, to tell them "He is not here, He has risen." They hasten to tell others. Peter comes to the tomb and also finds it empty. Here Christianity gains its core: a crucified savior who, as the Son of God, rises from the dead.

The places of crucifixion, burial, and resurrection are now enclosed within the enlarged Old City as rebuilt by the Romans in the second century and defined by Suleiman's Wall, erected in the sixteenth century. These sites are incorporated within the sprawling, massive, indescribable complex of columns, great arches, chapels, and reliquaries collectively called the Church of the Holy Sepulcher (Photo 14). On the day I visit the Church of the

Photo 13. The Via Dolorosa crowded with tourists.

Holy Sepulcher, my first day in Jerusalem, the crowds are so thick that I almost suffocate. I leave with only one impression I wish to remember: a tomb, quite hidden and little marked, that supposedly is the family tomb of Joseph of Arimathaea. This is not billed as the burial place of Christ. Had it been, I would never have been able to get near it.

During the forty days Jesus remains on earth after his resurrection, he appears to many people, most notably to Mary of Magdala on Easter *Forty* morning, to travelers on the road to Emmaus, and to his disciples, *days* either on the shores of the Sea of Galilee or in a house in Jerusalem *later* (the Gospel accounts vary). The ascension of Jesus is witnessed by his disciples.

I note the site of Emmaus on the drive from Jerusalem to Tel Aviv. It lies at a place where the hills meet the coastal plain. The area appears to be extremely fertile and fairly prosperous, as it must have been at the time of Christ.

I am troubled by the inconsistencies in the Gospel accounts of where the disciples are to meet Jesus following the resurrection and where the ascension takes place. Matthew says they are to hasten to Galilee, where he will show himself, but Galilee is a good eighty miles away through difficult hill country. By fast public bus, it takes me the better part of three hours. Mark says nothing on the subject. Luke and John indicate that Jesus appears to the disciples in Jerusalem, but John also recounts a later appearance on the Sea of Galilee. Matthew has the ascension taking place on a hill in Galilee. Mark does not give a place but says the event happens while the disciples are gathered with Jesus around a table. Luke says the ascension takes place outside Jerusalem, "near Bethany," which he confirms in Acts as the Mount of Olives. John does not mention the ascension. I know I should let such inconsistencies alone, but I am too place-oriented to avoid such musings. Here is one of so many bits of evidence that dates and places in the Bible are of only minor concern to the writers. What is important to the writers are the events themselves and their significance. Clearly, the Bible cannot be read as strict history, and its geography is often sketchy. Nevertheless, its time/place framework is intact, even if the details are not.

16
The New Faith Spreads

*Jesus the Jewish prophet…was executed by the Romans
in a manner so hideous that his followers could never
forget it…[But] their small Palestinian sect grew into a
movement that spread like
scattered seeds through the Roman world…*
Thomas Cahill
Desire of the Everlasting Hills

*In the case of those who were denounced to me as
Christians…I first interrogated these; those who confessed
I interrogated a second and a third time, threatening them
with punishment; those who persisted I ordered executed…
There were others possessed of the same folly; but because
they were Roman citizens, I signed an order for them to be
transferred to Rome.*
Pliny the Younger
*Governor (111-113 CE) of Pontus/Bithynia
[in what is now Turkey] to the Emperor Trajan
Letters 10.96-97*

Just before his ascension, Jesus proclaims what Christians have
since called *The Great Commission*. His followers are to go into
all the world to tell everyone the Good News, to "make disciples
of all nations," and to baptize them into the new faith. In other
words, Christianity is to be a missionary religion, spread by its followers.

Following on the publication and widespread dissemination of
the Septuagint, Judaism too is becoming a missionary religion, in

effect if not by design. Thousands of converts in the Graeco-Roman world now worship together with their diaspora co-religionists. Those who do not fully comply with Torah requirements (i.e. especially the strictures concerning circumcision and dietary laws) are called "God-Fearers," and they exist on the margins of Jewish religious society, attending worship services at synagogues: curious, sympathetic, no longer pagan, but not entirely Jewish either.

Pentecost

Ten days after the ascension, the disciples are gathered in Jerusalem. There, according to the account in the Book of Acts, they receive a sign, a tongue of flame resting on the head of each *Fifty* disciple, signifying that they have indeed been chosen to spread *days* the Good News. To this end, they are now able to speak in several *after* languages. They begin to tell of Jesus and of their experiences with *Easter* him to the Jews (and probably some "God-Fearers" as well) who are in Jerusalem at this time of year, on pilgrimage from many parts of the Mediterranean world for Pentecost. Pentecost, originally a "first fruits" harvest festival (for the harvest of winter wheat), has by this time come to mean for the Jews the celebration of the Mosaic law given by God on Mount Sinai fifty days after the first Passover. The term is Greek, the festival ancient. Jewish Christians begin to give new significance to the meaning of Pentecost, coming as it does fifty days after Easter. As the Jewish pilgrims return home, the news spreads. Meanwhile, the new religion – perceived at the time as a variant or reform of Judaism – takes root first in Jerusalem.

Paul

Gradually, the disciples and their followers understand that their mission is not only to fellow Jews but also to Greeks, Romans, and all others. The word spreads, as new ideas will. At first, the spread is slow, impeded at every turn by Jewish ecclesiastical leaders, of whom Paul – a devout Jewish scholar and Roman citizen from Tarsus, near the southern coast of what is now Turkey – is one. Paul, living in Jerusalem, tries to identify and wipe out the followers of the new faith. On one such mission, he travels north to Damascus, the northernmost of the Decapolis cities. But on the road to Damascus,

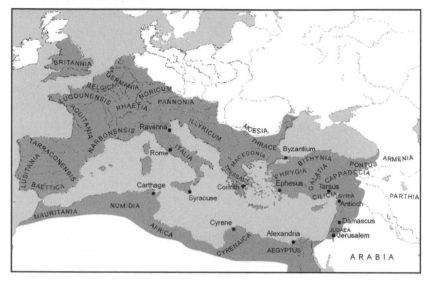

Map 23. The Roman Empire, ca. 40 CE.

Paul is felled by a blinding light, encounters Christ in a vision, and is himself converted. Paul becomes convinced that the message of Jesus is to Gentiles (non-Jews) as well as to Jews, and he wins the argument with Jewish Christians in Jerusalem that gentile converts need not follow Jewish dietary laws nor undergo circumcision. Many God-Fearers within the Jewish community are subsequently won over to Christianity.

The Pax Romana and the Spread of Christianity

ca. 37-67 CE

Paul changes from a persecutor of those who follow the new faith to an inspired proponent and missionary. The first believers are from the Jewish community, not only in Jerusalem but throughout the eastern Mediterranean and Rome. But the perception of Christianity as a religion distinct from Judaism grows, especially as the new faith takes root in Asia Minor among both Jews and non-Jews.

Paul and other missionaries travel with relative ease along Roman roads and in Roman shipping lanes. They establish communities of new believers as they go, not only in such Greek cities as Ephesus, Corinth, and Philippi, but also in Rome. Eventually, some of the early missionaries pay for their faith with their lives, for as the number of Christians grows, the Romans perceive that Christians are not merely a nuisance but a threat to their own state religion. Paul is held prisoner for two years at Caesarea, the Roman port city and administrative center in Palestine. He is sent to Rome for trial, is shipwrecked on the island of Malta, touches at Syracuse in Sicily, then remains for two years under house arrest as a prisoner in Rome. Finally, in 64 CE, Paul is set free for lack of evidence. By tradition, he meets death during the persecutions of Nero in 67 CE.

The Book of Acts (The Acts of the Apostles), written by the same author as the Gospel of Luke, tells the story of the early spread of Christianity, beginning in Jerusalem. Most of the other *ca.* books of the New Testament, other than the four Gospels, are *30-* letters from Paul and other early missionaries to various Christian *100 CE* communities in the Greek-speaking world. In addition to the places documented in the New Testament, tradition places the early spread of Christianity as far as India, Ethiopia, Spain, Britain, and to wherever Roman legions are posted. Given the stability and intercourse facilitated by the *Pax Romana,* none of these traditions can be easily dismissed. Wherever Christianity spreads, Jerusalem and Palestine begin to take on almost a sacred aspect, a holy destination, where pilgrims can "walk where Jesus walked."

17
Sites of Pilgrimage

Thanks to Constantine's mother,
the Christian tradition today has as many
holy sites and shrines in Israel
as do the Jews and Muslims combined.
To be sure, some of the sites which Helena pointed out were
already considered holy shrines commemorating specific
events in Jesus' life. Helena...
lent a great deal of legitimacy to the original traditions; no
one was arguing with the mother of the emperor of Rome.
David E. Lipman
Gates to Jewish Heritage

Aside from the New Testament accounts and the ever-growing archaeological record, pilgrims owe their understanding of life in Palestine in the first century CE to the Jewish historian *70-80 CE* Flavius Josephus, who writes in the seventh decade of that century. Josephus mentions Jesus, but his is the only historical source to do so, and he is not interested in pinpointing sites connected with Jesus' life. So the authentication of the sites must rest on tradition. Is tradition reliable?

I am able to visit most of the sites associated with the life and ministry of Jesus, with the exception of Tyre and Sidon, which are in Lebanon. At first, I am deeply skeptical of the authenticity of the sites. But the more I learn, the more I have reason to believe that most of the sites of pilgrimage actually do mark places at or quite near to where Gospel events occur. I come to believe that tradition carries with it a good deal of reliability.

Most of the sites that Christian pilgrims visit, sites connected with the life of Jesus, begin to be places of pilgrimage within a hundred years or less of Jesus' death and resurrection. The Acts of the Apostles *ca.* and the letters of Paul bear witness to the growing number of people *100-* who are willing to identify themselves as Christians. Certainly less than *300* *CE* three generations separate the events from the desire of the devout to visit these sites. Oral tradition may thus be considered fairly reliable.

Later, when Helena, mother of the first Christian Roman Emperor, Constantine, comes to the Holy Land in the early fourth century to arrange for the building of churches on the sites, she and her advisors take as much care as possible to authenticate the sites. Helena commissions the Church of the Holy Sepulcher to be built on the site of Jesus' crucifixion and tomb. Although it is desecrated and partially destroyed under the Fatimid caliphs in the late 10th century, Helena's church is later rebuilt by Crusaders and greatly renovated in the nineteenth century. Its basic Byzantine architectural features persist but with Gothic and neo-Gothic overlays. Today, like most heavily visited sites in the Holy Land, the site of the Church of the Holy Sepulcher is backed by long and unbroken tradition of pilgrimage.

It is recorded that the execution and burial take place outside the city wall. How, then, can the massive, sprawling Church of the Holy Sepulcher within the Old City of Jerusalem possibly contain the authentic sites? That is the problem that Oxford archaeologist Kathleen Kenyon attempts to solve in the 1960s and 1970s. She knows that the Jerusalem of the first century is smaller than the area of the present walled city. After exhaustive research, she finds evidence of a quarry where executions take place and of tombs hewn from limestone caves nearby. She authenticates that the Church of the Holy Sepulcher is indeed located on this site. Roman Catholic and Orthodox scholars, and most Protestant scholars as well, accept this finding. However, on a hill outside the present city wall, in a spot that seems to fit all preconceptions, a group of English Protestants maintains a garden and an ancient tomb. A guide points to a nearby hill site as the place of crucifixion. Some tourists prefer to think that this quiet site, not the impossibly complex and – yes – gaudy Church of the Holy Sepulcher, is where they should concentrate their devotions.

Covered with churches, the pilgrimage sites now bear almost no resemblance to how they must have appeared in Jesus' time. I find that it

145

Photo 14. The Church of the Holy Sepulcher.

helps to refresh my hazy knowledge of Palestine in Roman times and to have a map at hand at all times. In this way, I can try to reconstruct in my mind the sites and the people associated with them as they appeared when Jesus walked in Palestine. I had expected to be repelled by the proliferation of structures that everywhere commemorate, and in a sense desecrate, the sites. I find instead that I can respect the fervor and piety of those who erected these churches of so many different styles, representing such varied liturgical traditions and aesthetic values. My twenty-first-century aesthetics would tear it all down and try to restore it to its original appearance. But who am I to impose my values on those pilgrims of the past who came to memorialize the pilgrimage sites, all in their own way?

18

The Jewish Revolts and the Diaspora

So he gave order to the soldiers
both to burn and plunder the city...
They slew those whom they overtook without
and set fire to the houses
whither the Jews had fled,
and burnt every soul in them.
Flavius Josephus
Antiquities of the Jews, Book 20

These Jews have penetrated to every city,
and it would not be easy to find a single place
in the inhabited world which
has not received this race.
Strabo
Geography

History is fortunate to have the accounts of Flavius Josephus. A leader of the Jewish Revolt that starts in Caesarea and spreads to Galilee in the year 66, Josephus is captured the *66-73* following year. He determines that the revolt is a lost cause and ill-advised, *CE* and casts his lot with Rome. Of priestly heritage, Josephus now devotes his life to making Jewish traditions comprehensible to the Graeco-Roman world. For the remainder of the Jewish revolt, he stays on the scene as an interpreter, ingratiating himself with the Roman authorities.

Destruction of the Temple

70 CE

Josephus chronicles the seminal events of the year 70 CE, when the Romans under Titus utterly destroy the Second Temple – the one rebuilt in 515 BCE by the Judeans who returned from Babylon and greatly enlarged by Herod the Great. They carry temple artifacts to display in triumph in Rome, along with thousands of Jewish prisoners. The only part of the Temple the Romans leave standing is a portion of the massive Herodian retaining walls. This remnant is known as the Western Wall. Today, Jewish pilgrims come from all over the world to pray in front of it, some silently, some chanting aloud. Israeli soldiers come here as well, linking arms as they lean against the wall in grim resolution that "this shall not happen again."

As I approach the platform of the Haram al-Sharif, I have to climb steps that ascend the still visible and still massive Herodian retaining wall. At the Western Wall, and from a respectful distance, I train my camera on the men whose hands hold Scripture and who sway back and forth as they pray aloud. I sense the intensity of their emotion (Photo 10).

Masada

70-73 CE

Josephus gives an account of how a small band of Jewish zealots captures the imperial fortress of Masada, west of the Dead Sea, and defies the Romans for an additional three years. The fortress of Masada is being partially restored, enough so that visitors can get an idea of how extensive it is and how difficult to access. Strongly built by the Romans both to withstand a siege and to serve as a comfortable retreat for the proconsul, Masada sits on a flat-topped knoll to the west of the Dead Sea. The zealots capture the massive fortress at a time when the Romans are concentrating their efforts elsewhere. The zealots still have adequate food and water when, three years later, the Romans finally complete a ramp that gives them entrance to the fortress. The night before the Romans enter, the defenders choose suicide rather than submit to capture. Today, Israeli Jews, whose religion forbids suicide, are ambivalent about the Masada heroes. Although young soldiers in training are taken to the fortress to internalize the heroism of the first century Jewish defenders, the final suicidal act is not condoned.

Photo 15. In the distance, the ancient "Snake" ascent; in the foreground an aerial tram, a sign of the attraction of Masada for Holy Land tourists.

A narrow path aptly called "The Snake" gains entrance to the fortress by a steep 1,500-foot climb of switch-backs. While in control of Masada, the Romans bring in all supplies over this tortuous route. Today, an aerial tramway affords tourists a much easier route. Foolishly, I descend by the snake. The view is spectacular, across the turquoise Dead Sea and toward the haze-filtered cliffs of the Jordan plateau to the east. But because I am concentrating so strongly on braking my legs and urging unused muscles forward, I have no time or inclination for photography. The descent takes a half hour, the most precipitous half hour of my life. For the next several days, my thigh muscles complain incessantly. I sympathize with the soldiers and slaves who long ago had to travel up and down the Snake to supply the fortress.

After the Jewish Revolt, the Romans send Josephus to Rome to write history. He writes several multiple-volume works. One, *The Jewish War*, is an account of the revolt, prefaced with a brief survey of the previous two hundred years of Jewish history, all of it extra-Biblical. A second, *The Antiquities of the Jews*, records in considerable detail the history of the Jews in what is now known as the first century of the Common Era. Throughout, Josephus blames

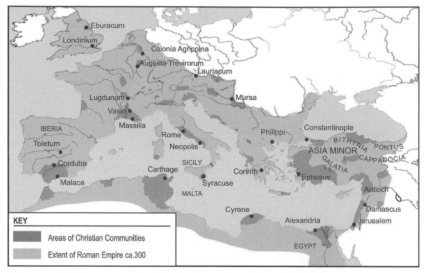

Map 24. The spread of Christianity by 300 CE.

the Jewish Revolt on a fanatical minority. Ill-conceived the revolt may have been, but it takes the Roman legions seven years to put it down. After the destruction of the Temple, the Romans expect no more trouble from their unruly Jewish subjects.

Judaism and Christianity in First Century Palestine

In the lifetime of Jesus and during the rest of the first century, the Jewish community in the Holy Land is divided between traditionalists, who still wait for a promised Messiah, and Messianists, the followers of Jesus. The traditionalists are divided into several camps as well: there are the Pharisees, who are legalists, and who believe in an after-life, merited or deserved by behavior in the present; the Saducees, also legalists, but without holding to a future after death; and the Essenes, committed to living ascetically and without a structured hierarchy. To the scholars of organized Judaism who treasure their monotheism, Jesus' claim to be the Son of God is blasphemy. Not all Jewish traditionalists oppose the Messianists, however, and for a time both worship together in the synagogues.

30-100 CE

During the Jewish Revolt, attitudes begin to harden. The Messianists in Jerusalem take no part in the revolt, and they flee Jerusalem for more tolerant communities in the north and across the Jordan River (Pella, the Decapolis city, harbors hundreds of Messianists at this time, undoubtedly saving their lives). Angry with the Messianists

150

for deserting their cause and deprived of their beloved Temple, Jewish scholars begin to rethink the nature of their heritage. What does it mean to be a Jew? The Messiah is still awaited. Those who consider Jesus as the Messiah are misguided. Jewish scholars eventually decide that they cannot worship together with the followers of Jesus, and they expel Messianic Jews from their synagogues.

From this time on, Jewish Christians worship chiefly in home-based communities, for the concept of a church as a structure does not yet exist. From this time on, also, Jewish communities no longer welcome the half-committed God-Fearers, and Judaism becomes a faith that encompasses and ministers to its own, without missionary aspirations. Before the end of the first century, Judaism and Christianity have split irrevocably. Matthew, Mark, and Luke write before the split has solidified; John's Gospel is completed after. It is significant that only John names the Jews specifically as being responsible for the crucifixion of Jesus (Matthew, Mark, and Luke speak of "the people" or "the crowds"). In subsequent centuries, the account in the Gospel of John, taken literally by Christian zealots, will bring untold grief to Jews.

The Bar Kokba Revolt

Toward the beginning of the second century, the Romans decide to rebuild Jerusalem. The desecration of the Temple Mount, with *132* statues of the emperor as a Roman god, provokes one last Jewish revolt *CE* in 132 CE. After this revolt, known as the Bar Kokba Revolt, Jews are forbidden to set foot in Jerusalem and Judea.

Talmud and Mishnah from Galilee

The remaining Jews now live chiefly in Galilee, the northern province. There, over the next two centuries, the Jews and the Romans *100-* develop a *modus vivendi:* The Jews promise to obey Roman law, and *300* the Romans agree to consider their religion legitimate. This is a period *CE* of rich scholarship among the rabbis of Tiberias and Sepphoris. A collation of rabbinical studies of the Torah, known as the *Talmud,* and commentaries on Jewish law, known as the *Mishnah,* emerge from this period. Through the centuries Jewish scholars in Palestine and elsewhere continue to contribute to the Talmud and Mishnah, and their writings

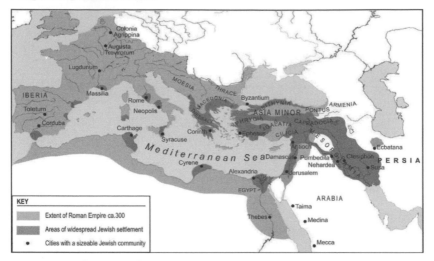

KEY

- Extent of Roman Empire ca.300
- Areas of widespread Jewish settlement
- Cities with a sizeable Jewish community

Map 25. The Jewish Diaspora, ca. 300 CE.

find their way to the scattered Jewish communities everywhere, helping to maintain cohesion in belief despite widespread separation.

Diaspora

After the fall of Jerusalem in 70 and the Bar Kokba Revolt in 132, the Romans take thousands of Jewish captives back to Rome and to other cities in the Empire. Many other Jews subsequently flee in terror, leaving the Holy Land forever. As we have seen, this is not the first Jewish *Diaspora* (a word that can mean both the "scattering" of a people and, collectively, all the places where they settle). Already there are Jewish colonies in many cities of the Roman world, and the emigrants seek safety among their fellow Jews outside Palestine. Some join their co-religionists in Mesopotamia, descendants of the Jews who remain in Babylon instead of returning to Judea. Others go to Arabia, Egypt, the farther reaches of northern Africa, Spain, Greece, and the Italian Peninsula. Still others go to the northern fringes of the Roman Empire, where they carve out a new life amid Germanic peoples.

If the Jews merge with the local population (and some do), history hears no more of them. But in most parts of the Diaspora, the Jews maintain themselves as a separate people. Many are skilled and educated and readily find a place in the economies of foreign lands. Gradually, the Jewish settlers blend their tongue and many of their customs with those of their neighbors. Religious leaders (rabbis, or teachers) in each community keep the knowledge of the ancient Hebrew texts alive. In western lands, the Jews in the Diaspora follow the Torah in the Septuagint version and subsequent vernacular translations. By the sixth century, Jewish scholars in the Holy Land have assembled all the Hebrew and Aramaic writings, from the Torah through the second century books of Daniel and Esther, into a codified whole, known as the Masoritic Text, that sets the canon and standardizes the arrangement of the Hebrew Scriptures. By this time, too, the Christians have accepted the various writings in the Hebrew Scriptures as the Old Testament.

Under most Roman emperors, the Jews of the Diaspora are allowed to practice their religion without harassment. Wherever they go, however, they look to Jerusalem as their spiritual homeland, and they voluntarily tax themselves to send money back to the Holy Land. Before 70 CE, the tax goes to maintain the Temple in Jerusalem. After, it helps to maintain rabbinical leadership and scholarship among the remnant of Jews left in the Holy Land.

The Romans designate a new name for the region that the Jews consider their homeland. Henceforth, it is to be known as *Palestina*, a name coined from the now-defunct "Philistine" and designed to break forever any tie to Jewish occupancy. The people who live in Roman Palestine are an eclectic people, descendents of all who have occupied, traded, farmed, or grazed their flocks in the region in past times: remnant Jews, Nabateans, Arabs, Romans, Greeks, Phoenicians, Persians, Scythians, Egyptians, Chaldeans, and others—all the peoples attracted through the centuries to the lands at the western end of the Fertile Crescent.

19
The High Point
of Empire

*[From ancient historical sources]...we can learn a great
deal about the relationship
between the Greek population of the Decapolis cities...
and the Jewish population, which was dispersed in the
townlets and villages along the shores of the Sea of Galilee
and on nearby Golan Heights.*
Arthur Segal
*Hippos-Sussita Excavation Project:
The First Season 2000*

*During the third season of excavation [at Hippos] it was
decided to expose the remains of the eastern city gate located
at the east end of the Decumanus Maximus*
Arthur Segal
*Hippos-Sussita Excavation Project:
The Third Season, 2002*

Roman occupation of the Holy Land reaches its zenith
in the second and third centuries CE. It is a time of
rapid urban growth and city planning with a main street,
100-300 CE or *cardo,* intersected at right angles (wherever the topography
allows) by a side street, or *decumanus.* Columns line the
streets, supporting a roof beneath which merchants conduct
every manner of business. A temple sits on the highest place,
dedicated to whichever god the city adopts as its protector.

154

Roman Construction

Roman architects and engineers display dazzling feats of construction, craftsmen beautify public places by covering stone with white marble, and mosaic artists create pictures out of tiny stone fragments in an array of colors. There is provision for entertainment, with theaters for plays, amphitheaters for chariot races and coliseums for bloody spectacles, and aqueducts to bring water from distant springs for public and private baths.

My first encounter with Roman construction in the Holy Land is in the ancient port city of Caesarea, where a long aqueduct designed to bring water from Mount Carmel is still standing. So also is a theater, formed of limestone from a nearby hillside. Later, in the Decapolis cities that I visit, I see spectacular ruins, some partially reconstructed. They speak to the wealthy, commercially thriving, and thoroughly hedonistic society that exists in Palestine at the height of Roman occupation.

The Decapolis Cities

During the first and early second centuries, the *Decapolis* is a regional name widely accepted within Roman Palestine. It is a loosely defined league of cities but not an official governmental unit. The Decapolis consists of ten or more cities (depending on the source) that occupy prime sites on trade arteries. In later years of the Empire, the cities exist as separate entities, not as members of a league of cities and not as part of a definable region. Most of the sites are in Jordan, two are in Israel, and two are in Syria (including Damascus).

On a previous trip to Jordan, I visit two Decapolis sites: Philadelphia (now Amman) and Gerasa (now Jerash) on the high road from Damascus to Philadelphia. Jerash is being magnificently restored as a United Nations Heritage Site. On this Holy Land journey, I visit five more Decapolis sites, three in Jordan and two in Israel:

- Pella in Jordan, just east of the Jordan River. Pella is now undergoing extensive excavation and restoration. The Jewish community

Photo 16. Restored colonnade on the site of ancient Gerasa (Jerash), in Jordan, near Amman.

in Pella shelters early Jewish Christians when the Romans raze Jerusalem in 70 CE.

- Scythopolis (once and now again Beit Sha'an), the ancient site in Israel that controls the Jezreel Valley passageway between the Jordan River Valley and Mediterranean seaports. It is the only Decapolis site lying west of the Jordan River.

- Gadara, the focus of much current archaeological activity, occupying the most spectacular site of all. From a hilltop in northern Jordan, it overlooks the deep gash of the Yarmouk River Valley, where today the borders of Jordan, Syria, and Israel are tangent.

- Abila (east of Gadara, also in Jordan), where archaeology is still in its early stages, but a few standing columns speak to the buildings they once supported.

- Hippos, high on a hill overlooking the Sea of Galilee from the east, and almost pristine in its grass-covered piles of toppled columns. Once fortified but now totally abandoned, Hippos is now beginning to be developed as an archaeological site.

At each of these sites, I see fallen columns, areas that were once marketplaces, and streets paved with stone. In all, I can trace a cardo, and in most, I can also see the intersecting pattern of cardo and decumanus that represents the Roman sense of urban order.

156

Photo 17. Columns in Hippos toppled by earthquakes.

Jerusalem Rebuilt and Renamed

In the second century, Jerusalem is thoroughly rebuilt as a Roman city. It takes the Romans three years to put down the Bar Kokba Revolt and settle the city sufficiently so that building can begin. The new Roman city is named Aelia Capitolina, but this name does not outlast Roman suzerainty. Most of the layout of the present Old City of Jerusalem is derived from the Roman street grid overlaid on the pre-existing city in the second century. Streets intersect rather than wind (Photo 18). Today, Israeli soldiers stand guard at these intersections.

As I walk through the streets of the Old City, I can recognize the original Roman layout. Near the Jaffa Gate, the entrance to the Christian Quarter, stands a fortress-like building known as the Citadel, whose original construction dates from Hasmonean times. Herod the Great uses it as his palace. Through the centuries all of Jerusalem's rulers have had a hand in changing and enlarging it. The stone Citadel has now been converted into one of the most effective museums I have ever seen. It chronicles the history of Jerusalem from the time of David to the present, leading me from one chamber of the old palace/fortress to another, up and down stairs on three or four levels, and past gardens enlivened this

Centennial year with glass sculpture of all colors, shapes, and sizes from the workshop of the American glassmaker Dale Chihuly. Fortunately, I see this museum on my last day in the Holy Land, giving me a good opportunity to process what I have been experiencing.

Two severe earthquakes shake the region of the Decapolis and Jerusalem in the sixth and eighth centuries. Afterward, much of the glorious work of the Roman builders lies in ruins.

20
The Byzantines

*Starting in the reign of Constantine the Great, practically
every site of biblical fame became, as we would say today, a
tourist attraction. From every corner of the Christian world
people poured into Palestine:
some as transient pilgrims, others on a longer-term basis.
Monasteries of every nationality sprang up like mushrooms
in the desert next to the Dead Sea.*
Cyril Mango
Byzantium, the New Rome

As Rome weakens from incursions of Germanic tribes and
Roman rule faces repeated threats from the east, the emperor
Constantine moves his capital to Byzantium, the ancient Greek
city situated across the Hellespont (the Bosporus) from Asia Minor.
He renames the city Constantinople. Historians have given the name
Byzantine to the era in which rule is centered in Constantinople.

315-
638
CE

By the beginning of the 4th century, Christians are still only a
minority within the Empire, but a growing minority. Constantine's
mother is a Christian. Constantine becomes convinced that the God
of the Christians has aided him in battles against his Roman and tribal
rivals, and in 315 he proclaims that the state religion of the Roman
Empire shall from henceforth be Christian. In Palestine the Byzantine
Christian era lasts about three hundred years, but a remnant of the
empire remains in Constantinople until 1453.

Before Constantine the Christian imprint on Palestine occurs
gradually and surreptitiously. After, Christianity is officially endorsed,

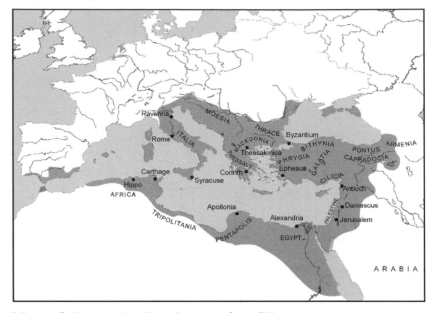

Map 26. Byzantine Empire, ca. 600 CE.

protected, and supported within the Empire. Where before it is dangerous to openly practice Christianity, now the onus is on those who still continue their allegiance to Roman gods.

Constantine is early bothered by the doctrinal controversies that are surfacing within the Christian church. Insisting on unity, he calls a conclave of Bishops at the northern city of Nicaea in Asia Minor in 324, and from this assemblage come the Nicene Creed, a statement of fundamental Christian belief that guides Christianity in all subsequent centuries down to the present. Christians whose understandings do not concur with the Nicene Creed are branded as heretics within the empire, and they are suppressed no less than non-Christians. Under the Byzantines the state church officially achieves unity. By the fourth century it also reaches near-final agreement on which of the many written records from the first century shall be incorporated within the New Testament. The last book, Revelation, does not make it into the canon until the fifth century, after nearly being permanently rejected because of conflicting understandings of its difficult imagery and symbolism.

The Byzantines continue life much as before, enjoying theaters and baths, importing the luxuries that come over the trade routes, but eschewing the grisly amphitheater entertainment that the Romans

ΗΑΓΙΑΠΟΛΙCΙΕΡΟΥCΑΛΗΜ

Photo 18. Fragment of the Madaba mosaic map, showing Jerusalem.

craved. Byzantine architects leave rich traces of their vision and skill as they build churches throughout the Holy Land, including the land *500 CE* east of the Jordan River. In some cases Greek and Roman temples are converted to Christian basilicas. In other cases temples are torn down, and their stones are used to build new churches. The floors of churches and the homes of the wealthy are richly adorned in the Roman manner with mosaics. It is these mosaics, more than the temples and churches, that survive the devastation of subsequent earthquakes.

The Madaba Map

In Madaba, a Jordanian town halfway between Amman and Mount Nebo, a modern church has been built to incorporate within its nave an impressive mosaic map of the entire known Eastern world, from the Nile River to Mesopotamia. The mosaic map is lost under rubble for nearly 1,500 years. Unfortunately, much of this map is torn up by unknowing workmen in the late nineteenth century as they excavate the site. However, the greatest gem remains intact: In the center of the map (which took more than a million tiny cut stones to complete) is a detailed plan of the city of Jerusalem. From this source more than

161

any other, people today can get a good idea of what Jerusalem looked like in the sixth century, at the time the map was created. An east-west *cardo* is clearly visible, and the city is encompassed within a wall. The Madaba Map is an invaluable world treasure.

In Madaba, I visit a workshop where young artists are attempting with much success to learn and employ the art of creating mosaics. An enlarged photograph of the Jerusalem portion of the Madaba Map now covers a wall in the Old City, and it is this image that later I am able to photograph (Photo 18).

The Byzantine Record

In Byzantine times, most of the Decapolis cities, as well as the cities west of the Jordan River, are ecclesiastical sees, with bishops, basilicas, and scores of smaller churches. Roman temples disappear as their stones are recycled. The former Temple Mount becomes a builders' quarry, and the statues of Roman gods and emperors disappear. Weeds cover the area that was once the center of Jewish worship.

So feverish is church construction that on a former visit in Jerash, I can identify the mosaic floors of three separate churches within a two-block area.

The Byzantine era is a difficult time for the Holy Land's Jews. Official government policy requires that all subjects adopt the Christian creed. In effect, Jews are required to convert. Some do, some retain their Jewish faith in secret, and some leave for lands beyond Byzantine jurisdiction, such as Arabia or Persia, adding to the Diaspora. By the year 350 CE, thirty-five years after Constantine adopts Christianity, it is estimated that ninety-five percent of all Jews are living outside the Holy Land.

By the beginning of the seventh century, Rome is no more, and even Constantinople is overextended. There is not enough tax revenue to keep up the roads that tie the Empire together, and there are not enough funds to rebuild after the earthquake that devastates almost the entire region of Palestine in the mid-sixth century. Many urban areas, including the Decapolis cities (Damascus and Philadelphia/Amman excepted), gradually slip into obscurity.

21
The Coming of Islam

True piety is this: to believe in Allah,
and the Last Day, the angels,
the Book, and the Prophets,
to give of one's substance, however cherished,
to kinsmen, and orphans, the needy, the traveler, beggars,
and to ransom the slave, to perform the prayer,
to pay the alms.
The Quran
Sura II: 170-175

Surely they that believe, and those of Jewry,
and the Christians…whoso believes in Allah and the Last
Day, and works righteousness…
no fear shall be on them, neither shall they sorrow.
The Quran
Sura II: 59

In all of the years covered by the Biblical account and the Roman years afterward, the Arabian Peninsula exists as an almost silent backdrop to the events taking place in Palestine. Arabs are of the same Semitic stock as Jews. Traditionally, Arabs take their beginning from Abraham's first son, Ishmael. Biblical mention of Arabia is rare and often vague, for the Biblical writers seem to consider all of the desert to the south and east as "Arabia" and most desert dwellers as nomadic herders. Both Esau and Moses, who flee to Midian (which lies within the Arabian Desert), spend time as herders.

163

Trade Routes in Ancient Arabia

Fragrant frankincense and myrrh from the Hadramaut – the southern coastal area of the Peninsula, now within the countries of Oman and Yemen – are valued in the Holy Land and figure strongly in trade between the two regions. Traders moving between Arabia and the ports at the eastern end of the Mediterranean Sea use a route along the moist Hejaz, the mountainous western region of the Arabian Peninsula. Solomon receives a famous wealthy visitor from Sheba (now a part of Yemen), who rules in the higher and wetter southwestern portion of the Peninsula. Another tradition, however, places the home of the Queen of Sheba in Ethiopia. Whether from Yemen or Ethiopia, the Queen of Sheba would have traveled at least part of the way on this ancient trade route.

200 BCE-200 CE From the second century BCE to the first century CE, and thereafter as part of the Roman Empire, the prosperous trading kingdom of Nabatea operates from the almost impregnable fortress of the capital city of Petra in the northern reaches of the Arabian Desert. From Petra, the Nabateans can control the trade that passes both north and south, and westward to Egypt as well. The Nabateans are farmers as well as traders, and in the desert they use water conservation practices that the Israelis imitate in the Negev two thousand years later. Although the Romans conquer the Nabateans, they continue to value their skills and knowledge as traders. Archaeologists digging in Decapolis cities often find Nabatean coins as well as images of Nabatean gods.

Hiking in the desert south of Petra, in the area known as Wadi Rum, I come upon ancient rock art, crude but recognizable representations of camels and donkeys. The beasts have mounds on their backs, presumably goods, and underneath are messages in an incised script that bears little resemblance to Arabic. I am told the script is not Nabatean but is much older. The desert's mysteries await decoding.

The Arabians and Their Gods

At the beginning of the seventh century CE, most of the people of the Arabian Peninsula are not traders, however, but oasis farmers or nomadic desert dwellers. Most are Bedouin tribesmen, desperately poor, superstitious, and constrained by the tradition of blood feuds. They fear and try to placate a host of local gods of whom the most prominent is Al-lah. Al-lah is the god of Mecca, the trading city near the east coast of the Peninsula. He is worshipped at the Kaabah, the black cloth-covered cube that houses in one corner a meteorite. In ancient (pre-Islamic) times Arabians in and near Mecca believe that Al-lah and the meteorite are one. They circle the Kaabah in homage to Al-lah. But Al-lah has no moral authority; the ancient god does not offer a way for people to relate to one another. Al-lah is not *the* god of the Arabs, only one of many. Each tribe has its own god. As yet, the Bedouin have developed no theology, no sense that they are a god-inspired people. Nor have they ever been unified.

In Mecca, Medina, and other towns in Arabia, new ideas reach the Peninsula along the trade routes. There are communities of both Christians and Jews in these cities, foreigners who worship one all-powerful God. Although urban Arabs show little inclination to adopt the strangers' ways of thinking, they are not unaware of monotheism.

Muhammed

Muhammed is born into this milieu in the year 570. Muhammed's father dies before Muhammed is born, and he loses his mother when he is three. An uncle raises him. His family belongs to a *570* minor branch of the powerful Quraysh tribe, who control the trade in *CE* Mecca that has made them wealthy. The Quraysh, once desert-poor, are now urban dwellers, dissolute in their prosperity, and without moral restraint. Muhammed, who grows up to be a contemplative young man, realizes that his fellow tribesmen will come to no good if they continue in their ways. He worries about this but has no answer, no way of speaking truth to his tribe. Muhammed marries Khadija, the widow of a rich merchant, fifteen years his senior, and with her wealth he can now engage in trade himself.

Muhammed gains some familiarity with the Jewish and Christian faiths. He learns of Abraham, Moses, and Jesus, and of the God who once spoke powerfully to both the Jews and the Christians. How and where he learns of Judaism and Christianity is not clear. The most likely way would be through encounters with Christians and Jews in

Mecca. But he is often away on trading ventures. His travels probably take him northward into the land of the Byzantines, and there, too, he could gain fragments of Judaism and Christianity. On the way, he could encounter Arab tribes on the fringes of the Byzantine empire who have converted to these faiths. By tradition, Muhammed can neither read nor write, but probably in caravansaries by candle light, he listens to stories that Christian or Jewish traders tell, and he carefully stores them in memory. In long, lonely hours on the trail and in month-long retreats in a cave at the base of Mount Hira, a few miles north of Mecca, he contemplates the ideas of monotheism and contrasts them with the dissolute ways of his fellow Arabs under polytheistic worship.

610 CE Muhammed longs for a God who will speak directly to the Arabs, as the God of the Hebrews and the Christians once spoke to the people of Palestine. In his fortieth year, in the cave at the base of Mount Hira, where he has retreated, Muhammed is visited by the angel Gabriel. Gabriel tells him that there is one God only and gives him many other messages that he must "Write!" He retains the messages in memory, but according to an early tradition, he fears for his sanity. He goes home to tell his wife, Khadija, what has happened, and she reassures him: He is a good and righteous man, and it is Al-lah who has spoken to him. Muhammed now becomes convinced that Al-lah, the god of Mecca, is the same as the God of the Jews and the Christians. His only word for God is Al-lah (eventually to become written in English as Allah). Over the next twenty-two years Muhammed receives his angelic visitor again and again in dreams or visions, and he narrates to scribes what the angel – God's messenger – tells him.

What the scribes write reflects considerable knowledge of Jewish and Christian tradition. The Quran refers to Adam and Abraham, Ishmael and Isaac, Jacob, Moses, David, Solomon, Mary, and Jesus. All of these personages from the Jewish and Christian scripture, many of them prophets, are forerunners of the final revelations that Muhammed believes he receives directly from Allah through Gabriel. "He has sent down upon thee the Book with the truth, confirming what was before it, and he sent down the Torah and the Gospel aforetime, as guidance to the people." (Sura III, 3)

Eventually, these writings are assembled as the Quran – The Book – a compact collection of 114 individual Suras, or revelations, that together are shorter than the New Testament. In the Suras, Allah tells believers how they shall live, how they shall worship,

166

how they shall conduct business, how they shall treat one another, how they shall treat other "People of the Book," and how they shall treat unbelievers. Muhammed sees himself as the final prophet of Allah, and the Quran as God's final revelation.

The Hegira

From the outset, Muhammed's wife believes in his visions and in his mission. So also do a small group of his immediate family and followers, especially his faithful friend Abu Bakr and his cousin (and later, son-in-law) and confidant Ali ibn Abu Talib. After Khadija dies, Muhammed takes other wives. He lives in a polygamous society, but his Quranic revelations decree that his followers may have no more than four wives, and they must be able to provide well for each, and her children. Muhammed, however, marries eleven times. Through the centuries his followers have difficulty explaining Muhammed's many wives, of whom the youngest and ultimately the most powerful is his favorite, Aisha, who is only eighteen when he dies. Aisha takes a strong dislike to Ali, a dislike which eventually will have great consequences not only for Ali but for all of Islam.

Muhammed begins preaching in Mecca, but the Quraysh want nothing to do with his new religion. Fights ensue, his followers are in danger. Some who want to convert he sends instead to temporary safety in Ethiopia, knowing that the Christian king there will protect them. In Mecca Muhammed fears for his life. In the year 622, Muhammed and his small group of followers flee to Medina, an oasis city about 200 miles to the north. The flight is termed the *Hegira*, and Islam dates its calendar from this year. *622 CE*

In Medina, Muhammed meets with a group of Jewish leaders and attempts to join his new faith with theirs; in fact, he directs the believers in Allah, who Muhammed now believes to be the God of Abraham, to bow toward Jerusalem, following Jewish custom. Then he learns from the Jews in Medina a local tradition that Ishmael, Abraham's first-born son, is taken by his mother to Mecca, and that Abraham comes to Mecca to help his son build the Kaabah. When the Jews fail to recognize Muhammed as a prophet or to equate Allah with the God of their fathers, Muhammed directs his followers to bow toward the Kaabah instead. Now he has what he needs: Ishmael and the Kaabah tradition give Muhammed a strictly Arab

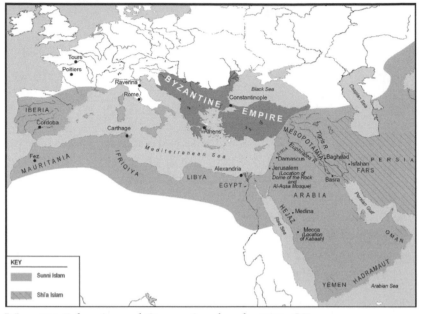

Map 27. Islamic and Byzantine lands, 850 CE.

connection. Allah is universal, but through Muhammed's revelations, it is the Arabs who are elected to bring him to the world and the Arab language the medium by which the knowledge shall be conveyed.

With these new understandings, Muhammed gains followers in Medina, assumes political and military leadership of the city, and with an army formed also of Bedouin tribesmen, he challenges the Quraysh. By 630 he has won over the Quraysh, partly through persuasion and partly through military victory. At one point during the struggle, Muhammed accuses the Jews of Medina, who have gained his distrust by their decision not to join with him, of opening the gates of Medina to Muhammed's enemies. For this act Muhammed orders that all the male Jews of Medina be slain, the wives and children be sold into slavery, and further orders that no Jews be allowed to live in Arabia. The Quranic revelations that come in the Medina years reflect Muhammed's growing negativism toward Jews. Several Suras are aimed against Jews and Christians, and these underlie harsh attitudes toward Jews and Christians that Muslim rulers who are fanatics display in coming centuries. More than that, these verses in the Quran are the basis for widespread antipathies toward non-Muslims that surface today among Islamists (See Chapter

28). But the Quran also has other things to say that exhort tolerance toward People of the Book, as we shall see.

Before his death in 632, Muhammed has joined all the Arab tribes of the Peninsula into a new unity, a unity based on faith in Allah, the One God, and allegiance to Muhammed, his Prophet. One of the last revelations Muhammed receives is, "Know ye that every $^{632}_{CE}$ Muslim is a brother unto every other Muslim, and that ye are now one brotherhood." The Muslim brotherhood, the world of Islam, is called the *Umma*. Membership in the Umma brings with it both duty and privilege.

The Pillars of Islam

Borrowing from the stories contained in Jewish and Christian Scripture but with elements closely keyed to his Arab desert experience, Muhammed gives his followers a new and strict code for living and a new sense of self-worth. The Quran calls their faith *Islam*, which means *submission*. To be a Muslim, a member of the body of Islam, one must say in Arabic, "I bear witness that there is no God but Allah, and that Muhammed is his Messenger." This is the first requirement, or pillar, of the faithful. There are four others: to pray five times daily, turning toward the Kaabah in Mecca; to give to the poor; to take no food or drink from sunup to sundown during the month of Ramadan; and to make a pilgrimage, a *Hajj*, to Mecca. This last requirement need happen only once in a lifetime, and only if the believer is physically able to do so.

The Quran teaches that the One God has been from eternity and has been revealed gradually by the prophets. Muhammed has been given the final and complete revelation. Jews and Christians have also been given knowledge of the One God, but they have fallen from purity of worship. By saying that Jesus the Prophet is the Son of God, Christians are blasphemers. But Jews and Christians are, nevertheless, People of the Book, people to whom the One God has been revealed. They should be allowed to live in Muslim lands (except Arabia), and to freely practice their faith. They will live among Muslims as a protected class, a *dhimmi,* with a status less than that of the followers of Muhammed. All dhimmi must pay the ruler or magistrate a *jizya,* a head tax. Through the centuries, the jizya collected especially from Jews becomes a predictable source of revenue in Arab lands, the homeland of millions of Jews (but few Christians). For further coverage of this subject, see Chapter 25.

The Night Visit to Jerusalem

A tradition called *The Night Visit*—not explicitly laid out in the Quran but based on the veiled meaning in one sura—holds that early during Muhammed's revelations, before the Hegira to Medina, the angel Gabriel takes Muhammed from Mecca to Jerusalem to the site where Ishmael (Isaac in Jewish and Christian tradition) was once offered for sacrifice. From this place, the Rock of Abraham, Muhammed ascends briefly to heaven. There he meets Abraham, Isaac, Moses, Jesus, and other prophets. He returns to earth, and to Mecca, with new understanding and new empowerment. In the *Hadith*, a collection of sayings of the Prophet and those who knew him, his wife Khadija is quoted as saying that on the night of the Night Visit Muhammed never left her bed, and as a result many followers interpret the Night Visit as a dream or a vision. Many others believe that The Night Visit was corporeal. Whether bodily or a vision, the tradition magnifies the significance of the Jerusalem site for all Muslims. But Jerusalem is not the most holy site in Islam. This is reserved for Mecca. It is toward the Kaabah in Mecca that every Muslim all over the world prays, and it is to Mecca that Muslims make their pilgrimage, following a tradition that among Arabs is far older than Muhammed.

The Spread of Islam

The certainties of their new faith energize Muhammed's followers, who set out to make converts. Desert tribesmen, willing enough to proclaim that Muhammed is the Prophet of the One God, are nevertheless new to the fine points of the faith. Raiders by tradition, they are motivated by the prospect of booty, and they willingly link up with the Muslim military leaders. Desert-hardened, the Arab tribes begin to unite and move out, westward into northern Africa, northward into the Holy Land and beyond, extending eastward into Persia and Central Asia, and southward into Yemen. Like Christianity, Islam becomes a missionary religion, its spread an act of piety, a Jihad. *Jihad*, the Arabic word for Holy War, means *to struggle for God*. (Its meaning can refer also to a believer's inner struggle for self-improvement, the meaning moderate Muslims choose today.) Before the century is over, the followers of Islam have crossed into Spain to the west and reached the Silk Road to the east. Where converts do not readily accede, the Bringers of Islam use the sword. But to the Christians and Jews they conquer, they give special status as People of the Book. The followers of the Torah and of the New Testament may keep their faith as dhimmi, so long as they pay the jizya. From the beginning, Muslims are ambivalent about Christians and Jews. The Quran enjoins a form of tolerance, but it also points out why their status must be below that of Muslims.

Muhammed dies in 632. Shortly after, his close friend and companion, Abu Bakr, is chosen to be the first caliph, or leader. At first the headquarters of the Caliphate is in Mecca. By 661, however, successors of Abu Bakr are established in Damascus, and their period of rule beginning in that year is known as the Omayyad Caliphate. *632-661 CE*

Some of Muhammed's followers do not accept Abu Bakr or his successors as legitimate. They feel that the succession should have gone to Muhammed's cousin, Ali ibn Abu Talib, whose father raised Muhammed, and who eventually married Muhammed's daughter Fatima. Like Abu Bakr, Ali too is numbered among the Prophet's companions. For a time Ali goes along with Abu Bakr's leadership, but eventually his supporters urge him to revolt. Aisha, Muhammed's favorite wife, leads the resistance to Ali for his refusal to support her marriage to Muhammed. She joins the Omayyad army that fights against Ali. In the year 662 Ali ibn Abu Talib is murdered in Persia by his Omayyad rival for the caliphate, a wealthy member of the Quraysh tribe.

With Ali's death, a split occurs in Islam that never heals, between the Sunnis and the Shi'ites. Sunnis support a line of succession that begins with Abu Bakr. Shi'ites believe the legitimate heir of Muhammed is Ali. When later Ali's son (and Muhammed's grandson) Husayn, is also murdered, the split becomes irrevocable. Nevertheless, the split within

Islam is political, not doctrinal. Shi'ites are found mainly in Iran and regions on its borders, such as southern Iraq. The tombs of Ali and Husayn are in Iraq, where they draw millions of Shi'a pilgrims.

In the century after Muhammed's death, people who knew him, or even who receive second-hand or third-hand information about his life, recount what they know of the Prophet's life and of his sayings other than those revealed in the Quran. A collection of these sayings and traditions concerning his life becomes the treasured text of Islam known as the *Hadith*.

Islam in the Holy Land

638 CE In the Holy Land, Byzantine ways gradually become fused with those of Islam. The only real battle fought for control of Palestine occurs in the Yarmouk Valley near Gadara in 638. The Arabs win decisively over the Byzantines, and gradually the new religion of Islam begins to prevail in the Holy Land. In Jerusalem early Arab rulers complete the magnificent Dome of the Rock (Photo 23) on the site where Ishmael (not Isaac, according to Muslims) is once trussed for sacrifice, and where Muhammed ascends to heaven. The Dome of the Rock, together with the Al-Aqsa Mosque opposite it on the Haram al-Sharif, becomes Islam's third holiest site, after Mecca and Medina. The flattened hilltop in Jerusalem, sacred originally to Jews, and within view of a score of Christian churches, becomes the province of Islam.

661-909 CE Christians, Muslims, and Jews live side by side in the Holy Land at first, recognizing their common heritage as People of the Book, and respecting each others' holy places. Christians and Jews, as *dhimmi,* are protected from forcible attempts at conversion, but they must pay the head tax, the *jizya,* from which Muslims are exempt. Otherwise, there is no overt persecution. Gradually, many Christians and Jews are absorbed into the Muslim Arab milieu but without coercion. This is true both under the Omayyad caliphs (661-750), who have their capital in Damascus, and the Abassid caliphs (750-909), who rule from Baghdad. The principal change is that under the Abassids, the Holy Land sinks into neglect, and even Damascus becomes a backwater.

Islamic Civilization

Arabic, the language of the Quran, is a holy language, so the Quran is not to be translated. (Indeed, modern translated versions cannot capture the power or even the precise intent of the Arabic, say scholars.) Believers not fortunate enough to have Arabic as their native tongue but instead speak Persian, Turkish, Farsi, Urdu, Malay, or a hundred other tongues, must devote years of their youth to memorizing the Quran in Arabic. Schools, called *madrasas*, are set up all over the Islamic world for this purpose.

The schools also appear in the Holy Land, giving such an education only to qualified believers. The sons of Christians and Jews do not qualify, so they must count on their own dwindling religious communities to pass on knowledge.

In their capitals, the caliphs encourage the decorative arts, almost always based on geometric patterns and words from the Quran. Intricate variations of Arabic script are inscribed on stone, wood, ceramics, and tile. Like Jewish religious art, but unlike Christian art, Islamic art does not include the human figure.

As Islam spreads into lands of Greek and Persian learning, its followers come to include mathematicians, poets, philosophers, and artists. Learned scholars, often Jewish or Christian, translate the writings of the Greeks and Romans into Arabic (thus helping to preserve them). In Muslim lands, Jews become merchants and bankers for Muslim clients, whose religion constrains them from earning interest.

Like all faiths, Islam can be interpreted in a number of ways and is sometimes used to back up pre-existing customs. The Quran does not marginalize women, for example, and only for Muhammed's wives does it require the veil. But as Islam is securing its place in the wider world, its adherents adopt the customs of the Persians, Byzantines, and Jews of the time, who require that women wear the veil and be secluded. Much later, Western civilization shakes off these restrictions, but much of Islam still retains them.

173

22
The Crusaders

*This royal city [Jerusalem] situated
at the center of the earth,
is now held captive by the enemies of Christ
and is subjected, by those who do not know God,
to the worship of the heathen.
She seeks, therefore, and desires to be liberated
and ceases not to implore you to come to her aid.*
Pope Urban II
***to the assembled Frankish nobles
at Clermont, 1095 CE***

*The presence of the crusader states in the Near East for
almost two centuries certainly destabilized Muslim power,
and therefore hindered unification
into a single Islamic state.*
Thomas Madden
The Impact of the Crusades

Although the Holy Land passes into Muslim rule, Christians
and Jews from all over the known world do not forget their
attachment to its holy sites. A few actually complete the
difficult journey, and Omayyad and Abbasid Muslim rulers respect
their journeys and their destinations. The advice and interpretation of
Jewish scholars who live in the Holy Land, particularly in the north,
in Galilee, is sought out by their co-religionists everywhere.

The weakening Byzantine Empire has a precarious hold on
southeastern Europe and the Anatolian Peninsula, but by this

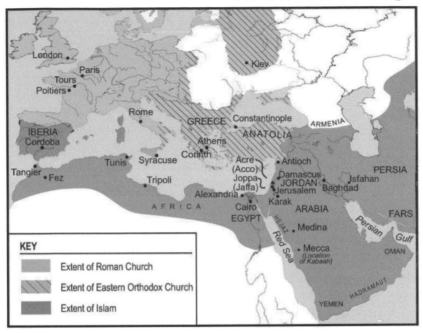

KEY

	Extent of Roman Church
	Extent of Eastern Orthodox Church
	Extent of Islam

Map 28. Europe and the Middle East at the time of the Crusades.

time there is little cooperation between the churches in Rome and Constantinople. As the sphere of Byzantine political rule shrinks in Asia Minor, the influence of the eastern orthodox hierarchy similarly wanes. Maintaining only with difficulty their ties to Constantinople, Greek- or Arabic-speaking Christians in the Holy Land have little or no contact with the growing power of the Latin church in Rome that effectively replaces political power in the west. The Christian community in the Holy Land shrinks but it does not disappear.

Reclaiming Lost Territory

In 909 CE a new and fervently orthodox Islamic power appears in *909 CE* the Holy Land, the Fatimids. From North Africa, the Fatimid rulers have little tolerance toward non-Muslims. Christian pilgrimage is thwarted. When historic churches are ravished, particularly the Church of the Holy Sepulcher, word reaches Rome. In 1096 Pope Urban II rallies Europe's feudal rulers to prepare for a war to recover the Holy Land.

The effort is termed a Crusade. Geographically, the idea of a Holy Land Crusade is a far reach for Europeans of this feudal time, but its motivation is not unique. A Holy Land Crusade will simply add

175

another front to an ongoing struggle to recover territory that Christians have lost to the Muslims. The first victory is at Poitiers in France, just south of Tours, where the Franks halt further Islamic penetration into Europe in 732 CE. By the time of the First Crusade, the Muslims have been ousted from northwestern Spain, and the 500-year *Reconquista* to recover the entire Iberian Peninsula has begun.

The First Crusade in the Holy Land, towards the end of the eleventh century, is an extremely bloody affair. When the European knights reach Jerusalem, they have two perceived enemies: the Muslims and the Jews. By contemporary accounts, the streets of Jerusalem are knee-deep in blood, as knights wield swords in their Holy War to recover the land that they believe belongs to Christians.

By the time of the Fourth Crusade, a hundred years later, the Roman and Eastern Orthodox churches have split, and the warrior knights from western Europe rampage through Constantinople and Asia Minor on their way to the Holy Land, adding Eastern Orthodox Christians to their list of enemies.

The Crusader Presence

1096-1290 CE

In Palestine, the Crusaders build Mediterranean harbors at Joppa (now Jaffa) and Acre (now Acco). From these protected ports, English, German, and French knights land their troops and weapons. For the next two centuries, Europeans are able to take and hold all or part of the Holy Land. They erect a string of forts, establish their families in feudal castles protected by the forts, and put yet one more cultural and genetic stamp on Palestine.

I visit two of these impressive forts, one at the site of the Crusader's Acre and one far south at Karak in Jordan on the ancient Kings' Highway trade route between Damascus and Arabia. The Crusader forts are true strongholds, Norman Gothic in style. Massively built, they exhibit great sophistication in architecture and engineering.

However, the Crusader forts cannot hold back the Seljuk Turks, recent converts to Islam who by 1144 have all but eliminated the Byzantines from Anatolia and have wrested the caliphate from the Fatimids. The Turks themselves become masters at fort building. Led by the brilliant Saladin, a Kurd and member of a recently conquered

Photo 19. The Crusader castle at Karak in western Jordan.

group, the Turks deliver strong blows to the Crusaders toward the end of the twelfth century. The Crusaders regroup, take Jerusalem once more, and are not finally defeated until the last of the knights departs Acre in 1290.

Legacy of the Crusaders

In all this time, the Muslims in Palestine do not use the term *Crusaders*. They think that they are fighting the *Franks*, and this is what their histories record. The events in Palestine during the Crusades have little more than local significance in most parts of the Islamic Empire. Baghdad, Fez, and Cordoba – centers of Islamic learning and culture – pay little attention to what is happening in the increasingly neglected backwater region of Palestine.

Only in the last two hundred years do the words "Crusade" and "Crusaders" come into Muslim vocabularies, learned in studies of Western history. These terms are now "red flags" among Muslims, a symbol of the time when Christians dared to impose their rule on the Holy Land. After the events of September 11, 2001, United States President George W. Bush realizes this to his consternation when he uses the word "crusade" in the modern sense to announce a war against terrorism. Muslims everywhere are offended.

While in Palestine, the Crusaders learn to blend the ways of the West with those of the East. The work of western scholars, laboring quietly in Cordoba to translate Arabic documents into Latin, now gets wider attention as the Crusaders pick up knowledge of Arab medicine and Arab geographical lore. What the Crusaders lose in territory, they more than gain in thirst for knowledge. Returning to Europe, they give vent to ideas that will lead to the Renaissance, the Age of Discovery, and the Reformation.

The Jews fare badly under the Crusaders. The knights of the First Crusade find only a few thousand Jews living in the Holy Land, and many of these they slay. For Christians of the Middle Ages, the Jews are the villains in the crucifixion story, and the Crusaders deem both Jews and Arabs as unworthy occupants of the Holy Land.

In regaining power, the Seljuk Turks are magnanimous toward the Christians. They respect the principle of the dhimmi. There is no wholesale slaughter of the remnant knights and their families as they depart. The Turks acknowledge that Christians may continue to come to the Holy Land, as individuals and as pilgrims. Meanwhile, a remnant of Crusader authority remains in the Holy Land to this day: the responsibility accorded by the Crusader popes to the Franciscan Order for maintaining the Holy Places. Franciscans are present at all of the pilgrimage sites that have come under Roman Catholic protection, and there has never been a time when their presence was not allowed.

23
The Turks

For six hundred years the Ottoman Empire swelled and declined. It advanced from...Anatolia to conquer the relics of Byzantium... It swept up the heartlands of Islam, controlling the thoroughfares which linked Europe to the Middle East. The empire was Islamic, martial, civilized, and tolerant. To those who lived outside its boundaries, it was an irritant and a terror. To its own subject peoples, however, it belonged in the Dar ul-Islam, or "Abode of Peace."
Jason Goodwin
*Lords of the Horizons:
A History of the Ottoman Empire*

Shortly after the Crusaders leave, the Seljuk Turks surrender power in the southern part of the Holy Land to the Mameluks, slave warriors from Egypt. Little happens under the Mameluks, and as they weaken, a brilliant new Turkish regime takes over.

The Fall of Constantinople

The Turkish ruler Mehmet II (1432-1481), a masterful strategist, finally brings about the fall of the almost-impregnable Constantinople in 1453. This ends the last trace of Christian rule in the East, and the last and much-altered vestige of Rome's once mighty Empire. *1453 CE* In the century following the fall of Constantinople, Europe is awed and terrified by the military might of Mehmet II, Suleiman the

179

Photo 20. One of the battle-scarred gates of Suleiman's Wall.

Magnificent, and their successors. The Turkish Empire, called the Ottoman Empire by European chroniclers, extends from northern Africa, into the Middle East, and into eastern and southeastern Europe. As late as the mid-seventeenth century, it threatens Vienna.

The land link between the three parts of the Ottoman Empire is Palestine. However, the Ottomans rule an area that slowly turns into a backwater, Palestine with it. Overland caravan trade along the route of the Silk Road and the Fertile Crescent, the source of Turkish wealth, gives way to maritime trade on the world's oceans. The ports at the eastern end of the Mediterranean Sea fall into disuse.

The Holy Land under the Ottomans

Suleiman the Magnificent (1520-1566) takes great interest in Jerusalem and rebuilds the wall of the ancient city, giving a new definition to its boundaries. He directs that the Dome of the Rock be refurbished. But after Suleiman, the fortunes of the Turks decline, and the Holy Land experiences centuries of partial neglect under Ottoman rule. Cities shrink into towns, and towns disappear. Arab *1520-* flocks graze the hillsides, and trees are cut for firewood. Malarial *1918* swamps border the Jordan River. Roads are neglected, and brigands make travel dangerous.

180

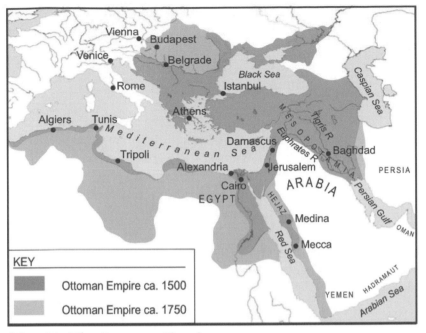

KEY

- Ottoman Empire ca. 1500
- Ottoman Empire ca. 1750

Map 29. The Ottoman Empire.

Palestinian townsmen ply ancient crafts, carry on trade, and perform clerical services for the Ottoman rulers. But the Ottomans do not allow them self-rule. Monks and nuns from both Roman and Orthodox traditions oversee and maintain the places of pilgrimage, and European travelers make sketches that illustrate the extent to which the lands of the Bible have been neglected.

A small number of Jews continue to live in the Holy Land, in the towns of Galilee and in places holy to their faith – Jerusalem, Hebron, Shechem. Since their expulsion by the Romans in the first and early second centuries, the remnant left in Palestine constitutes a gradually eroding and politically powerless minority.

In cities of the Ottoman Empire, the Jews are tolerated and generally not ill-treated; their experience especially in banking and finance is valued. Originally by decree but later by convention or preference, the Jews in Ottoman cities live in a separate Jewish Quarter. There they carry on their customs and worship and pass on their traditions to their children. This is the origin of the Jewish Quarter in the Old City of Jerusalem. Today about one-third of the city within Suleiman's Wall is occupied by the Arab Quarter. The remainder is divided among the Jewish Quarter, Christian Quarter, and Armenian Quarter. The character of each is distinctive, no less today than during the period of Ottoman rule.

Beginnings of Modernity

Within the limits of their vision, the Ottomans manage to keep order in Palestine and even make early attempts at building a modern infrastructure. They govern Palestine as a part of a much larger territory that extends from Arabia to the southern border of what is now Turkey. Late in the nineteenth century, they build a rail link between Mecca in western Arabia and Damascus in Syria.

I retain an image of Ottoman military barracks erected at the site of the ruins at Gadara. Jordanian authorities have decided that these Ottoman period pieces should come down so that the focus can be on the Roman character of the site. I feel they should stay so that visitors can get a feel for Gadara's more recent history. The truth is there is almost no evidence of nearly five centuries of Ottoman rule, either in Israel or Jordan.

Toward the end of the nineteenth century, Protestant and Catholic organizations from Europe and the United States come to the Holy Land to establish hospitals and schools. Among the Palestinian Arabs, there is now the beginnings of a Western-educated professional class. At the turn of the twentieth century, Ottoman Palestine is overwhelmingly Arab (largely Muslim but also Christian) and largely rural. Jerusalem is the cultural center of Palestine, but the center of Turkish rule is Damascus.

During World War I, the Arabs in Palestine side with the British against the moribund Ottoman Empire, which casts its lot with *1914-* Germany. T. E. Lawrence parleys with the Arab sheiks of the Hejaz *1918* (western Arabia) at Wadi Rum, the desert redoubt in what is now southern Jordan. He leads them into battle against the Turks, and they cut the rail lines between Mecca and Damascus.

At the end of World War I, the Ottoman Empire is no more. Its only remnant is the modern country of Turkey, where a revolution led by Kemal Ataturk installs a new and viable state in 1923, secular and on the road to modernity. The rest of the Ottoman Empire must be reordered. Officially, the task falls to the League of Nations. But in reality, it is the British and French who are on the scene.

182

24
The Mandate Years and After: Roots of Arab Anger

His Majesty's Government views with favour the establishment in Palestine of a national home for the Jewish people and will use their best endeavours to facilitate the achievement of this object, it being clearly understood that nothing shall be done which may prejudice the civil and religious rights of existing non-Jewish communities in Palestine...
Arthur James Balfour
British Foreign Secretary, in a letter to Baron Lionel Rothschild, November 2, 1917

Out of the eastern remnants of the former Ottoman Empire, the League of Nations creates the modern states of Jordan, Lebanon, Syria, and Iraq. Palestine is also intended for statehood, but circumstances there will frustrate the creation of a single national state.

Before World War I, Arab nationalist underground movements are forming throughout the region, opposing Ottoman rule. When the Sharif of Mecca and the Bedouin of the Hejaz (the western mountainous fringe of the Arabian Peninsula) cast their lot with the British against the Turks, they receive widespread support from Arab underground members. The hope among the Syrians, especially, is that out of the defeat of the Ottomans a strong Arab state will emerge.

But the British and French have other ideas. In an agreement kept secret from the Arabs, they partition the Arab states into British *1919-* and French spheres of influence, and by 1923 these are confirmed *1923* by the League of Nations. The former Ottoman province of Greater Syria (which included Palestine) is divided into British- and French-ruled areas and eventually becomes four separate entities: Palestine, Trans-Jordan, Syria, and Lebanon. The League awards a mandate over Palestine and Trans-Jordan to the British and a mandate over Syria and Lebanon to the French. Egypt is already a British Protectorate. At the end of the war, the British also control Mesopotamia, and from this position, they secure a League of Nations mandate over Iraq. The League specifies that the mandates are not to be turned into colonies. Instead, they are to be prepared for self-government. But the effect of the mandates is to solidify the British and French presence and to keep the region politically fractured.

There is little or no Arab input into League decision-making, and League planners seem unaware of the impact that the foreign mandates will have on Arab nationalism. In a real sense, Britain and France, working through the League of Nations, lay the groundwork for the resentment toward the West and the political turbulence that has since plagued the region.

The British Sphere: Egypt, Trans-Jordan, Palestine, and Iraq

Egypt. The British presence in Egypt goes back to the mid-nineteenth century. Britain's interest lies in protecting the Suez *1882-* Canal. An Egyptian royal family from an Albanian line, installed *Prsnt.* by the Ottomans, is corrupt and unpopular. Britain rules Egypt as a Protectorate from 1882 until 1922, when it officially recognizes Egypt's independence under the Ottoman-installed king. But Britain continues to maintain control over Egypt's administration and over the Canal. When a popular revolt occurs in 1952, bringing to power General Gamal Abdel Nasser, Britain is ousted. In 1956, Egypt takes control of the Suez Canal. The British, allied for this purpose with France, try unsuccessfully to take it back, and in this context, Israel invades Egypt and acquires Gaza and (temporarily) the Sinai Peninsula. Anti-British and anti-Israeli sentiment runs high, and because the United States is allied with both Britain and Israel, Egyptian anger also turns toward the U.S. Following the 1967 war Egypt loses the Sinai to Israel,

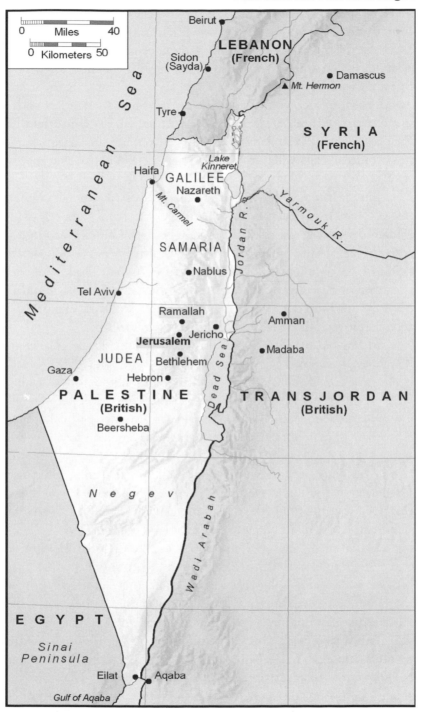

Map 30. The League of Nations Mandates, 1920-1945.

and Egyptians are outraged. In 1978, through the mediation of President Jimmy Carter, Egypt's president Anwar Sadat and Israel's Prime Minister Menachem Begin work out a landmark agreement: Egypt and Israel establish diplomatic relations, and Egypt regains the Sinai Peninsula. But a militant Islamist underground in Egypt assassinates Sadat and works (so far unsuccessfully) to topple the Egyptian government and to install *Sharia* (Quranic) law in its place. At present, in sympathy with the cause of the Palestinians, Egypt has broken almost all diplomatic ties with Israel. Ties with the United States, a major benefactor, remain strong nevertheless.

Jordan. After World War I, Britain receives a League of Nations mandate to rule over Palestine and the largely desert land to the east of the *1919-* Jordan River, called Trans-Jordan. Britain places as king of Trans-Jordan *Prsnt.* Abdullah ibn al-Hussein, the prince of the Hashemite tribe that is loyal to Britain in the fight to oust the Ottomans from Arabia. The Hashemites trace their lineage directly to Muhammed. The father of King Abdullah bears the title Emir of Mecca, King of the Hejaz, and King of the Arabs. (A title Ibn Saud disputes: see **Saudi Arabia**, below.)

In 1946 Trans-Jordan gains its independence as the Hashemite Kingdom of Jordan. The present ruler, King Abdullah (1999-Present), is the great-grandson of Jordan's first king. Jordan goes to war against Israel in 1948, and although it takes over the West Bank and the Old City of Jerusalem, it pays dearly in the war's aftermath, as Palestinian refugees swell its population and create political problems for the young state. Between 1970 and 1971 Jordan's King Hussein, grandson of King Abdullah, cracks down hard on Arafat's Palestinian Liberation Organization and forces the PLO to relocate its headquarters. It is at this point that the PLO goes to Lebanon. With the political situation stabilized, Hussein sets about to build Jordan's economy.

Jordan establishes diplomatic relations with Israel in 1994, as one of the results of the Oslo Accord. Unlike most of the other Oslo provisions, Jordan's diplomatic ties with Israel have not been broken since, and Jordan is often a conduit through which Israelis and Palestinians can initiate or maintain negotiations.

Palestine. From the beginning of the mandate, Palestine presents Britain with a situation quite different from the Trans-Jordan *1919-* Mandate. It is more urban and its population more diverse, with a *1948* small but growing number of Jewish immigrants. Britain is committed simultaneously to allowing Jewish immigration into Palestine and protecting the rights of Palestine's Arabs, a task which it carries out by carefully enumerating and limiting the number of Jews who are allowed into Palestine. At the same time, as the Mandate prospers economically, new job opportunities result in an influx of Arab immigrants from adjacent countries, and these immigrants are not counted. The overall population of Palestine grows. At the end of the Mandate it is about one-third Jewish, two-thirds Arab.

As Nazi persecutions of Jews accelerates in the 1930s, Britain honors what it feels is its commitment to the Arabs and does not increase the number of Jews it allows into Palestine. While frustrating and angering the Jews who live under the Mandate, Britain's policy toward Jewish immigration fails to mollify the Arabs. During the entire period of the Mandate, Arabs are unhappy with the British, for they feel that Palestine should be their country and that Britain has no right to allow Jewish immigrants to settle there. Arab underground leaders regularly attack Jewish settlements. A Jewish underground responds with measures both defensive and offensive. People are killed on both sides.

In this volatile situation Britain rules Palestine directly, hoping to set up a parliamentary form of government but with no workable vision for forming a Palestinian state. Arab underground leaders fume; their compatriots in Jordan and Iraq have their own government, and they blame the Jews for the lack of progress in setting up a self-governing Palestine. With Jewish Holocaust refugees flooding into the Mandate after World War II, and with no ability to stop the violence between Arabs and Jews, Britain has painted itself into a corner. It turns the problem over to the United Nations, which comes up with a way of dividing Palestine into an Arab state and a Jewish state, based on where most Arabs and most Jews live (Map 2). The division is to take place in October of 1948. Arab countries bitterly oppose this division and their armies mobilize to fight. They mass on the Mandate's borders. Jewish leaders in Palestine decide they dare not wait. On the day that the British Palestinian Mandate officially ends, May 14, 1948, Israel declares independence and the first Arab-Israeli war begins.

Iraq. Iraq becomes part of Britain's sphere when the British defeat the Ottomans in Mesopotamia in World War I. Afterward, *1921-* the League of Nations awards Iraq to Britain as a mandate. Aware of *Prsnt.* oil in the region, the British want to continue to govern. But popular

187

uprisings in Iraq force the British to set up the state of Iraq, and a king is elected in 1921 by plebiscite. King Faisal is a Hashemite, a brother to Abdullah of Trans-Jordan. In 1932, the British Mandate is officially terminated and Iraq enters the League of Nations as a monarchy. In effect, however, the British continue to exert influence over the Iraqi king.

A series of coups, spawned by nationalist military leaders, topple the monarchy in 1958 and by 1979 bring to power a military strong man named Saddam Hussein. Hussein, a leader in the (largely Sunni) Ba-ath Arab Socialist Party, uses oil revenues to flex and undergird his power. Although as Baathists they share common aims of secularism, socialism, and Arab unity, Saddam Hussein and neighboring Syrian president Hafez Assad (after his death, his son Bashar Assad) are rivals. Like Assad, however, Saddam Hussein opposes Israel, supports the PLO with weapons, and bears deep grievances toward the West. He sees Baghdad as a rival to Cairo as the intellectual capital of the Arab world. But in subsequent years he makes too many enemies for this to occur. He leads Iraq into a war with Shi'ite Iran in the 1980s over rival claims to territory in the Shatt al-Arab (the delta region fronting on the Persian Gulf); he wins this war but takes huge losses in manpower. In 1990 he invades neighboring Kuwait and loses the subsequent war with the United States and allied powers.

Iraq has three main ethnic groups: the Kurds in the oil-rich north, who are Sunni Islam, have strong separatist aspirations and represent 20 percent of Iraq's population; the Arab Sunnis, centering on Baghdad and central Iraq, whose 20 percent of the population gains absolute political control of Iraq under Saddam Hussein, and the 60 percent majority group, the Arab Shi'ites, mostly in the south, who are suppressed by Hussein. Ruling by terror, Hussein reveals to the world community his willingness to use weapons of mass destruction (WMDs) even against his own people.

During the 1990s Saddam Hussein becomes a world pariah as he frustrates UN searches for suspected WMDs. Banned from normal world trade, he diverts humanitarian aid to building up personal wealth and advantage for his Sunni followers. In 2003 the United States and Coalition partners invade Iraq. Militarily defeated, Saddam Hussein is captured and is now in Coalition hands. Meanwhile, the United States and its Coalition allies are struggling to rebuild Iraq's economy and to lead Iraq toward effective self government. Several factors combine to slow efforts at rebuilding: the perception and consequent resentment among many Iraqis that Coalition troops are an occupying force; the push among the Shi'ites for quick direct elections, which would then concentrate power in the hands of the much-aggrieved Shi'ites and might precipitate civil war; the efforts of the Kurds to take back property wrested from them by the Sunnis in the oil-rich north; and the covert resistance from underground movements sparked by Saddam's Hussein's former followers and by foreign Al Qaeda-trained terrorists who are slipping through Iraq's porous desert borders with Syria.

The French Sphere: Syria and Lebanon

Syria. At the end of World War I, France, like Britain, is faced with Arab resistance to its mandates. The Syrians feel betrayed by the British/French agreement to partition Arab lands. Syrian Arab *1919-* underground independence movements attempt to thwart French rule, *Prsnt.* and the French have a tough time keeping order in Syria. Syria finally achieves independence at the end of World War II. A series of military coups leave the country unstable for twenty years. Meanwhile, the Ba-ath Arab Socialist Party gains strength in Syria as in Iraq and in 1970 brings General Hafez Assad to power. His son, Bashar Assad, is Syria's president today. Syria actively opposes Israel, wants the Golan Heights back, refuses to offer citizenship to Palestinian refugees living in Syria, and continues its Baathist commitment to socialism, secularism and Arab unity. Syria is suspected of allowing Al-Qaeda operatives to filter across the Syria/Iraq desert border. From its capital in Damascus, Syrians are the defacto rulers of Lebanon. After Lebanon's protracted civil war (see **Lebanon** below), Syria enforces peace on Lebanon and still keeps a strong military presence there, despite UN resolutions calling for Syria's departure from Lebanon.

Lebanon. Until the beginning of the French Mandate in 1923 Lebanon is considered to be part of Greater Syria. France creates Lebanon essentially to give a voice to the only substantial Christian *1919-* population in the Middle East. The border with Syria runs along the *Prsnt.* crest of the mountains shared by the two countries. The new Lebanon, which includes both the Muslim coastal areas and the Christian hill country, has an Arab population that at the beginning of the Mandate is about 60 percent Christian, 40 percent Muslim. When Lebanon becomes independent in 1943 it is prospering and has a strong framework for democracy. Most of the leaders of the republic that emerges are Christian. Lebanon becomes the banking and cultural capital of the Arab Middle East. However, the Muslim population, with a higher birthrate, begins to exceed that of the Christian, and Muslims demand a voice in the government proportionate to their population. A shared-rule policy is developed but fails to create stability.

In 1948, when Israel becomes a country, a large number of Palestinians come as refugees to Lebanon. Many continue to live there, about a third still in United Nations refugee camps. Their presence, as well as Arab Muslim dissatisfaction with minority Christian rule, precipitates a civil war that rages for much of the time between the late 1950s and the late 1980s. Syrian military forces intervene in 1976, temporarily imposing peace. They are still in Lebanon (see **Syria**, above). In 1971, after Jordan expels the Palestine Liberation Organization, the PLO transfers its headquarters to Beirut. The Hezbullah party, based in southern Lebanon among Shi'ite Muslims, makes common cause with the PLO, and–supported both by Syria and by Shi'ite Iran–launches terrorist raids into northern Israel. To counter, Israel invades Lebanon, bombs the Muslim areas of Beirut, and ceases military action only after a multinational force of United States and Western European troops arrives to protect Muslim and Palestinian civilians and to move the PLO headquarters to Tunisia.

The multinational force withdraws after a barracks bombing kills 300 U.S. and French troops in 1983. The preceding year, following a Muslim terrorists' assassination of Lebanon's Christian president-elect, Israeli-backed Christian militia massacre hundreds of Palestinian civilians in two refugee camps. The horror of this massacre turns world opinion against the Israelis, who then withdraw to southern Lebanon to counter Hezbullah attacks. Israel stays in southern Lebanon until 2000, when it withdraws its troops. Since the early 1990s, Lebanon has known an uneasy peace. With the rebuilding of its capital of Beirut, it may yet again resemble the Jewel of the Eastern Mediterranean it formerly was.

The Arabian Peninsula

Saudi Arabia. The Bedouin of central Arabia take no part in World War I, nor are they in league with the Hashemite tribes of the

Hejaz who fight against the Ottomans and are rewarded when their titular leaders receive the thrones of Jordan and Iraq. In 1902, Abdulaziz ibn Saud captures Riyadh and sets out on a 30-year campaign to unify *1902-* the Arabian Peninsula. His grandson rules in Saudi Arabia today, and *Prsnt.* his progeny and their children command the vast wealth that begins to come to the Peninsula with the discovery of oil on Arabia's Persian Gulf coast. A British advisor, an ex-spy angry at his own government, turns ibn Saud in the direction of United States rather than British oil interests. By 1932 it is the joint-venture of an American oil consortium (Standard Oil, Texaco, and Mobil) and the Saudi family, called the Arabian American Oil Company (ARAMCO) that begins to extract the oil from Saudi Arabia's fabulously productive Persian Gulf field. In the beginning Saudi princes run through vast oil fortunes, but by the 1960s they begin to use their oil wealth to build an impressive infrastructure in what was once a land of Bedouin nomads and oasis dwellers.

The Saudis adhere to an extremist Islamic sect, the Wahabbis, named after its founder, an eighteenth century Muslim religious leader. Saudi Arabia is an Islamic state, governed by *Sharia* law based entirely on the Quran. It accepts responsibility for maintaining the pilgrimage sites of Mecca and Medina, and with its oil money (the oil industry is now nationalized, and there is no longer an Arabian American Oil Company), it funds madrasas in all Muslim countries, where young boys learn the Wahabbi extremist brand of militant Islam. Saudi-funded madrasas in Pakistan and Afghanistan, for example, often serve as the only schooling young boys receive. In Indonesia, traditionally religiously tolerant, Saudi-financed schools and mosques have now spawned a militant Islamism that is precipitating religious wars.

To protect his oil resources during the Gulf War with Iraq in 1990-1991, the Saudi king allows the U.S. to deploy its military forces within the kingdom. By doing this, he intensely angers a rich young Saudi named Osama bin Laden, who believes that because the Arabian Peninsula was the home of the Prophet Muhammed, the presence of U.S. troops defiles holy Saudi soil. He leaves for Afghanistan to fight the Russians, then stays on in Afghanistan to establish and train terrorists for his Al Qaeda network, aimed at destabilizing countries of the West and overthrowing both the Saudi government and moderate Arab regimes. Bin Laden sees Israel as a cancer in land that belongs to Arabs, and he reserves his greatest vitriol for the United States, because of its support for Israel.

United States' relations with Saudi Arabia become problematical with the events of September 11, 2001, when 14 of the 19 hijackers are found to be Saudi citizens. As members of Al Qaeda, the hijackers are among those committed to overthrow the Saudi regime. But their carefully planned attacks in New York City and Washington DC require support from many sources, some of which are traced to leading Saudi families and charities. The Saudi government has since cracked down hard on terrorists within its borders. Meanwhile, the United States military has little remaining presence within the Kingdom.

Saudi Arabia unites with other Arab countries in opposition to Israel and helps to fund the Palestinian Authority. In 2002 Saudi Prince Abdullah, the nominal head of state, joins in the international effort to bring about peace between Israel and the Palestinians. Abdullah proposes a variant of U.N. resolution 202, which would pledge all Arab states to give diplomatic recognition to Israel following Israel's return to pre-1967 boundaries. This proposal represents a significant shift in Saudi policy, which since 1947 has been unwavering in opposing Israel's right to exist.

The Gulf States. On the fringes of the Arabian Peninsula in the Persian Gulf, and extending south of the Straits of Hormuz, are a number of Arab Bedouin states that early in the past century welcome British advisors, who are on the spot as oil is being discovered beneath their desert domains. With good advice, and an abundance of oil to finance their venture, a group of Sheiks join to form the United Arab Emirates, whose oil wealth is now prodigious. Other former Bedouin sheikdoms likewise evolve into the modern countries of Kuwait, Bahrain, Qatar, and Oman. Bahrain, the oldest of the oil-rich Gulf states, has developed into a sophisticated center of international banking.

Capitalizing on their spectacular good fortune, the Sheiks in each of these countries, who rule with absolute authority, direct a good part of their wealth toward building cities with spectacular architecture, port facilities as advanced as any in the world, modern four-lane highways cutting through the desert, and desalinization plants, giving their coastal desert domains the appearance of highly developed nations. Their citizens need pay no taxes and receive free education and medical care. Gradually a cadre of Gulf States citizens is being trained abroad for present and future leadership. Meanwhile, foreign workmen from Pakistan, India, Bangladesh, and the Philippines do most of the hard labor involved in construction. The Gulf States support the Palestinians and are no less determined than Saudi Arabia in their opposition to Israel, but unlike the Saudi kingdom they give critical logistical support to coalition forces in the 2003 war to topple Saddam Hussein.

Yemen. The southwestern portion of the Arabian Peninsula is occupied by Yemen, a very old country that may have been the home of the fabled Queen of Sheba. Or the Queen of Sheba, if she existed, may have come from nearby Ethiopia, with which Yemen maintains close contact for thousands of years. Coffee is said to have originated in the highlands of either Yemen or Ethiopia, and Yemen's ancient Jewish community may well have been the origin of the Jewish community in Ethiopia. From Yemen's Arabian Sea desert coastlands come the frankincense and myrrh that once dominates caravan trade. The greatest part of Yemen is desert, but Sana, its capital, is centered in the better-watered highlands at the south end of the Hejaz, which rise to 8000 feet. Yemen has no oil or other resources on which to build a modern state, and most of its population are farmers. It ranks among the world's poorest countries. Nevertheless, the wealthy family into which Osama bin Laden was born originated in the highlands of Yemen. The country today has a reputation for harboring terrorists, although officially it opposes the Al Qaeda movement. In Yemen's port of Aden, a United States naval vessel is severely damaged by terrorist action in 2000. (Yemen's once sizeable Jewish community is no longer welcome after 1948 and is transported to Israel. Yemeni Jews form a conservative bloc in the Israeli parliament, and they infuse an exotic element into Israel's ever-evolving popular culture.)

25

The Roots of
Modern Israel

J' Accuse!
Emile Zola
Public Letter to French Authorities in defense of
Captain Alfred Dreyfus, 1894.

If you will it, then it [Zionism] is no dream.
Theodor Herzl

Now is the time to make plans to come home to
Israel. Today you can pick up the telephone and make
arrangements to move to Israel. Today you can sell your
home for a fair price. Today you can leave with all your
money, your belongings and your family.
Tomorrow may be too late.
Ahavat Israel Web site

What of the people of the Diaspora? By the middle of the fourth century, only five percent of all the world's Jews remain in Palestine. This percentage continues to decline in succeeding centuries. As we have seen, there have been many Diasporas, beginning with the Assyrian conquest, when ten ancient Hebrew tribes are scattered and lose their identity. But ever after, in the scatterings brought about by the Babylonians and Romans, or in voluntary emigration through the centuries, Jews everywhere retain their sense of themselves as a separate people, a chosen people, a people whom God once led out of captivity into the

ca 100- 1900 CE

194

Promised Land. Though without a temple in Jerusalem or a central place of worship, the Jews of the Diaspora nevertheless ritually say, at the end of every Seder (the commemorative family meal that begins each Passover observance), "Next year in Jerusalem." Jerusalem is a state of mind, an affair of the heart, and together with the Torah, the Talmud, and the Mishnah, it forges an enduring Jewish identity.

The Diaspora in the Middle East and North Africa

Much of the time following the Roman Diaspora (initiated in 70 CE), the Jews in northern Africa, Arabia, Mesopotamia and Persia live in peace with their neighbors. Until the Romans adopt Christianity, they recognize Judaism as a legitimate religion even while they persecute the Christians. After Christianity becomes the official religion of the Empire, the Jews have a more difficult time, and most leave the Holy Land. Under Islam, the words in the Quran as given to Muhammed guarantee that Jews, as People of the Book, will have dhimmi status; they will be allowed to live in Muslim lands and practice their religion, so long as they pay a special head tax, the jizya. In succeeding centuries, as Islam spreads to North Africa and into Spain, to Western and Central Asia, and eventually to southeastern Europe, how Jews are treated depends on the whims and piety of the Muslim ruler. Any ruler who internalizes the strictures against Jews that are part of the Quran will find ingenious ways to denigrate the Jews in his domain: he will decree that Jews must wear strange, even ridiculous, garb so they can be clearly identified, or that Jews must keep their eyes down when they meet an Arab. Fortunately, fanatic rulers, such as the Almohads in Spain, from where the great twelfth century Jewish philosopher and physician Maimonides is forced to flee, are an exception.

Most Muslim rulers are not troubled by the presence of Jews in their midst. They welcome the revenue from the tax that Jews must pay, and they value the skills of Jewish scholars, physicians, merchants, bankers, and craftsmen who provide valuable service in Muslim cities. A tradition of the cultured Jew—scholar, poet, and administrator—serving alike the ruler and his own Jewish community, comes to the fore and is honored especially by those majority Jews whose status as dhimmi forever marks them as less than full participants in Muslim society. Because Jews are not allowed to own land, almost none make their living by farming. Jews, in other words,

	1948	1968	2001
Aden	8,000	0	0
Algeria	140,000	1,500	0
Egypt	75,000	1,000	100
Iraq	135,000	2,500	100
Lebanon	5,000	3,000	100
Libya	38,000	3,750	0
Morocco	265,000	5,000	5,700
Syria	30,000	4,000	100
Tunisia	105,000	10,000	1,500
Yemen	55,000	500	200
Total	856,000	31,250	7,800

Source: The Jerusalem Report, Jan. 12, 2004

Chart 4. Population of Jews in Arab countries, 1948-2001.

get along in Muslim lands because they recognize the limits imposed on their lives, and they operate within these limits, maintaining their own identity. For most Jews living within the *umma*, Arabic or Persian or Turkish becomes a mother tongue.

But after Israel becomes a country, in 1948, everything changes, as Arab countries vent their anger over the founding of the state of Israel. Jews are no longer welcome in Arab lands. In some cases they are literally "thrown out," unable to take with them any possessions but what they can carry. In other cases, they leave of their own volition, because Arab countries no longer present a comfortable environment. The only two Arab countries where there is still a recognizable Jewish presence are Morocco (5,700) and Tunisia (1,500), and neither of these countries adopt expulsion as government policy, as do all other Arab countries. Except for Morocco and Tunisia, Jews number 100 or less in all Arab countries today. The "In-Gathering" brings in a

ca 1948-1968

196

total of nearly 600,000 Jews from Arab lands, whom Israel considers are no less displaced than the Palestinians who lose their homes to Holocaust survivors in Israel in the late 1940s. The largest Jewish presence in the Middle East today, outside of Israel, is in the non-Arab Muslim countries of Turkey (26,000) and Iran (30,000), whose Jewish communities (like the former Jewish communities in Arab lands) go deep into history and form an important segment of the merchant and professional class.

The Diaspora in Europe

Jews form colonies throughout the Roman Empire in Europe, and it is to Jewish synagogues that Paul goes first when he reaches any Greek or Roman city. Most first century Christians, in Europe as well as in Palestine, are Jews. Trouble begins for Jews in Europe after the Roman Empire adopts Christianity as a state religion, and church leaders take literally the accounts in the Gospel of John blaming Jews for the crucifixion of Jesus. Jews who hold fast to Judaism and maintain their own customs and traditions are often persecuted. The behavior of the Crusaders towards Jews in Palestine mirrors their massacre of Jews in Europe in the early stages of their march. There is no dhimmi status in European lands. The Inquisition is aimed as much at Jews as at apostate Christians. Nevertheless, Jews and Christians find an accommodation, and the Jews do not leave. They perform the same services in European lands, especially as merchants and moneylenders (later, bankers), that are valued in Muslim lands, and sometimes they act as go-betweens when Europeans and Muslims need to do business.

In the ninth century CE Judaism becomes the religion of the ruler of the Khazars, a powerful kingdom that occupies territory on the grasslands between the Black and Caspian Sea. The Khazars are a Turkic people who come originally from Central Asia, but by this time include among their population also many Persian and Semitic peoples who have come north from Mesopotamia. The Khazar kingdom includes followers of Islam, Judaism, and Zoroastrianism (a Persian religion), as well as primitive religions. Some of the people who reach the region in earlier times may well have been Jews from the Babylonian or Roman or Byzantine diasporas, but this is only conjecture. At any rate, for a century or more Judaism is the official religion of the Khazar kingdom, and during this period Judaism is widely adopted not only among the Khazars, but also among Slavic tribesmen to the west, whom they conquer. By the end of the twelfth century the Khazar kingdom is no longer politically significant. But when eventually, two centuries later, Jewish settlers in central Europe begin migrating eastward into Slavic lands, they find a few pockets of existing Slavic Jewish communities. There is now no way of telling to what extent Khazar roots exist among the once-extensive Jewish communities in eastern Europe, Russia, and Ukraine, but it is probable that they do. As the tools of genetic research progress, there is great interest among scholars in exploring such mysteries.

Unlike Jews who live for many centuries in Arab lands and Western Europe as city-dwellers, many Jews in Slavic lands become farmers. Many also become merchants and professionals and craftsmen in the cities. During most of their history in Eastern European lands, as well as in Western lands, Jews become an under-class. Under Czarist Russia, as elsewhere, Jews seek to live among their own in Jewish sectors of cities and in farm villages as well. But under the Czars (as later under the Nazis) restriction to ghettos is often imposed. Persecution under the Czars is always heavy, and from time to time a Czar orders a pogrom, an organized military raid on Jewish communities. His orders are usually carried out with enthusiasm, for the Russian and Polish peasant – steeped in what is at the time an Orthodox or Roman Catholic faith that blames Jews for the death of Christ – conscripted into the army, is all too eager to do his bit to exterminate the hated Jews.

In European cities also, Jews tend to live in sectors, often called the Jewish Quarter. Although the Ghetto may be mandated, for Jews it is to some extent a comfortable place where they can more easily preserve their customs and identity. Jews in diaspora eventually speak the language of whatever land they settle. But as the need develops for communication between German-speaking and Slavic-speaking Jews, a new language develops – part German, part Slavic, part Hebrew – called Yiddish. A language with its own body of literature, Yiddish is now fast disappearing, for Israelis have no need for it, and most Jews elsewhere in the world are now part of the main culture stream.

In 1492, the year Columbus sets sail for what is to be a New World, their Catholic Majesties Ferdinand and Isabella of Spain expel all Jews from their kingdom. Some among those expelled are descended from Jews who come to the Iberian peninsula in Roman days, but most are descended from Jews who come during the Arab centuries. Through the seven hundred years of the *reconquista*, of territories passing back and forth in battle, they learn to speak Arabic or Spanish, and usually both languages; as well, they evolve a special subculture, part Jewish, part Arab, part Spanish, with its own variant of the Spanish language called *Ladino*. They take this language and culture with them when they flee from Spain.

Jews who once lived in Spain and speak Ladino come to be known as Sephardim, in contrast to those in Western and Eastern Europe, known collectively as the Ashkenazy, most of whom speak Yiddish as well as the language of the country where they live. A large number of Sephardic Jews in southeastern Europe retain their unique Ladino-speaking Sephardic culture down to the twentieth century.

Not a few Sephardim ousted from Spain and Portugal (for Portugal mirrors Spain in its expulsion of Jews) find their way from Iberia to the New World, where under Spanish or Portuguese rule they can live as *conversos,* converts to Roman Catholicism, or die if they backslide into Judaism and are found out. In a quirk of history, Jewish merchant bankers in Central Europe, servants of the Holy Roman Empire whose king also rules Spain, underwrite much of the early exploration in the New World.

In Western Europe, the nineteenth century brings a welcome tolerance towards Jews, who become integrated into the fabric of society. Anti-Semitism exists but seldom overtly surfaces. But in Eastern Europe persecution becomes institutionalized as rulers unleash their armies on Jewish villages in sanctioned *pogroms.*

The Diaspora widens as more than four million Jews leave Europe in the nineteenth and early twentieth centuries, joining other Europeans seeking opportunities in the United States, Canada, Middle and South America, South Africa, and Australia. In the United States the biggest wave of Jewish immigrants comes in the late 19th and early 20th century, from among the Ashkenazy of Eastern Europe, who, seeing opportunity, set about first to learn the language of the adopted country and then become merchants and professionals in cities all over the United States.

Some six million European Jews are killed in the Nazi Holocaust *1940-* in Europe between 1940 and 1945. Survivors of Nazi death camps *1945* form the initial group of refugees who begin arriving in the Palestine Mandate, then Israel, after 1945. Today there are only tiny remnant Jewish communities in Germany and countries under Nazi rule in World War II.

The apology of Pope John Paul II for past sins of persecution and intolerance by the Roman Catholic Church toward Jews, made in Rome in the millennial year and reiterated by the Pope during his visit to the Holy Land, is of the utmost historical significance. Some in Israel feel that the Pope did not go far enough, and that he should have specifically admitted Rome's responsibility in the Holocaust, through its failure to act, and worse, by documented evidence of complicity. But it would have been impossible to embark on an almost endless litany of evidence of past barbarism, of which the Holocaust is now the most keenly felt.

The Jewish community in Britain, never large, and never subject to the Holocaust, is thriving. The large Jewish community in Russia, persecuted under the Czars and forbidden religious observances under the Communists, suffers now only latent Russian anti-Semitism. In the past two decades since emigration from Russia has been allowed, one million Jews have left Russia for Israel.

Zionism and Early Zionist Settlers

In a sense, Zionism is as old as the Babylon Captivity, when Judeans far from their homeland long for Jerusalem and their destroyed Temple. The term Zionism is derived from "Mount Zion," the rise within the southwest part of the Old City of Jerusalem where David built his palace. A low ridge connects Mount Zion to Solomon's Temple Mount (the Haram al-Sharif) in the eastern part of the city. Throughout history "Zion" among Jews becomes a metaphor for Jerusalem, and for keeping alive the traditions and beliefs that started in ancient Judea. Not until the middle of the 19th century, however, does the idea of Zionism as an organized movement take root. And it gets its start not from within the Jewish community but in England, among Protestant Christians.

ca. *1850*

Christians in England, bothered in their conscience by the treatment of Jews in Europe, begin to explore an alternative, the creation of a homeland for Jews in Palestine. Artists by this time have made Jerusalem and the Holy Land well known to Europeans; but the pictures they sketch show a land that is essentially treeless, and with few people, an image that reflects the condition of much of the Holy Land, particularly the central plateau, towards the end of the Ottoman Empire. Artists seldom sketch the fertile and more populous lands of the coastal plain and of Galilee. And so the impression gained by well-meaning but insufficiently informed visionaries is that Palestine is a largely vacant land which could favor settlement. Zionism as a movement is born. It gets further impetus from a belief among some Christians that a return of Jews to the Holy Land and a cataclysmic struggle there must precede the Second Coming of Christ, understandings gained from a literal reading of the Book of Revelation, the final book of the New Testament. Prime Minister William Gladstone, a fervent Methodist, a fervent Zionist, keeps alive the idea of a homeland in Palestine for Jews.

A fund is started, and contributions come also from wealthy Jewish banking families, on the continent as well as in England. When Czarist Russia seeks to hunt down socialist revolutionaries – many of them highly educated Jewish professionals – trying to overthrow the established order, a haven in Palestine is held out, and funds are available for purchasing land from Turkish landholders. The first European Jewish settlers reach Palestine in the late 1870s. The pioneer settlers establish the idea of a *kibbutz*, a communal farm where work and property are shared. They also plan that the language of the new land, soon to welcome Jewish settlers speaking a variety of tongues, shall be Hebrew, the ancient liturgical language which they work to adapt to modern usage and vocabulary.

In the 1890s, Zionism becomes an organized Jewish movement. It is started by Theodor Herzl, an Austrian Jewish journalist and playwright who sees Zionism as a possible answer to the still-existent anti-Semitism that he witnesses in France while covering the Dreyfus Affair. In 1894, Captain Alfred Dreyfus, a French army officer and a Jew, is unjustly accused of treason and sentenced to the French penal colony on Devil's Island, amidst ugly anti-Semitic signs displayed at that time on the streets of Paris. The Dreyfus Affair splits France. The government, the army, the Church, and the conservative press are allied against Dreyfus, despite the fact that the real traitor – a member of the French aristocracy, and a Roman Catholic – is known to many. The writer Emile Zola champions Dreyfus's cause and later helps to secure his release from Devil's Island.

Appalled by the blatant anti-Semitism he has witnessed at the Dreyfus trial, Herzl perceives that Zionism can offer Jews a political alternative to enduring persecution, and in 1895 he writes *The Jewish* *1895* *State: A Modern Solution to the Jewish Question.* The following year he founds the World Zionist Organization, a movement that divides the world Jewish community. Some support it and devote their lives to its cause; others reject the political implications of Jewish settlement in the Holy Land. The world Christian community is likewise ambivalent. Some (for theological as well as moral reasons) give outright financial support to the cause of Zionism, but most reject the idea as politically unworkable and, in the "enlightened world" at the beginning of the twentieth century, indeed unnecessary. Meanwhile, in Eastern Europe and Russia, pogroms continue in Jewish villages and Jewish urban ghettos.

By the turn of the century, the Zionist movement is supporting a trickle of Jews from Eastern Europe and Russia who come to live in Palestine. The movement aids their immigration and funds their land purchases. Official Ottoman policy forbids Jewish settlement in Palestine. But local Turkish functionaries, their palms greased, look the other way as absentee Arab and Turkish landholders demand inflated prices for degraded land that has long since ceased to bring in much income. Most of the early settlements are on the coastal lowlands, the area between Tel Aviv (a modern city that grows with the settlers) and Haifa. Arab tenants who live on this land as subsistence farmers or herders must leave. Or they can stay as workmen on land they formerly considered theirs. The seeds of resentment are sown. Meanwhile, settlers on pioneer kibbutzim and *moshavs* (cooperative settlements permitting private ownership) begin to plant trees on slopes that are long denuded by grazing, a practice that continues in Israel to this day and has transformed the appearance of the land.

There is an overwhelming difference, a great infusion of green, on slopes in Israel since I first saw the country more than forty years ago.

Among other crops, the early settlers plant orange trees, and very early the large sweet Jaffa oranges are introduced to the European market. Against overwhelming early odds, the pioneers hold on and begin to prosper. Labor is in short supply, and Arab workers are needed. Word begins to get around to Arabs who have long since left Palestine: There is work to be had on Jewish farms, and in Jewish enterprises in Tel Aviv and Haifa. Arab immigration into Palestine outpaces Jewish immigration.

Through the early decades of the twentieth century, Jewish settlement in the Holy Land grows gradually from a trickle to a flow, particularly after the British Mandate takes over from the Ottomans. Not all of the early Jewish immigrants become farmers. Some employ skills learned in Europe as merchants or craftsmen in the relatively cosmopolitan and growing port city of Haifa, located at the foot of the ridge known as Mount Carmel, midway between the ruins of ancient Caesarea and the Crusader's Acre. Skilled diamond cutters from Amsterdam and Antwerp set up in Haifa, the beginnings of a new world center for the diamond industry. Another group of pioneer immigrants in Haifa is a German community, whose solidly built houses and shops dating from the early twentieth century indicate they prospered. No other sign of that community remains today.

Haifa today is a thriving industrial city and Israel's chief port. It is not particularly attractive, but it has one of the country's leading universities, and it has a beautiful formal garden leading to the tomb and shrine of the founder of the Baha'i faith, the 19th century Persian mystic called Baha'u'llah, who dies in exile in Ottoman Palestine. One enters the shrine in total silence, out of respect for a teacher who nobly tried to synthesize the teachings of all the world's great religions.

Britain's Palestine Dilemma

Midway into World War I, Britain's Foreign Office attempts to deal with the problem of the growing number of Jewish settlements in Palestine, for the British fully expect that they will be governing postwar Palestine. *1917* The British are torn. On the one hand, they are sympathetic to the cause of Zionism, which originates in Britain. On the other hand, they are now the champions and allies of the Arabs. Jewish Zionists in England are alarmed: what will become of the Zionist Movement? Baron Rothschild, leader of the Jewish Zionist community in London, sends a memo to Lord Arthur Balfour, Britain's Foreign Secretary, asking for clarification of British policy. Balfour's reply, soon formalized into government policy, follows:

His Majesty's Government views with favour the establishment in Palestine of a national home for the Jewish people and will use their best endeavours to facilitate the achievement of this objective, it being clearly understood that nothing will be done which may prejudice the civil and religious rights of existing non-Jewish communities in Palestine.

The British government has now committed itself to a policy that thirty years later will doom the prospects for self-government in Palestine. At one and the same time, Palestine shall be a homeland for Jews, and Arab rights shall not be infringed.

By the 1920s, Palestinian Arabs begin to react to the presence of Jewish settlers in their midst. Arab tenant farmers and farm workers are losing their homes and jobs as absentee landowners sell their properties to Jewish settlers. Arabs are beginning to fear that what is still a trickle of pioneer Jewish settlement may soon pose a threat to their homeland. Scores of Jewish settlers are killed in an Arab underground action in the mid-1920s, and thereafter Jewish underground groups organize to counter the threat. Both sides use brutal tactics. But at this stage the British are still able to keep peace, for the most part, in the Palestinian Mandate. Both Arab and Jewish underground members risk imprisonment.

In the years between the end of World War I and World War II, the British try hard to rule their Palestine and Trans-Jordan Mandates *1918-* with fairness. They improve on the Ottoman infrastructure, and they *1940* begin water projects to divert Jordan River water for irrigation. But as more and more Jews come to live in Palestine, Arabs become increasingly resentful. In the 1930s application of Jews to emigrate to Palestine steps up as Hitler begins to reveal his plans for exterminating Europe's Jews. As the Jewish refugees from Nazi Germany begin arriving, Arab resentment escalates. Settlers are attacked, and the Jewish underground retaliates. Meanwhile, the British try to keep both the Arab and Jewish undergrounds at bay. To mollify the Arabs, the British deliberately hold down the number of refugees from Hitler's Germany who are allowed to settle in Palestine.

Many young Jews volunteer for World War II service in Britain's Jewish Brigade. Few Palestinian Arabs do. They view the British as *1940-* their enemy and the Mandate as a hindrance to statehood for Palestine. *1945* They deeply resent the fact that other Arab Mandates are headed for independence.

As World War II ends, the full extent of the Holocaust is revealed. Jewish leaders in Britain and the United States struggle over their *1945-* response. Not all are inclined toward Zionism, but all are in deep *1948* mourning over the tragedy. The American Jewish Congress is formed to offer an alternative to Zionism: that resettlement must occur in many places in the world, including Palestine, but that in Palestine Arabs and Jews together should form a democratic society. Arabs should not have

Photo 21. Holocaust memorial tree dedicated to Raoul Wallenberg at the Yad Vashem Holocaust Museum.

to leave their homeland. This more moderate voice, which originally appeals to Reformed Judaism in the United States, is eventually hushed as frantic and organized Zionist appeals open purses of Jews in the United States who survive the war in safety.

In Palestine, events rush faster than the British can contain them. Holocaust survivors pour into Palestinian lands. The Jewish underground movement, operating as the highly effective and secretive Haganah and Irgun, assists the Holocaust settlers. It forcibly takes over land and property from Arab families, and tells the Arabs to leave. No longer is there payment for land taken. Forced out, the majority of Arabs do leave, over the period from 1946 to 1949. The Israelis put out the word that the Arabs flee of their own free will. And flee some do, uneasy and intimidated. But Israeli historians have since documented the land takeover, and Israel no longer denies it. At the same time, it makes uneasy justification in terms of the urgency of the time. The roots of Arab anger today revolve around the displaced Palestinian Arabs.

The Arabs flee to neighboring Arab states, and the Arab states prepare for war. On May 14, 1948, Israel declares independence. The British pull out, and Arab armies move in. The Arab-Israeli war rages for over a year until the UN armistice is signed.

1948

With its borders delineated, and most of the world's countries, conscience-heavy over the Holocaust, recognizing its existence (Arab countries excepted), Israel begins the task of nation-building. Like the warriors of Joshua long ago, the new Israelites (now called Israelis) claim the Promised Land, wresting it from its present owners. Now they must hold on to it. And they must step up their appeal to Jews in the United States, who will bear much of the financial burden.

"Never Again"

Despite continuing territorial conflicts, the Israelis have succeeded in creating a homeland for Holocaust survivors and for Jews the world over who want to live in what tradition tells them is their Promised Land. In the Yad Vashem Holocaust Museum, the story of the Holocaust lives, and Israelis do not want the world to forget. A group of unevenly truncated square stone columns represents the children who were victims at Auschwitz, Buchenwald, or Dachau.

At the entrance to the Yad Vashem Museum, a walkway is lined with gnarled trees, each holding stones lovingly placed at the nook where the tree branches. Each tree is dedicated to someone whose courage saved lives. One of these is in honor of Raoul Wallenberg, the Swedish diplomat who helped thousands of Eastern European Jews to escape the Nazis, only to lose his own life in Russian captivity. One leaves the museum sick at heart, aware that gross inhumanity is not an isolated occurrence, that it has happened, could happen again, and requires the constant vigilance of democratic societies.

Israel continues to assuage the horrors of the Holocaust in a furious and successful effort to build a viable political entity. At the same time, it has assimilated more than 3.5 million immigrants from many different languages and cultures who with great difficulty must learn Hebrew as the ancient/modern common language.

Photo 22. Truncated columns at Yad Vashem represent child victims of the Holocaust.

Israel vows "never again." Never again shall there be a Holocaust. Never again shall Jews be forced to leave their homes. To keep this vow, Israel has what may be the world's best-trained, most-effective military force. Every Israeli male must give three years to the military; every female must give nineteen months. The army is a force for assimilation, and as such has helped Jews from many different cultures and cultural backgrounds to work together.

Wherever I go — on buses, in restaurants, in a northern spa, in the Old City — I see young Israeli military personnel, always with rifles slung over their shoulders. Some wear the small skullcaps that mark an observant Jewish male, but not all do. They are of every hue and of many different genetic strains.

By having its soldiers ride public buses, Israel reduces the need for military transport. In the event of war, the buses can be commandeered. Many Israeli families point to pictures on their walls of their sons or daughters who have died defending their country. Army service can be hazardous, for the frustration and anger of the Palestinians — whose losses in the Intifadeh exceed those of Israelis by a ratio of more than three to one — remain high.

26
Sharon and Arafat:
Antagonists at Seventy

For our part, we will honor our commitments...
Our participation in the great peace process
means that we are betting
everything on the future.
Yasser Arafat
on the signing of the Oslo II Accord
in September 1995 to implement Palestinian
rule over a portion of the Occupied Territories

I don't know anyone who has as much civilian Jewish blood
on his hands as Arafat since the Nazis' time.
Ariel Sharon
then Israeli Defense Minister,
October 1995

In the late 1920s, two babies are born some 200 miles apart into families with deep attachment to the Holy Land. Seven decades and more later, the two will take center stage as bitter antagonists in the Israeli-Palestinian conflict. Neither will keep his birth name.

In 1928 on a moshav north of Tel Aviv in the British Palestine
1928 Mandate, Shmuel and Dvora Scheinerman, who have immigrated from Russia six years prior, name their new son Ariel. The family drops "Scheinerman" and takes the name of the region where they have settled, the "Sharon" Valley.

In Cairo the following year, a successful Palestinian merchant and his wife name their son Muhammed Abdel-Rahman Abdel-Raouf Arafat al-Qudwa, but his family call him "Yasser."

Lessons in Hatred

Growing up, Ariel Sharon and Yasser Arafat have contrasting experiences that will forever color their viewpoints.

On the agricultural settlement where his family has settled, Sharon's father and mother are ostracized by the community *1930's* for refusing to participate in Bolshevist-style public revilement rallies. Ariel learns to live with rejection. His parents are rich in books but otherwise poor. They save so that Ariel can attend high school, a goal rare among moshav families of the time. When he is fourteen, he joins a paramilitary group whose duty is to protect the settlement from Arab raiders. His father gives him a knife. "The knife was symbolic," Sharon later writes, "to protect ourselves from our enemies. It was a lesson I have never forgotten." By age seventeen, Ariel has been inducted into the Haganah, the Jewish underground.

Arafat's mother dies when he is five, and he is sent to live with his uncle's family in Jerusalem. His uncle is among many Palestinians who want the British out of their land. He has been active in the underground. Yasser remembers British soldiers breaking into his uncle's house after midnight, beating members of the family and smashing furniture. By 1938, Yasser is back in Cairo, and eight years later, at age seventeen, he is smuggling arms to Palestine to be used against the British and the Jews.

The Cause

In the Haganah in 1945, Sharon works on missions to harry the British and bring Holocaust refugees into Palestine. He becomes an instructor of police, a regimental intelligence officer, *1940's-* and in the first Arab-Israeli War in 1948, a platoon commander *1950's* in the army. He studies history at Hebrew University and later receives a law degree. But he is never far from military service. He participates in each of Israel's wars, and in between he becomes an expert in gathering intelligence. He organizes and leads "Unit

101," an elite unit that makes bloody retaliatory strikes against Palestinian guerrillas infiltrating Israel.

Arafat is nineteen when Israel declares independence, and he desponds over the results of the first Israeli-Arab war, shocked that the Palestinians now do not even have the state and territory that could have been theirs had the Arabs agreed to the UN partition plan. Arafat (the name he takes after finishing engineering studies in Cairo) is consumed with two interlocking ideas: that Palestinians must have their own independent country, and that the state of Israel must go. Working in Kuwait, Arafat forms the Fatah party, dedicated to these ends. Fatah later merges with the Popular Front for the Liberation of Palestine (PFLP) to form the Palestinian Liberation Organization (PLO), and Arafat is chosen as PLO leader.

Terrorists

Leading both his Fatah party and the PLO, Arafat sets up a base in Jordan, where the largest number of Palestinian refugees *1960's*-live and where he can garner support and recruits. From Jordan *1980's* he directs efforts to destabilize Israel. He orders night raids across the border into Israeli settlements. He arranges for hijacking of international plane flights, and at one point his operatives throw overboard a Jewish tourist aboard an Italian cruise liner. As Arafat grows in power, his PLO becomes a threat to Jordan. Climaxing a two-year civil war, in 1971 Jordan's King Hussein throws out Arafat and his PLO. Arafat sets up shop in Beirut and in 1972 his PLO operatives manage to assassinate almost the entire Israeli Olympics team in Munich. From Beirut, Arafat directs new assaults against Israel with the help of Hezbullah guerrillas infiltrating across Israel's northern border.

Sharon has had enough. In 1982 he invades Lebanon, and his troops quickly reach Beirut. He wants to assassinate Arafat, and he bombs Arafat's headquarters. But Arafat escapes. United States and French troops land in Lebanon to escort Arafat and the PLO to Tunisia, and Sharon is left to deal with Lebanon's ongoing civil war between Muslim and Christian factions. Muslim terrorists assassinate the Christian President-Elect. In senseless retaliation, which Sharon does nothing to prevent, Christian militia raid two Palestinian refugee camps, slaughtering hundreds. (The shock reverberates internationally, and in 2002 Sharon is sued by survivors in court action in Brussels on the charge of a crime against humanity. Although it is determined that the court does not have jurisdiction, and nothing comes of the effort, the memory of the 1982 refugee camp atrocity is kept alive.) Because it happens on his watch, and the outraged Knesset says he should have prevented the massacre, Sharon is called home in disgrace. But first he must pull his army back to southern Lebanon, where they can keep watch on Hezbullah guerrillas. At home and out of uniform, Sharon remains popular with right-leaning Israelis. He is given government posts responsible for building Israeli settlements within the West Bank.

From Tunisia, Arafat continues to direct terrorist moves against Israel. He endorses the first Intifadeh that begins (probably spontaneously, with rock-throwing) in 1988 and abets its escalation. But he is aware that Hamas and the Islamic Jihad are having a greater role than the PLO in directing events. He wants to get back into control. From Tunisia he gains the attention of the United Nations, at a time when a Labor government in Israel is willing to negotiate.

The Oslo Peace Process starts, but Sharon will have none of it: "No one will touch Judea and Samaria [the occupied West *1988-* Bank]. They belong to us. They have been ours for thousands *2000* of years, eternally." In Israel, Sharon is a hero to the right, an obstacle to peace to the center and left. He craves leadership, but it is repeatedly denied him. He is too controversial. Arafat, on the other hand, gains prestige and legitimacy, both within his county and outside of it.

The Statesmen

In 1988, Arafat addresses the United Nations, representing the PLO, and in this address, he changes course. He declares that the PLO renounces terrorism and supports the right of both Israel and a Palestinian state to exist. Sharon publicly questions Arafat's sincerity. But at this point Arafat becomes a world statesman. He signs the Oslo Accord in 1993, receives the Nobel Peace Prize (together with Israeli Prime Minister Yitzhak Rabin), and begins negotiations that after Oslo II (signed in Washington in 1995) create the Palestinian Authority. He returns to Palestine and assumes the Authority's presidency, by popular acclaim. In Palestine he rules absolutely, paying little or no attention to his elected parliament. His source of strength remains the leadership of Fatah and its military wing, Tanzim. The help he gets from Arab countries he mismanages, and his government is widely recognized as corrupt. Meanwhile, he stashes money in European bank accounts, enough so that his wife—living in Paris—can withdraw a million dollars at a time.

*2000-
Prsnt.*
Sharon, distressed and angry at the terms of the Oslo Accord that a left-leaning Labor government has signed, believes that the Israeli government has sold out. He publicly decries the Oslo Accord. When a conservative government returns to power, he joins it and resolves to do all he can to delay Palestinian Authority progress. Resuming the role of director of settlements that he held in the 1980s, Sharon disregards the directives of the Oslo Accord and continues adding to the Jewish population in the West Bank and to the infrastructure supporting the settlements. In 2000 he assumes the post of Defense Minister.

By September of 2000 Arafat is despairing. It is apparent that further negotiations with Israel are going nowhere. The Sharon faction in Israel does not trust him, and Arafat doubts Israel's sincerity. Within the Authority, he must deal with the growing power and popularity of Hamas and the Islamic Jihad, as well as with the PFLP leadership within his own PLO. He has been unable to wrest East Jerusalem from the Israelis, his fragmented Palestinian Authority is almost ungovernable, the Israeli military under Sharon's direction is constraining his people, and his own people are questioning his leadership.

In that same month, Sharon, whose house in the Arab Quarter of Jerusalem—heavily guarded and flying the Israeli flag—is a daily provocation to Arabs, undertakes another provocation as he walks on the Haram al-Sharif (see Chapter 3). He knows what he is doing. To the religious Jewish right the Temple Mount is and must always be Jewish. Here, someday, the Jews will rebuild their Temple. His act is deliberately symbolic.

The Intifadeh begins. Arafat reacts predictably, and so does Hamas and the Islamic Jihad, sending young men and women to turn themselves into suicide bombs. As the Israeli army retaliates with tanks and helicopter raids, Sharon gains strength. In 2001 Israelis finally vote in Sharon as Prime Minister. Meanwhile,

Arafat organizes a new terrorist organization, the Al-Aqsa Martyrs Brigade, under his personal authority. He is desperate to be seen by Palestinians as the man in charge, rather than the leaders of Hamas or the Islamic Jihad.

Both Sharon and Arafat say publicly that they want peace, but each on his own terms. Sharon wants an end to terrorism, assurance that Jewish settlers beyond the Green Line can live in safety, and Israeli sovereignty over all of Jerusalem. Arafat wants an end to all Israeli occupation of the West Bank and Gaza, a Palestinian capital in East Jerusalem, and right of return for Palestinians who once lived in Israel.

Sharon accuses Arafat as masterminding the Intifadeh and refuses to negotiate further with him. He destroys part of Arafat's headquarters in Ramallah, cordons off the rest with tanks, and totally restricts Arafat's movement. Arafat can communicate with other parts of the Authority only by phone, fax, and email. But as the months proceed, suicide missions and retaliation continue. Arafat's popularity with his own people, and his ability to control his Fatah group, its armed wing, the Tanzim, and the Al-Aqsa Martyrs Brigade, remains strong, in spite of his growing bank account in Switzerland and his inability (or unwillingness) to achieve peace through negotiation. Sharon too remains popular, despite the shadow of allegations that he may have taken bribes, allegations which if proven would put an end to his political career. Sharon refuses to talk with Arafat directly. Arafat appoints two successive prime ministers to negotiate with Sharon. They are both ineffective, partly because Sharon yields nothing and partly because Arafat refuses to empower his ministers to halt terrorist strikes.

At seventy-five, both Sharon and Arafat seem truly to represent the majority of their people. And neither seem to harbor hope that negotiation can bring a viable plan for stopping terrorist attacks and the reprisals that follow. Sharon says Arafat does not have the will to stop terrorism. To the extent that Arafat may still be committed in his heart to the destruction of the state of Israel, Sharon may be right. And to the extent that Sharon is committed to protect the rights of Jewish settlers in the West Bank, and to retain Jerusalem as Israel's capital, Arafat too may be right. There is little basis for negotiation, despite the fact that the world urgently demands it and Arab countries, President Bush, and an unofficial Israeli-Palestinian group put forth plans.

213

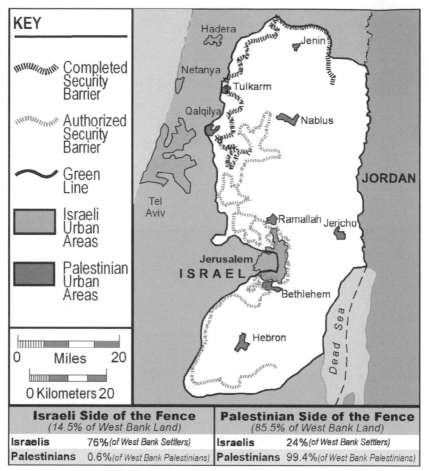

KEY

⬛ Completed Security Barrier

⬛ Authorized Security Barrier

〰 Green Line

⬛ Israeli Urban Areas

⬛ Palestinian Urban Areas

0   Miles   20

0 Kilometers 20

Israeli Side of the Fence (14.5% of West Bank Land)		Palestinian Side of the Fence (85.5% of West Bank Land)	
Israelis	76% (of West Bank Settlers)	Israelis	24% (of West Bank Settlers)
Palestinians	0.6% (of West Bank Palestinians)	Palestinians	99.4% (of West Bank Palestinians)

Source: Israeli Ministry of Defence, Israeli Ministry of the Interior, Palestinian Central Bureau of Statistics, CIA World Factbook, BBC website.

Map 31. The Israeli Security Barrier.

So for the time being Sharon decides to give up on negotiation. He is building a Security Barrier, one-third finished at this writing: a 20-foot high concrete barrier in densely settled areas, and in open stretches a tangle of barbed wire flanked by a wide plowed berm. The fence snakes deeply into the West Bank, appropriating 14.5 percent of Palestinian territory to shelter three-fourths of all settlers. The other fourth Sharon would like to protect as well, and there are rumors that he may want to run the fence in the Jordan Valley, totally surrounding the Palestinians. But that is not going to happen. Sharon knows that taking 40 to 50 percent of Palestinian territory would guarantee the demise of Palestine as a viable entity. Palestinians would then have to give up the idea of an independent state, become a dissident minority within an expanded Israel, and look forward to a time in the not too distant future when Arabs would have the majority vote. At this point Israel would have to decide whether to give up its cherished democracy and become a dictatorship in order to preserve its Jewish identity. None but the most rabid Israeli nationalist want to go that route, and Sharon would not want to lead them there.

So Sharon will finish the security barrier as now planned, and probably will pull settlers out of Gaza and the unprotected parts of the West Bank. Then, he assures Israelis, Palestinian terrorism will stop because, unilaterally, he has done what had to be done to make it stop. Israel and Palestine will be separate entities, on Sharon's terms. At seventy-five, Sharon is probably taking the biggest gamble of his life.

Meanwhile, until the wall is completed, Arafat gambles with the martyrs that his rhetoric continues to produce. And he appeals to the international community, once again, to halt Israeli aggression. He will not negotiate. And Sharon will not negotiate with him.

Sharon and Arafat, lifetime adversaries, in a sense are holding the whole world hostage, because their struggle has been co-opted.

Holy Land, Whose Land?

Part III
Today:
In the Vortex

I didn't realize, when I was last in the Holy Land in the spring of 2000, how fortunate I was. The interminable conflict was simmering, but it was not flaring. Life seemed normal. I was able to move safely and at will. Israeli soldiers were everywhere, giving me a sense of security. But they are everywhere today, and security is so uncertain that most Israelis now admit that military action alone will not let them feel safe.

Israelis and Palestinians have a significance way out of proportion to the land they occupy. What is happening in New Jersey-sized Israel and in the would-be Palestinian state (about the size of Northern Ireland) reverberates in the world at large, forcing awareness, polarizing allegiances, and underlying a wider conflict.

219

27
A Shattering of Dreams

One martyr in the Holy Land is worth
seventy martyrs anywhere else.
Yasser Arafat
in a message to Palestinians,
December 20, 2001 (cited in New York Times)

A compromise over Jerusalem would lead to uncontrollable
violence in the Middle East...No Arab or Muslim can
relinquish rights to East Jerusalem or its holy sites.
Hosni Mubarak
President of Egypt, 2001

[In building the Security Barrier]...
Sharon implies that he
does not foresee any end to the conflict with Arabs.
James Bennett
New York Times, February 4, 2004

The Al-Aqsa Intifadeh, which begins in September of 2000, escalates quickly from stones and rocks to mortars and 2000 bombs. The delivery medium shifts, too, as young Palestinians strap on belts loaded with explosives and blow themselves up in Israeli cafes and busses. In response, using helicopters and artillery, Israelis bomb suspected terrorist cells in Palestinian cities. But retaliation is not always precise, and innocent lives are taken. Palestinians respond yet again. Sporadically Israelis freeze border crossings, so that Palestinians who have jobs within Israel cannot get to them. Each side charges the other with aggression. Casualties mount, but the toll among Palestinians is higher by far.

Both Israelis and Palestinians are as frustrated now as at any time in the past. The hope of the Oslo Accords has collapsed. Neither Israelis nor Palestinians can go about their lives in safety. Arafat's Islands are barricaded. The Palestinian dream of a sovereign state with East Jerusalem as its capital is still only that, a dream. In Israel support for the liberal parties, traditionally more inclined to Land-for-Peace negotiation, is yielding to the uncompromising position of the parties of the far right.

Negotiation is repeatedly stalled or broken off. Arab countries, led by Saudi Arabia, propose a recognition of Israel in return for Israeli pullout from all settlements, a halt to Palestinian attacks, restitution for refugees, and a form of shared sovereignty over Jerusalem. President Bush, backed by European countries, offers a Road Map to Peace similar to that proposed by Arab countries, but joins Prime Minister Sharon in refusing to negotiate with Yasser Arafat. Disclosures reveal that Arafat himself is steeped in corruption. Much of the monetary aid sent by European and Arab countries to the PLO finds its way to Arafat's accounts in Swiss banks. While revelations of corruption cause moderate Palestinians to despair and others increasingly to align themselves with Hamas and the Islamic Jihad, Arafat nevertheless retains control of all channels of power. He succeeds in undercutting the ministers he appoints to negotiate with the Israelis.

With negotiations going nowhere, Sharon takes a different tack, a unilateral approach. Work continues on a 425 mile Security Barrier that snakes into Palestinian territory to encompass seventy-six percent of all West Bank settlers. Early in 2004 Sharon suggests publicly that some settlements will probably have to be abandoned. He announces an intended (no date given) total pullout of settlers from the Gaza Strip and a partial pullout of settlers in the West Bank, those whom the security barrier will isolate. The barrier, and the high concrete walls that are its most egregious symbol, can come down or be moved when and if a lasting peaceful settlement is achieved, Sharon insists. The Palestinians fume. This is not the kind of pullout they have demanded, and the boundary the security barrier is effecting is appropriating nearly 15% of West Bank territory. As lines harden on both sides, the door to negotiation becomes increasingly hard to pry open.

In the spring of 2004 Sharon goes to Washington and comes back with what he seeks: an endorsement from President Bush of the planned pullout of Gaza settlements, and with it the President's endorsement of the retention of "some" West Bank settlements, presumably those being enclosed within the Security Barrier. Although Sharon's program of desperation wins a powerful ally, the United States' pragmatic recognition of Israel's West Bank settlements sets off a firestorm of opposition, not only in the Arab world but also in Europe. It does not help matters when immediately on his return to Israel Sharon steps up a campaign to wipe out the leadership of Hamas, and possibly also of PLO militants.

The way Sharon sees it, Israel's very survival rests on its ability to neutralize the terrorists that threaten it. The way most of the rest of the world sees it, Israel must draw back to the Green Line, leaving the Palestinians to create a viable state. Increasingly, however, the way Islamist militants see it, Israel has no right to exist. In the Arab world today, the Israeli/Palestinian issue underlies everything.

28
The Wider Conflict

*Bin Laden changed the game. We need a different
engagement with cultures of the world…
We must acknowledge that religion is a component of most
political conflicts in the world today.*
Douglas Johnson
*President, International Center for Religion
and Democracy, 2001*

*Osama bin Laden achieved his aim: 9/11 sparked real
tensions between the Judeo-Christian West and the Muslim
East…Whether these tensions explode into a…clash of
civilizations will depend a great deal on whether we build
bridges or dig ditches between the West and Islam in…
Israel-Palestine.*
Thomas Friedman
The New York Times, January 11, 2004

The Israeli-Palestinian conflict is no longer a regional problem
only, if indeed it ever was. From some unknown hideout on
the Afghan-Pakistan border Islamist renegade Osama bin
Laden, and his chief tactician and planner, the Egyptian surgeon and
Islamist Ayman al-Zawahiri, call on all Muslims to fight a *Jihad*, a
Holy War against Israel and the West. Arab television, most especially
widely-watched independent station Al-Jazira, based in Qatar,
broadcasts messages from bin Laden and al-Zawahiri, and young
Muslim men in distant places rally to his call. At this writing they
are slipping through porous desert borders in Iraq and Afghanistan.

They target not only United States and other Coalition military personnel but increasingly the locals who are working to bring order out of the chaos that has accompanied the destruction of the Taliban and the regime of Sadaam Hussein. Their immediate aim is to get the United States and its allies out of the Middle East, not because the United States supports democracy and human rights, but because the United States supports Israel.

Exploiting Arab Bitterness

Bin Laden and al-Zawahiri see themselves as leaders of an Arab world that history has wronged. They evoke the power and cultural leadership once held by Arabs and link the fall from power to what they see as a turning away from the purity of Islam. Their message resonates. Long-held Arab bitterness toward the West stems from Europe's seaborne ascendancy beginning in the sixteenth century, from the British-French closet agreements that carve up Ottoman lands after World War I, from the humiliation of colonial or mandate occupation, from the British support of Jewish immigration to Palestine, and from the support that the West, and especially the United States, has given to Israel. Thus Al-Qaeda's commitment to a Holy War is aimed not only against Israel but also against the West and especially the United States.

Present economic disparities between Arab lands and western countries only heighten Arab frustration that Al-Qaeda exploits. Arab governments are stressed internally. As they work toward modernization, their poor and poorly-educated, embracing extremist versions of Islam learned in madrasas, are left behind, jobless, aggrieved and embittered. Al-Qaeda and linked terrorist organizations enlist the aggrieved in their cause, using them as they try to destabilize existing regimes.

The Holy Land is one issue on which most Arabs can unite. Most people in Arabs countries, early learning a vocabulary that slanders Jews, and absorbing state-sanctioned views against Jews in their schoolbooks, deeply resent the presence of a Jewish state in their midst. They resent the fact that the founding of Israel leaves many Palestinians homeless, Palestinians who are now living in surrounding Arab lands. In truth, most Arab countries view the Palestinians as something of a nuisance, taking up space and continually agitating. For this, they blame

Israel. The spectrum of Arab states' attitudes toward Israel runs from measured accommodation (Jordan and Morocco) to guarded minimal contact (Egypt since the Al Aqsa Intifadeh), to refusal to recognize Israel's right to exist (Algeria, Tunisia, Libya, Lebanon, Syria, Iraq, Saudi Arabia, Yemen, Oman, and the Gulf States).

Because in their effort to gain support within the Arab world bin Laden and al-Zawahiri have taken the Palestinians' cause as their own, Al-Qaeda has strong attraction to frustrated Palestinians. Young Palestinians reach Al-Qaeda training camps and return with expertise in the ways and weapons of terror. Arafat denies Al-Qaeda connections, but both Hamas and the Islamic Jihad receive financial help and training from Al-Qaeda, and Sharon charges that Arafat too gets help from this quarter.

Oil-wealthy Arab rulers, eager to deflect populist grievances away from themselves and toward Israel, also support the Palestinian uprising. Bin Laden's role is complex; he wants the West out of the entire Middle East, and he blames Arab rulers for consorting with the West. Particularly, he blames the Saudi rulers for allowing American troops on Saudi soil, which he views as holy soil. He holds to the same Wahabbi view of Islam that pervades all of Saudi life, but he charges the Saudi princes with turning their back on the mandates of the Quran. The Palestinian cause serves his purpose, but it puts him in bed with the very regimes he wants to oust. Al-Zawahiri, like bin Laden, started with a deep hatred for the existing regime in his own country; a leader of the Islamic Brotherhood, he has served time in Egyptian prisons. But through Al Qaeda, al-Zawahiri now casts his mission in a larger frame: the ousting of "decadent" regimes everywhere in the Muslim world, the defeat of Israel, and the destabilization of western countries that are to blame for the ills in the umma. The Palestinian cause also serves Al-Zawahiri's aims.

Most leaders in the Arab word are aware of Al-Qaeda's power game. They recognize it as being as much a threat to their own regimes as to Israel, and they reject its use of terror. But many of their people are powerfully attracted to charismatic Muslim leaders who promise to redress wrongs.

Most Muslims say they reject the Islamist views that motivate Al-Qaeda. (The term *Islamist* is not to be confused with *Muslim*.) The Islam they espouse, they say, is a religion of peace. For moderate Muslims, *Jihad* refers to a continuing personal struggle for moral betterment, not to a religious war. They may oppose Israel, and most do, but they deny that their opposition has anything but a political base. But in the Israeli-Palestinian conflict, as in all conflict where cultures clash, motivations blur and are difficult to separate. Many moderate Israelis, too, would deny that their Jewish faith or ancient tradition has anything to do with their desire to strengthen the state of Israel and to make it secure.

Monotheistic Links

So far in this book we have been able to trace direct ties among the world's three great monotheistic religions, as well as the emotional ties to the Holy Land shared by all People of the Book. The God of Jews, Christians, and Muslims is the same God, revealed through Abraham and the Prophets, which all three acknowledge. The name Al-Lah that prior to Muhammed refers to an Arabic tribal deity, becomes for Muslims simply the Arabic word for God, Allah. All three faiths are divided into many strands, but each has a common core.

Jews consider that God has made them his chosen people, beginning in the promise made to Abraham. The ancient story that unites Jews everywhere revolves around Moses, who leads Israel from captivity in Egypt, receives the Ten Commandments, and prepares the descendents of Abraham to conquer the Promised Land. The Hebrew Bible records the words and deeds of the prophets, kings, and priests who direct the Israelites in the millennium following the conquest. Jews honor Jesus as a teacher and moral leader who lived as a Jew in Palestine 1300 years after Moses. But Jesus is not their promised Messiah, whom they still await. Jews are scattered all over the world, but though scattered most retain their faith and identity. About two-fifths of the world's Jews live today in Israel. Most Jews today have little concern for the concept of life after death. Led by sages who through the centuries continue to interpret their Scriptures, most feel they are under obligation to direct their energies to create a better world here and now.

Christians believe that Jesus was indeed the Messiah whom the Hebrew Scriptures foretold, sent by God as his Son to redeem the world. They adopt early Jewish tradition as an integral part of their own, a prelude to the appearance of Jesus on earth; Jewish history

227

as recorded in the Old Testament is part of the Christian Bible. For Christians no less than Jews, the Holy Land is sacred space. The redemption offered by Jesus is spiritual, not political. It directs followers to do good, to love one another, and to look forward to a life after death. Unlike Judaism during most of its history, Christianity from the first is a missionary religion. For Christians, the message of Jesus Christ, that God is Love, is meant for everyone. Christians, too, consider themselves chosen by God, but they are under obligation to spread the blessings of their faith. Today Christianity is the world's most widespread religion, with the leading number of adherents.

Muslims acknowledge all of the prophets of the Old Testament as part of their own tradition. For Muslims, Jesus too is a prophet, as well as the greatest of teachers and moral leaders. They cite his teachings. But they believe that God's final revelation comes through the Prophet Muhammed to his chosen people, the Arabs, whose descent they trace to Abraham. Parts of the Holy Land associated with the prophets are sacred to Muslims, but Jerusalem holds special meaning. What Jews once called the Temple Mount is now Islam's Haram al-Sharif. For Muslims, Jews and Christians are People of the Book. Muslims acknowledge the sacred scriptures of Jews and Christians, but believe that the word of God as given to Muhammed and recorded in the Quran is the final revelation. The duty of Muslims is to spread Islam, submission to the One God. Every Muslim is obliged to observe the five pillars of his faith: to acknowledge that there is only one God, to pray daily, to give to charity, to observe a month of fasting, and to make a pilgrimage to Mecca. The reward for a good life will be an afterlife in Heaven. Islam is the world's second religion in terms of numbers of adherents, and currently the fastest growing.

All three religions provide their believers with a common core of rules by which humans should live together. All ask that believers treat one another as they themselves would wish to be treated. All have also through the centuries picked up a good deal of cultural baggage which bears little or no relation to the core concepts of their teachings, but to which adherents are fiercely attached. Such, for example, is a veil, an ikon, or a yarmulke. Outward observances or appearances that mark differences can thwart opportunities for exploring the similarities at the core of the three faiths.

Differences

Unfortunately, it is the differences, not the similarities, that fire zealots, who point to their holy writings to back up their zealotry. For some forty years after Christ's ascension, Messianic Jews and traditional Jews continue to worship side by side in synagogues in Judea and Galilee. But after the Romans destroy the Temple in 70 CE, Jews lose the geographic focus of their identity. Angry at the Messianic Jews who refuse to take part in the rebellion against Rome, and needing to reassess their identity, Jewish leaders make a critical decision. The Messianists will have to go. The followers of Jesus will no longer be welcome in the synagogues. The Gospel of John is completed thirty or more years later, when traditional and Messianic Jews are no longer communicating, except as adversaries. The account of the trial and crucifixion in the Gospel of John says that it was the Jews—not "the crowd" or "the people" of the earlier Gospel accounts—who crucified Christ. Although most Christians today believe that it is all sinners who bear responsibility for the crucifixion, this portion of John's Gospel has been used to justify unspeakable past actions and underlies anti-Semitism among some Christians even today.

Literalist Muslims point out that the Hebrew Scriptures assail the Jews of ancient times for not remaining faithful. Can the Quran do less? Christians commit the ultimate blasphemy when they say that the Prophet Jesus is the Son of God. From Morocco to Indonesia most Muslims believe that the Quran is the revealed word of God and must therefore be taken literally, and the Quran has some provocative things to say about Jews and Christians: The Jews try to introduce corruption (Sura 5:64), have always been disobedient (Sura 5:78), and are enemies of Allah, the Prophet, and the angels (Sura 2:97,98). Take not the Jews ...for friends (Sura 5:51). The Christians say, "The Messiah is the Son of God"...God assail them! (Sura 9:30). Referring to Jews and Christians, the Quran asks believers to "fight and slay the infidels wherever you find them." (Sura 9:5).

A Matter of Interpretation

Should followers of Islam take literally such Quranic directions? Or should they follow instead the implied tolerance in the Quran

Photo 23. The Dome of the Rock on the Haram al-Sharif.

that singles out Jews and Christians as People of the Book? Most Muslims believe that because everything written in the Quran was revealed directly to Muhammed by God, and because the Arabic text has not undergone compilation or change, everything in the Quran is true and relevant as written. A literal reading of the Quran, however, sometimes poses a problem for moderate, educated Muslims, who see their faith as one that promotes caring, self-discipline, peace, compassion, love, mercy, tolerance, modesty, and justice. *Islam* means submission to the will of God. *Jihad* is a personal struggle for betterment. Rarely does it mean a Holy War against others, either People of the Book (Jews and Christians) or unbelievers.

Young Muslims learn piety from their parents, but they learn the Quran in religious schools, verse by memorized verse, in Arabic. In poor societies, they may receive no other education. To Muslim fundamentalists, a Holy War declared against Israel and its Christian allies is sanctioned, even urged, by the Quran.

Most readers of the Hebrew Scriptures view the accounts of bloody battles and harsh treatment of enemies in the distant past as archaic, certainly not as a template for action today. But fundamentalist Jews interpret their Scriptures literally when it comes to such matters as imposing Sabbath regulations on the modern Jewish state or determining who can be considered a Jew (for Israeli citizenship). For Orthodox Jews (and

230

fundamentalist Christians as well), the very existence of the state of Israel is supported by a literal interpretation of God's promise to Abraham and Moses: God has set aside the Promised Land for his chosen people, the Jews.

Hebrew and Christian Scriptures can be read in the original Hebrew or Aramaic or Greek, or in translations in hundreds of languages. Meanings change subtly in translation, and through the centuries interpretations change. Jewish and Christian scholars have continued to examine their texts and to make changes when justified by scholarship. Further, customs change – customs that are not critical to the core of faith – and, therefore, most Jews and Christians can interpret their Scriptures as relevant in today's world without taking literally the portions that are relevant to another time and place.

Judaism undergoes two severe and formative trials in its history, both leading to the re-formation of faith and tradition that has enabled it to endure: the Babylonian Captivity and subsequent return, in the sixth century BCE, and the destruction of the Temple in 70 CE. For Christians, the great cataclysmic upheavals and regenerations are the Renaissance, the Reformation and the Counter-Reformation, leading to the Enlightenment, through which human reason takes on a "new birth of freedom" with the scientific and democratic revolutions as its outgrowth.

Islam has had no such regeneration. The Reformation begins barely fifteen centuries after the death of Christ. Islam is as old now as Christianity was when the Reformation begins. But in Islam it is still widely accepted that to apply critical scholarship to the Quran would be to question God himself. Movements that early split Islam into two major factions (Sunni and Shi'a) and scores of offshoots are largely politically motivated, with little effect on the faith. The Quran is interpreted much the same today, everywhere, as it was in the seventh century. That is both its strength and its weakness.

Haram al-Sharif / The Temple Mount

Religious fundamentalists of all three faiths approach the Israeli-Palestinian conflict from their own eschatological view. Eschatology is the system of belief that concerns the End-Time. For many believers, whether Jewish, Christian, or Muslim, eschatology centers on the Temple Mount, the Haram al-Sharif.

Orthodox Jews (who are only a minority in Israel but hold the controlling swing vote in the government) believe that the rebuilding of the Temple must happen because it is foretold in prophecy. When the Temple is rebuilt (but not until then), the Messiah will finally be revealed, and Jews will enter a long-awaited period of righteousness and fulfillment. The ultra-Orthodox believe that with the rebuilding of the Temple will come a restoration of the power of the priestly caste, clerical rule, and animal sacrifice, following literally the Iron-Age practices that prevailed after the Hebrews occupied the Holy Land.

The rebuilding of the Temple cannot happen until the Dome of the Rock and the Al-Aqsa Mosque are no more, because the Temple must be rebuilt in the same location it formerly occupied. A tiny minority of ultra-Orthodox Jews believe that they should hasten the destruction by militant action, and several times in recent decades there have been attempts to bomb the Dome of the Rock. Although most Orthodox Jews believe that God in his own good time will arrange the destruction, their views strongly underlie Israel's refusal to negotiate on Jerusalem. When Ariel Sharon, whose motivations are always political but rarely religious, walks on the Haram al-Sharif in September of 2000, his act is calculated and symbolic. Sharon's strongest support in Israel has always come from the religious right.

Sharon also gets strong support from those Christian fundamentalists, particularly in the United States, who also believe that the Temple must be rebuilt, but for a different set of eschatological reasons. Fundamentalist Christians base their end-time scenario on the opaque and highly symbolic prophesies in the Book of Daniel and the Book of Revelation. Pre-Millennialist views strongly underlie the thinking of most Christian fundamentalists. Many Christians hold the belief that Christ will return again to earth at the end of time, and will reign for a thousand years of peace. Pre-Millennialism provides the scenario for the events that must occur in the Holy Land before Christ's return. Of these events, two have already happened: the nation of Israel has been restored (1948), and the Old City of Jerusalem has become a Jewish city (1967). Only one event remains before end-time events are triggered: The Jews must rebuild the Temple. A charismatic leader, whom the Jews will revere as their long-awaited Messiah, will lead in the seven year project of rebuilding, but after three years the leader will reveal his true nature as the anti-Christ, and the period known as the *Tribulation* will begin. The anti-Christ will desecrate the Temple and turn against the Jews. He will then lead a series of attacks on the Jews, aided by world military forces from many parts of the earth. The whole world will be in turmoil, but true believing Christians will not know the agony, because they will be *raptured* or taken up to heaven, at the time the Tribulation begins. In the climactic battle, to be fought north of Jerusalem on the hill called Armageddon (the archaeological site known as Meggido), almost all of the combatants will be killed. After this battle, Christ will return to reign on earth – from Jerusalem – for a thousand years. He will bring with him the raptured saints, who will live in an earthly paradise. With them will be the 144,000 Jews who survive the battle and become believers. The end of the world will come after this thousand-year reign, when the dead will rise again, and Christ will be their judge. This scenario is the backdrop of the phenomenally successful twelve novels in the currently popular *Left Behind* series, whose authors are reaping the latent interest in the Pre-Millennialist end-time view. Like ultra-orthodox Jews, fundamentalist Christians differ in how the initiating event, the destruction of the Dome of the Rock, shall come about. A tiny minority believe it should be hastened by violence.

Almost all fundamentalist Christians, whether Pre-Millennialist or not, are in sympathy with Zionism and thus with Israel. They see the immigration of Jews to Israel, and the events of 1948 and 1967 as divinely ordained steps toward the prophesied End. In Israel an organized contingent of Christian Zionists, called the International Christian Embassy in Jerusalem, has strong ties to fundamentalist Christian groups in the United States and elsewhere. Many fundamentalist Christian congregations lend financial support to Israeli causes. Some target their help specifically toward financing the emigration of Jewish settlers from Russia and other countries to Israel, on the assumption that immigration is the key to Israel's survival as a Jewish state, an assumption with which most Israelis would agree.

Although ultra-Orthodox Jews and Pre-Millennialist Christians differ greatly in their theology, the Israeli right cultivates and encourages all possible support from Christian fundamentalists and openly admits its value. In the United States, where according to one poll forty-six percent of all Americans believe that the establishment of Israel is the fulfillment of biblical prophecy, the views of fundamentalist Christians regarding the Israeli-Palestinian conflict have inevitable political overtones. United States support for Israel, which many defend on strategic and logistical terms alone, is probably motivated far less by the so-called

"Jewish lobby" than by the eschatology of fundamentalist Christians in the electorate.

Christians who do not hold pre-Millennialist views generally eliminate eschatology from whatever stand they take on the Israeli-Palestinian conflict. Although they are sympathetic to all efforts to redress the horrors of the Holocaust, they tend to be more critical of Israel and more sympathetic to the cause of the Palestinians than their more fundamentally-inclined co-religionists. They realize and understand that tourism in Israel is geared to the interests of those who come as pilgrims, to walk where Jesus walked. But they realize, too, that visitors to Israel get little or no opportunity for contact with the struggling Arab Christian community in the Holy Land.

The Israeli military gathers the intelligence that so far has enabled them to foil all attempts on the part of either Jewish or Christian zealots to damage the Dome of the Rock. To the disappointment of fundamentalist Christians and Jews, when Israel takes over all of Jerusalem in 1967, it restores control of the Temple Mount to the Waqf, the Muslim authorities who manage the temple grounds. Israel's only terms require that people of all faith have access to the Haram al-Sharif, an access that Jordan denies to Jews during the period between 1948 and 1967. Until the beginning of the present Intifadeh the agreement holds; at present Jews are again restricted from entering the Haram al-Sharif.

Muslim traditions concerning the end-time echo those of Christians and Jews, but the players have different roles. Wars and moral corruption will herald the *Hour* (the Muslim term for the End Time). A false messiah will conquer the world. He will be a Jew, leading an army of Jews from the east. At last Jesus will return to defeat the deceiver in a battle near Jerusalem. All Jews and Christians will be killed. With peace restored, the dead will rise and all will face judgment next to Jerusalem's walls. Many Muslims believe that on the Last Day believers will ascend directly to heaven from the Dome of the Rock.

The Islamic significance of the Haram al-Sharif is grounded partly in eschatology and partly in Arab—most specifically, Palestinian—nationalism (as can be said for the Jewish view of the Temple Mount as well). Whether on the Night Visit Muhammed literally ascends to heaven from the site of the Dome of the Rock, as most Muslims believe, or merely experiences the Heavenly Visit in a dream, the Dome of the Rock has strong religious connotation for all Muslims. The Rock, of course, is the Rock of Sacrifice, where Ishmael was trussed, by Muslim belief. Since 638 CE the Haram al-Sharif has been in Muslim hands. The Dome appears as a logo on most publications that come from the Palestinian Authority. For Palestinians, continued and permanent Arab occupancy of the Haram al-Sharif is non-negotiable. This stand underlies Arafat's insistence that East Jerusalem (the Old City), and no other site, must be the capital of the Palestinian state.

Radical Islam has a ready explanation for the wrenching defeat suffered by the Arabs in the Six-Day War in 1967. It is the result of the moral decay of modern secular Arab society. After 1967 religious extremism in the Muslim world begins to focus on the Haram al-Sharif, the site of the coming Hour. Organizations such as the Islamic Jihad begin to swell with adherents. In no small sense, the attraction of bin Laden's Al-Qaeda network is an outgrowth of this defeat.

Viewpoints on a Spectrum

To the horror of moderates everywhere, extremists of all three faiths see the struggle for the Holy Land as a struggle between Islam and the Judeo-Christian West.

Secular Israelis, who for reasons of security are increasingly voting with the right, are not interested in such cosmic terms, but they are pragmatic; they accept the support of the Christian right, regardless of its motivation. Palestinians are frustrated and overwhelmed by their lack of security, which they equate with the Israeli occupation. Even moderate Palestinians are caught up in rhetoric that posits the total defeat of Israel. The majority of Palestinians, disillusioned with the lack of progress toward a Palestinian state, accept the necessity for Muslim extremist organizations within Palestine (Hamas, the Islamic Jihad, and the Al Aqsa Martyrs Brigade), as well as of extremist groups from elsewhere, such as Hezbullah and Al-Qaeda, dedicated to Israel's overthrow.

Moderate voices from the Palestinian community do surface occasionally, especially among members of the dwindling Arab Christian community. But Christians in the Palestinian Authority, in Bethlehem or Ramallah or elsewhere, are having an increasingly difficult time maintaining their programs, and Muslim extremists often unjustly accuse them of collaborating with Israel. Arab Christians within Israel generally do not ally themselves with the Christian right. As Israeli citizens who are both Arab and Christian, they are able to provide a needed bridge of understanding in an increasingly polarized society. Moderate Israelis and Palestinians, who are willing to negotiate Land-for-Peace, seek support and understanding from Christian, Muslim, and secular moderates everywhere. These are the people who, working behind the scenes, are searching for openings and encouraging dialog.

Towards the end of 2003 a group of Israelis and Palestinians — businessmen, politicians-out-of-power, and scholars — meet in Geneva, Switzerland to sign an accord that is the fruit of months of behind-the-scenes meetings. They agree, basically, that a two-state solution is possible, that most (but not all) of the Israeli settlements must go, that certain land now in Israel should be ceded to Palestine, that Jerusalem can be a divided capital, and that the "right of return" claimed by Palestinians whose former home was within Israel's borders must be changed to "right of restitution." They sign an unofficial Geneva Accord, and for a few days there is optimism, particularly within Europe and the United States. But their reasonable approach satisfies neither of the governments in power in the Holy Land. Even while they are meeting, as well as after, progress on the Security Barrier continues, suicide bombings make new Palestinian "martyrs," and settlers in the West Bank and Gaza threaten to riot if their homes are threatened.

29
The Only Way Out

Terrorism has no military solution.
Israeli security officer
cited in the New York Times, December 21, 2001

*The ultimate weakness of violence is that it is a descending
spiral. Instead of diminishing evil, it multiplies it. Hate
cannot drive out hate: Only love can do that.*
Martin Luther King, Jr.

The Al-Qaeda network has been severely crippled; it may no longer be a coherent unit led from a single source. But it has morphed, amoeba-like, into terrorist cells in many parts of the world, employing the fruits of common training, in touch with one another, but acting independently. Islamic fundamentalism and the internal political struggles within Muslim countries that give birth to Al-Qaeda remain. So long as the Israeli-Palestinian conflict is unresolved, the Holy Land will remain in the vortex of a destabilized world.

In the International War on Terrorism that is the declared response to the bombing of the World Trade Center September 11, 2001, the Israeli-Palestinian conflict is shoved repeatedly to the forefront. The United States must be able to count on its Arab allies – allies who are quite ready to tie their cooperation to a just peace in the Holy Land.

The definition of *just*, of course, depends on who answers the question posed in the title of this book. No agreement is ever totally just. Agreement can come about only through negotiation, through

237

the willingness of both parties to give. As I write, statesmen from the United States and Europe, as well as the United Nations, continue to prod the adversaries to the table, to tap the residue of willingness that remains on both sides.

Leading spokesmen both in Israel and Palestine now recognize publicly that the al-Aqsa Intifadeh and the harsh Israeli retaliatory measures have brought no gains whatsoever, to either side. Even as attitudes harden and negotiation becomes ever more difficult, and even as a Security Barrier designed to keep terrorists out of Israel snakes deeply into Palestinian territory, a growing number of both Palestinians and Israelis now realize that only through talking, and not through guns, can come the peace that both sides crave.

Israelis are in the Holy Land to stay. And so are the Palestinians. Both are deeply attached to the same land. Through negotiation, somehow they must squelch the fanatics among them and find a way to share that land. There will be pain on both sides, for neither will be satisfied with the compromises that they must eventually make. But the alternative, already underway, is what Martin Luther King has called the "descending spiral of violence."

Yitzhak Frankenthal, an orthodox Israeli and a religious Zionist, is the founder of the Bereaved Families Forum in Tel Aviv. He has met with political leaders on both sides, and with leaders of Hamas and the Islamic Jihad. "The current situation is dreadful for Israelis and Palestinians alike," says Frankenthal. "That's why there is no alternative to peace."

Ten year ago, at about the time the Oslo Accord is signed but before the first Intifadeh has been declared at an end, Frankenthal is traveling in the Gaza Strip with his nineteen-year-old son Arik, on leave from the army. The son senses the tension and bitterness on Gaza streets, and he tells his father that if he were a Palestinian in Gaza, what he would most want to do is kill an Israeli soldier. A week later, back in service in the West Bank, Arik is dead, kidnapped and slain by four young members of Hamas. Frankenthal, in his agony, drives back to Gaza. He searches for a family whose son has been killed by Israeli soldiers, and he finds that family. He embraces them, and they weep together. Then Frankenthal decides to form a league of the bereaved.

The Bereaved Families Forum is now 400-strong, its membership roughly half-Palestinian, half-Israeli. They have made a memorial display of hundreds of mock caskets, some draped with Israeli flags, some with

Palestinian flags, side by side, and they center their activities in a Tent of Peace in Tel Aviv's Rabin Square. They sponsor billboards, erected on both sides of the Green Line, proclaiming in Hebrew and Arabic: "Better the Pains of Peace than the Agonies of War."

There *is* common ground, in the suffering both sides endure, in the peace with security that all want, and in the tangent faiths they embrace.

In the words of the Prophet Isaiah:
*He shall judge between the nations,
and they shall beat their swords into ploughshares,
their spears into sickles.
Nation shall not lift up sword against nation;
neither shall they learn war any more.*

In the words of the Prophet Muhammed:
If they incline toward peace, incline thou also to it.

And in the words of Jesus:
Blessed are the peacemakers.

Shalom Peace Salaam

Epilogue:
From Suleiman's Wall

2000

It is the last day of my stay in the Holy Land. The late spring sun is already hot. As I sit in a shady niche on the Wall that surrounds the Old City, I am thinking of the three monotheistic faiths that claim Jerusalem as holy, their common ancestor Abraham, the prophets whom all three acknowledge, and Jesus of Nazareth – Messiah to Christians, Teacher to Jews, and Prophet to Muslims. Yes, I reassure myself, the teachings of Jesus about the common humanity of all people under One God have the power, even now, to form a basis for peace.

I use the time on the Wall to try to bring together and make sense of what I have experienced. I have benefited from a comprehensive itinerary that has let me trace the events of the Hebrew Bible, the interlude between Nehemiah and Matthew, the account in the Gospels of Jesus' life, the Jewish Revolt and the Diaspora, the coming and waning of the Byzantines, Islam's stamp on the Holy Land, the Crusaders' quixotic mission, Ottoman Rule, the impossible task of the British Mandate, the modern state of Israel and the impact it has made on the land, and, finally, the tragic conflict between Jew and Arab, between Israeli and Palestinian.

2002

Today, two years later, as I recall my time on the Wall, it seems as if it were long ago: before the breakdown of peace efforts between Israelis and Palestinians, before the renewal of the Intifadeh and the

240

daily wailing over caskets carried in disorderly procession through streets of angry mourners, before the concrete barricades and the terror and fear, before 9/11 and the International War on Terrorism with its ever-present side-bar in the Holy Land. Peace seemed near on that spring day in Jerusalem two years ago. But now, as so often in the past, peace in the Holy Land is once again elusive.

2004

I began writing this account while on the Wall and continued it over the ensuing months. Two years later it became a book, and now — an additional two years later — that book has been revised and updated. There have been additional happenings, and I have gained new insights, so that there are small or large changes on most pages. But one thing has not changed, indeed has been magnified: the urgency for peace in the Holy Land, a peace that both sides can live with.

Dorothy Weitz Drummond

Holy Land, Whose Land?

GLOSSARY: TERMS

ABBASSID CALIPHATE. The period [750-1258 CE] when the Arab Empire was ruled from **BAGHDAD**. In 909, the Abbassid Caliphate was succeeded in the **HOLY LAND** by the **FATIMIDS**.

ACTS, BOOK OF. The fifth book of the **NEW TESTAMENT**, properly titled The Acts of the Apostles, which records the activities of **PAUL** and other apostles from the third to the sixth decades of the first century. It was probably written by the author of the **GOSPEL OF LUKE**. (See **LUKE, GOSPEL OF**).

AGE OF DISCOVERY. The period beginning in the fifteenth century when Portuguese, Spanish, English, and Dutch maritime explorers began to map the world as they sought a water route from Europe to the Orient.

AL-AQSA INTIFADEH. The resistance movement started in September 2000 by stone-throwing **PALESTINIANS** protesting the presence of Israeli Defense Minister **ARIEL SHARON** (See **SHARON, ARIEL**) on the **HARAM AL-SHARIF** in front of the **AL-AQSA MOSQUE**. The Al-Aqsa Intifadeh was soon co-opted by militant Palestinian groups, whose suicide bombings in **ISRAEL** have been followed by Israeli retaliation. As of the date of publication, the Al-Aqsa Intifadeh has not abated.

AL-AQSA MARTYRS BRIGADE. Palestinian terrorist organization founded by **YASSER ARAFAT** (See **ARAFAT, YASSER**) in January, 2001 and under his control.

AL-AQSA MOSQUE. The **MOSQUE** located on the **HARAM AL-SHARIF** in **JERUSALEM** that dates to the seventh century **CE**.

ALLAH. Common rendering in English of the Arabic word **AL-LAH**, the **MUSLIM** word for God. Before **MUHAMMED**, the name of the god worshipped in the vicinity of **MECCA**.

AL-LAH. A god worshipped in the vicinity of **MECCA** from ancient times. Its name was appropriated by **MUHAMMED** to mean the One God, which **MUHAMMED** understood to be also the God of the **JEWS** and the **CHRISTIANS**.

AL-QAEDA. The international movement founded by **OSAMA BIN LADEN** (See **BIN LADEN, OSAMA**) that promotes terrorism in order to destabilize existing governments that it opposes.

AMERICAN JEWISH CONGRESS. The Jewish organization in the United States, particularly active after World War II, that advocated an alternative to **Zionism** for resettlement of Jewish refugees.

Annunciation, The. The event where the virgin Mary (See **Mary, Mother of Jesus**) learns she is to become the mother of the **Messiah**.

Anti-semitism. Antipathy expressed (consciously or unconsciously) by some non-Jews toward **Jews** as a group. Although **Hebrew**, the language originally spoken by the **Israelites** and now the language of Israel, is one of many **Semitic** languages, and the Israelites one of many Semitic peoples, the term anti-Semitism has come to be used only in a context referring specifically to Jews.

Antonia Fortress. The Roman-fortified tower and administrative center overlooking the **Temple Mount** where **Pontius Pilate** (See **Pilate, Pontius**) resided while in **Jerusalem**. It was destroyed in 70 CE.

Apocrypha. A body of texts written between the fifth and first centuries BCE, some in **Aramaic**, some in Greek, that was incorporated within the **Septuagint**. It is accepted as canonical by Roman Catholics and Anglicans but rejected by other Protestants as not being a portion of the **Hebrew Scriptures**.

Arafat's Islands. A nickname (somewhat derisive) for the fragmented territories of the **Palestinian Authority** resulting from the **Oslo Accord**.

Aramaic. A **Semitic** language introduced into the **Holy Land** by **Judeans** returning from exile in **Babylon** at the end of the 6th century BCE. Widely spoken in the area at the time of **Jesus Christ**, it was gradually replaced as a **lingua franca** by Arabic, beginning in the 7th century CE.

ARAMCO. Acronym for Arabian American Oil Company, a consortium of American petroleum companies (Standard Oil, Texaco, Mobil) formed to extract petroleum in **Saudi Arabia**. ARAMCO became 100% Saudi owned in 1980 and is now known as Saudi ARAMCO.

Ark of the Covenant. A vessel, resembling a chest, in which the ancient **Hebrews** kept the words of God given to **Moses** on **Mount Sinai** (See **Sinai, Mount**). The Ark was enshrined in the holiest portion of **the Temple** built by **Solomon**.

Armageddon. According to **Pre-Millennialism** belief, the climactic battle that will precede the **Second Coming of Christ**. It will be fought on an archaeological site north of **Jerusalem**, termed Megiddo.

Ascension, The. The term given to the last appearance of **Jesus Christ** on earth, when he rose upward and out of view of the disciples. **Luke** says this event took place on the **Mount of Olives**. (See **Olives, Mount of**).

Ba'ath Party. The Arab Socialist party that in the 1960s put into power the totalitarian ruling parties of **Iraq** and **Syria**. The Ba'ath Party in **Iraq** was defeated by the United States and other Coalition forces through military action in 2003. Its leader, **Sadaam Hussein**, was captured. In **Syria** the Ba'ath party is led by President Bashar al-Assad. (See **al-Assad, Bashar**).

Babylonian Captivity. The period from ca 597-533 BCE when, following the destruction of **Jerusalem** by the **Babylonians**, leaders and artisans of **Judah** were taken to **Babylon** and held there in captivity. After **Persia** conquered the **Chaldean** (or Neo-Babylonian) Empire, many of the former captives scattered throughout the **Persian Empire**. The period of captivity officially ended when the Persian ruler **Cyrus** authorized the **Judeans** to return to Jerusalem to rebuild their **temple**. Some did, but others remained in the east.

Babylonian Empire. The period (ca 1950 **BCE** to 1400 BCE) when the rulers of **Babylon** held sway over the entire Mesopotamian region and beyond. They were defeated by the **Assyrians**. In turn, by 625 BCE a **Chaldean** people, ruling from Babylon, had defeated the Assyrians and begun what is known as the Neo-Babylonian Empire, which also ruled in **Mesopotamia** and was defeated by the **Persians** ca 530 BCE.

Baha'i. A religion that holds that its founder, **Baha'u'llah**, is the most recent messenger of those (**Moses**, Krishna, Buddah, Zoroaster, **Jesus Christ**, and **Muhammed**) whom God has chosen to reveal his will to humanity. Baha'u'llah spent the latter part of the nineteenth century in **Palestine**, exiled from his homeland in **Iran**.

Balfour Declaration. The statement issued by Lord **Arthur Balfour** (See **Balfour, Arthur**), British Foreign Secretary, in 1917 supporting **Palestine** as a homeland for **Jews** but stating that Arab rights shall not be infringed.

Baptism. An ancient **Hebrew** rite in which water is symbolic of spiritual cleansing. At the beginning of his ministry, **Jesus Christ** was baptized by **John the Baptist** (probably an **Essene**) in the **Jordan River**. Baptism is now a rite practiced within all branches of **Christianity**.

Bar Kokba Revolt. The final and unsuccessful revolt of **Jews** in **Palestine** in 132 **CE**, protesting the Roman desecration of the **Temple Mount** where a statue of the Emperor as God was erected.

BCE, CE. Faith-neutral designations of historical time: Before the Common Era and Common Era, respectively. These are often used by historians to replace BC (Before Christ) and AD (taken from the Latin Anno Domini, or the Year of Our Lord). The point at which BCE becomes CE is the mistaken date formerly given for the year of the birth of **Jesus Christ**.

Bible. The sacred scripture of both **Jews** and **Christians**. For **Jews**, the **Bible** is the collection of books that form the **Hebrew Scriptures**, beginning with the first five books known as the **Torah**. For **Christians**, the **Bible** is the **Old Testament** – essentially the books of the **Hebrew Scriptures**, with some reordering – plus the books of the **New Testament**.

British Palestine Mandate. See **Palestine Mandate**.

Bronze Age. The period of pre-history marked by the use of bronze (a mixture of copper and tin) in weapons and items of decoration. Bronze is softer than iron, at whose discovery the Bronze Age was superseded by the **Iron Age**.

Byzantine. Pertaining to the Graeco/Roman/Christian civilization that characterized the eastern **Roman Empire** after the removal in 315 **CE** of the imperial capital from **Rome** to **Byzantium**. Byzantium, the Greek name for the city, was changed to **Constantinople** after the Emperor **Constantine** took up residence there. During Constantine's reign, the Roman Empire embraced **Christianity**.

Byzantine Era. The period when the **Roman Empire** was Christian and ruled from **CONSTANTINOPLE**. In **PALESTINE**, from 315 **CE** to 638 **CE**.

BYZANTINE EMPIRE. The eastern part of the **ROMAN EMPIRE**, and after the fifth century, its successor. The Empire was ruled from **CONSTANTINOPLE** from the early fourth century **CE** until the final defeat of Constantinople by the **OTTOMANS** in 1453.

CAMP DAVID ACCORD (1979). The agreement between **EGYPT** and **ISRAEL** in which **EGYPT** recognized the existence of Israel, and Israel agreed to return the **SINAI PENINSULA** to **EGYPT**. Negotiated by former U.S. **PRESIDENT JIMMY CARTER** (See **CARTER, PRESIDENT JIMMY**) in 1979 at Camp David, the presidential retreat outside Washington, D.C.

CAMP DAVID PROPOSAL (2000). An offer made by Israeli Prime Minister **EHUD BARAK** (See **BARAK, EHUD**) to give up ninety percent of the **WEST BANK** to Palestinian control. It was rejected by Arafat (See **ARAFAT, YASSER**) because **ISRAEL** would have retained control of all **WEST BANK** roads, as well as of **EAST JERUSALEM**.

CANAAN. The land promised to **ABRAHAM** and his descendents. Its boundaries are indefinite, but the region included essentially the land from the Mediterranean Sea to the **JORDAN RIVER** (and sometimes beyond), and from the slopes of **MOUNT HERMON** (See **HERMON, MOUNT**) to the northern **NEGEV DESERT**.

CARDO. The main street or way in a Roman-planned city.

CATHOLIC. See **ROMAN CATHOLIC**.

CHRISTIAN. See **CHRISTIANITY**.

CHRISTIAN ZIONISTS. Organized groups of **CHRISTIANS** who support the idea of **ZIONISM** as a precondition for the events that will trigger the **END TIMES**.

CHRISTIANITY. The name given to the community of followers of **JESUS CHRIST**. Christianity is the world's largest and most widespread religion. It is divided into three major branches - **ROMAN CATHOLIC**, **PROTESTANT**, and **EASTERN ORTHODOX**.

CIRCUMCISION. The removal of the foreskin of the penis. This covenanted rite was announced by God to **ABRAHAM** and is observed by both **JEWS** and **MUSLIMS**.

CITADEL, THE. A fortified complex inside **JAFFA** Gate in Jerusalem's **OLD CITY** (See **OLD CITY OF JERUSALEM**), first constructed by **HASMONEANS**, then repeatedly rebuilt and enlarged by all successive rulers. It is now a museum of the history of **JERUSALEM**.

CODEX SINAITICUS. The oldest existing copy of the **BIBLE**, dating to the mid-fourth century. It was written in Greek on parchment and preserved in the Monastery of Saint Catherine (See **SAINT CATHERINE'S MONASTERY**) until its discovery and removal to museums in Leipzig and St. Petersburg in the mid-nineteenth century.

CONVERSO. A Jew in **SPAIN** or its colonies who converted to **CHRISTIANITY**, following the expulsion of **JEWS** from **SPAIN** in 1492.

COPTIC. A branch of **CHRISTIANITY** followed in **EGYPT** and **ETHIOPIA**, dating to the first century, and by tradition introduced by **MARK THE EVANGELIST**.

COUNTER-REFORMATION. The moves taken by the **ROMAN CATHOLIC** church in the 16th and 17th centuries to reform certain controversial church practices.

CRUCIFIXION. A brutal method of execution practiced by the Romans in which the victim was nailed by the hands and feet to a cross beam probably placed on a stationary pole. **JESUS CHRIST** was executed in this fashion.

CRUSADES. A series of military expeditions undertaken by European knights in the eleventh, twelfth and thirteenth centuries to wrest the **HOLY LAND** from **MUSLIM** control. The **CRUSADERS** controlled parts of the **HOLY LAND** for almost two centuries, from 1099 to 1291.

DANIEL, BOOK OF. Probably written during the time of the **MACCABEAN** (See **MACABEAN REVOLT**) struggles against the **SELEUCIDS**, this book tells of the events of the **BABYLONIAN CAPTIVITY** 400 years previously. It is often read as the story of the clash of the kingdom of God with the kingdoms of the earth and the ultimate powerlessness of the latter.

DEAD SEA SCROLLS. Writings on parchment found beginning in 1949 in jars hidden in caves to the west of the **DEAD SEA**, near **QUMRAN**. Preserved in the arid climate, the writings date from the third century BCE to the first century CE. Fragments written in **HEBREW**, **ARAMAIC**, and Greek include portions of all the books of the **HEBREW SCRIPTURES**, as well as the records of a puritanical sect of **JUDAISM** known as the **ESSENES**, who compiled the writings.

DECAPOLIS. A region recognized in Greek and **ROMAN PALESTINE** (second century BCE to second century CE) consisting of the territories governed by ten (or more) semi-autonomous trading cities, all but one located east of the **JORDAN RIVER**. The **DECAPOLIS** is mentioned several times in the **GOSPELS**. Its culture was Graeco-Roman, in contrast to the culture of the Jewish communities of nearby **GALILEE**.

DECUMANUS. The grid of streets intersecting the **CARDO** in Roman-planned cities.

DEUTERONOMY, BOOK OF. The fifth book of the **TORAH** (the **PENTATEUCH**), Deuteronomy means "a retelling." It is by tradition the writings of **MOSES**, forty years after the **EXODUS**, in which he retells the story of the flight from **EGYPT** and the giving of the **TEN COMMANDMENTS**, and records the law that the **HEBREWS** are to obey as they take possession of the **PROMISED LAND**. Modern scholars ascribe to sixth-century compilers the version that exists in the **TORAH**.

DHIMMI. Historically, a protected status in **ISLAMIC LANDS** awarded to **JEWS** and **CHRISTIANS** as **PEOPLE OF THE BOOK**. All dhimmis were required to pay a head tax, or **JIZYA**.

DIASPORA. A term that means "scattering," Diaspora can refer to the dispersion of any group of people (e.g., the Palestinian Diaspora) but is usually used to mean the communities of Jewish people living outside the **HOLY LAND**. The term can refer both to the events that precipitated the scattering (as in the Roman Diaspora), and to the lands where **JEWS** (or **PALESTINIANS**, or other scattered peoples) settled.

DOME OF THE ROCK. Completed in 691, the Dome of the Rock is built on the **HARAM AL-SHARIF** over the rock where **MUSLIMS** believe **ABRAHAM** trussed **ISHMAEL** for sacrifice, and from where **MUHAMMED** in the **NIGHT VISIT** ascended to heaven. One of the earliest and most beautiful examples of

Islamic architecture. The dome was retiled in the mid-sixteenth century during the reign of SULEIMAN THE MAGNIFICENT. For PALESTINIANS the Dome of the Rock is a national symbol.

DREYFUS AFFAIR. Circumstances surrounding the 1894 trial and unjust sentencing in France of Army Captain ALFRED DREYFUS (See DREYFUS, ALFRED), a Jew, to the penal colony on Devil's Island on false charges of treason. His cause was taken up by the novelist EMILE ZOLA (See ZOLA, EMILE), who succeeded in winning his release. The ANTI-SEMITISM revealed during the Dreyfus Affair led Austrian reporter THEODOR HERZL (See HERZL, THEODOR) to found the international ZIONIST (See ZIONISM) movement in 1896.

EASTERN ORTHODOX. See ORTHODOX CHRISTIANITY.

END TIMES. The events that, according to prophecy, will be associated with the end of the world. (See ESCHATOLOGY).

ERETZ ISRAEL. The BIBLICAL PROMISED LAND, projected to the present by ORTHODOX JEWS in ISRAEL.

ESCHATOLOGY. That branch of theology or belief systems that deals with the END TIMES, or "last things."

ESTHER, BOOK OF. A book of the HEBREW SCRIPTURES (the OLD TESTAMENT), probably written in the third or second century BCE, that tells the story of a Jewish woman during the BABYLONIAN CAPTIVITY who becomes the queen of the king of PERSIA and subsequently saves JUDEANS of the kingdom from the designs of the wicked HAMAN. The story is celebrated by JEWS in the Feast of PURIM.

EXODUS, BOOK OF. The second book of the TORAH, which relates the story of the deliverance of the HEBREWS from slavery in EGYPT, the giving of the TEN COMMANDMENTS to MOSES on MOUNT SINAI (See SINAI, MOUNT), and the subsequent 40-year period of wandering in the wilderness of the SINAI DESERT, EDOM, and MOAB. Most scholars give a late sixth century date for the final compilation of the Book of Exodus in its present form, from written sources dating to the ninth century.

EXODUS, THE. The escape of the HEBREW tribes from EGYPT, where they had been held as slaves, an event (probably occurring in the thirteenth century BCE) for which there is strong evidence in tradition but none in archaeology or historical record.

EZRA, BOOK OF. A book of the OLD TESTAMENT where Ezra narrates the history of the JEWS from the return from BABYLONIAN CAPTIVITY in 538 BCE to about 458 BCE. It names the families that returned, tells of the rebuilding of the TEMPLE, and of the efforts of Ezra, a Jew in the service of the PERSIAN ruler, to restore the observance of MOSAIC LAW to ISRAEL.

FARSI. An Indo-European language spoken in IRAN.

FATAH. The leading Palestinian political party and the larger of the two groups which merged to form the PALESTINE LIBERATION ORGANIZATION (PLO). Founded by YASSER ARAFAT (See ARAFAT, YASSER), FATAH continues to exist as a separate entity within the PLO, owing its allegiance to its founder. Its military wing, TANZIM, acts as an unofficial army of the PALESTINIAN AUTHORITY.

FRANCISCAN ORDER. A monastic order within the ROMAN CATHOLIC Church founded by Saint Francis of Assisi. In the fourteenth century, a papal decree gave the Franciscans the responsibility for maintaining all Christian holy places in the **HOLY LAND**. Those under Roman Catholic care are maintained by Franciscans to this day.

FRANKINCENSE. A gum resin that seeps from a low, small-leaved thorny tree that is found in better-watered parts of the **HADRAMAUT**, in what is now southern **OMAN**. Frankincense was prized in ancient times for its scent when burned and for its medicinal and cosmetic qualities.

FUNDAMENTALISM. A rapidly growing global religious impulse that seeks to recover and publicly institutionalize aspects of the past that modern life has obscured. Fundamentalism in any religion insists on the literal truth of its sacred books. Fundamentalism tends to proclaim itself as the guardian of truth, usually to the exclusion of others' interpretations.

GENESIS, BOOK OF. The first book of the **HEBREW SCRIPTURES** and the **OLD TESTAMENT** containing accounts of the Creation, the Flood, and the **PATRIARCHS ABRAHAM**, **ISAAC**, and **JACOB**.

GOSPELS. The first four books of the **NEW TESTAMENT** , which tell of the life, ministry, death, and **RESURRECTION** of **JESUS CHRIST**. The **GOSPELS** are named **MATTHEW**, **MARK**, **LUKE**, and **JOHN**.

GRAECO-ROMAN WORLD. A term referring to the culture of the lands of the eastern Mediterranean following the conquests of **ALEXANDER THE GREAT** in the fourth century **BCE** and the subsequent rule by **ROME** beginning in the first century BCE. Although two hundred years of Greek rule was followed by Roman conquest, and later by **BYZANTINE** rule, in the eastern lands the Greek language continued to prevail and Greek culture blended with that of Rome. The Graeco-Roman world faded after the **MUSLIM** conquests of the seventh century **CE** but continued in **ASIA MINOR** until the coming of the **TURKS** in the twelfth century. Only with the fall of **CONSTANTINOPLE** in 1453 was it totally extinguished.

GREAT COMMISSION, THE. The missionary command of **JESUS CHRIST**, given just before his **ASCENSION**, telling his followers to go into all the world to preach the **GOSPEL**.

GREEN LINE. A term that refers to the pre-1967 border between the **OCCUPIED TERRITORIES** and **ISRAEL**.

HADITH. The sayings of **MUHAMMED** and those who knew him, and the traditions concerning his life, collected in books called the Hadith Books.

HAGANAH. An underground military organization of the Jewish community during the **PALESTINE MANDATE**.

HAJJ. The **PILGRIMAGE** to **MECCA** required of all **MUSLIMS** who are able. A person who makes such a **PILGRIMAGE** is thereafter accorded the title Hajji.

HAMAS. An underground organization operating in the **WEST BANK** and **GAZA STRIP**, formed in 1987. Hamas uses violent means, including terrorism, to pursue its goal of establishing an Islamic Palestinian state in place of **ISRAEL**. Hamas has an unknown number of hard-core members but tens of thousands of supporters and sympathizers. Hamas also carries on an extensive program of social services among **PALESTINIANS**.

HARAM AL-SHARIF. See **PLACES: HARAM AL-SHARIF.**

HASHEMITE. A tribe of **BEDOUIN** from the **HEJAZ** of **ARABIA** who aided the British in World War I. The kings of the **HASHEMITE KINGDOM OF JORDAN** are of the Hashemite royal line, whose lineage can be traced to **MUHAMMED.**

HASMONEAN KINGDOM. The period in Jewish history following the **MACCABEAN REVOLT** during which a priestly family known as the **HASMONEANS** ruled in **PALESTINE** as an autonomous part of **SYRIA** (142-129 BCE) and an independent kingdom (129-63) BCE until they fell to the Romans.

HEBREW. The language of modern **ISRAEL.** A **SEMITIC** language deriving from ancient **MESOPOTAMIA.** In ancient times, the language spoken by the **ISRAELITES** but reserved mainly for liturgical purposes after the **JUDEANS** returned from the **BABYLONIAN CAPTIVITY** using **ARAMAIC** as their **LINGUA FRANCA.** Restored to a modern common language by the first European **JEWS** who migrated to **PALESTINE** in the late nineteenth century under the impetus of organized **ZIONISM.**

HEBREW BIBLE. See **HEBREW SCRIPTURES.**

HEBREW SCRIPTURES. The books that collectively form the sacred writings of **JUDAISM.** The first five books of the **HEBREW** Scriptures are known as the **TORAH.** The canon of the **HEBREW** Scriptures was fixed in its present form about 150 BCE, but much of the work of assembly was accomplished following the return of the Jewish priests and scribes from captivity in **BABYLON** (See **BABYLONIAN CAPTIVITY**), in the latter part of the sixth century. The **OLD TESTAMENT** of the Christian **BIBLE** is essentially the **HEBREW** Scriptures, with slightly altered format.

HEGIRA. The flight of **MUHAMMED** and his followers from **MECCA** to **MEDINA** in the year 622 **CE.** **MUSLIMS** date their calendar from this year.

HELLENIC. A term used to describe Greek civilization as spread by **ALEXANDER THE GREAT** and his successors.

HEROD'S TEMPLE. An inaccurate term for the **SECOND TEMPLE,** as it appeared after the renovations ordered by **HEROD THE GREAT** toward the end of the first century BCE.

HEZBULLAH. A militant, armed anti-**ISRAELI** terrorist organization based in southern **LEBANON,** drawing its strength from the Shi'ite (See **SHI'A ISLAM**) community, its protection by **SYRIA,** and much of its financial support from **IRAN.** The Hezbullah (Party of God) carries on an extensive program of social services in addition to its military concerns.

HOLY OF HOLIES. The inner part of **THE TEMPLE,** which in **SOLOMON'S** time enshrined the **ARK OF THE COVENANT.** Said to have been built over the **ROCK OF ABRAHAM.**

HOLOCAUST, THE. The systematic slaughter by the Nazis of six million **JEWS** in Europe during World War II. Victims of the Holocaust are memorialized in many places, but most particularly in the Holocaust Museum in Washington D.C. and in the **YAD VASHEM HOLOCAUST MUSEUM** in **JERUSALEM.**

HOLY LAND. The land with associations sacred to three world faiths: **JUDAISM, CHRISTIANITY,** and **ISLAM.** Geographically, it includes all of present-day **ISRAEL**

and the OCCUPIED TERRITORIES, and also western JORDAN, southern SYRIA and LEBANON, and the SINAI PENINSULA.

HOLY SEPULCHER, CHURCH OF THE. A church in JERUSALEM established on the site where its founders, emissaries of the Emperor CONSTANTINE, had reason to believe the CRUCIFIXION and the burial of JESUS CHRIST took place.

HOLY WAR. A war considered by its perpetrators to be justified or mandated by God. For Christian knights the CRUSADES were a Holy War. In ISLAM a Holy War is termed a JIHAD.

HOLY WEEK. The week observed by CHRISTIANS that commemorates the events leading up to and including the trial, CRUCIFIXION and burial of JESUS CHRIST. It begins with Palm Sunday, when Jesus entered JERUSALEM in triumph, and ends with the dawning of Easter Sunday, which commemorates his RESURRECTION.

HOSANNA! The message shouted by people along the way as JESUS CHRIST entered JERUSALEM on Palm Sunday, the first day of what has come to be known as HOLY WEEK. An ancient HEBREW acclamation, accompanied by the waving of palm branches, its meaning can vary. A literal translation is "Lord, Save!"

HOUR, THE. A MUSLIM term for the END TIME.

IKON. A sacred image or picture, generally of JESUS CHRIST, but also of a saint, revered especially within ORTHODOX CHRISTIAN churches and by Orthodox CHRISTIANS in their homes.

IN-GATHERING. A term referring to the immigration of JEWS from lands of the DIASPORA into modern ISRAEL.

INQUISITION. Inaugurated in the twelfth century by the ROMAN CATHOLIC Church, the Inquisition was an attempt to rid Christendom of heresy. Many CHRISTIANS and JEWS suffered in the brutality of the Inquisition, particularly in sixteenth-century SPAIN.

INTIFADEH. An uprising of PALESTINIANS against Israeli rule in the OCCUPIED TERRITORIES. The first intifadeh began in 1988 and continued until the OSLO ACCORD was signed in 1995. The second, titled the AL AQSA INTIFADEH, began in September of 2000. Both started with stone-throwing and soon escalated to more violent resistance. The Al Aqsa Intifadeh has been characterized by suicide bombings. At publication, the Al Aqsa Intifadeh is ongoing.

IRGUN. A militant armed Jewish underground organization, founded in 1931 by dissident HAGANAH commanders in the PALESTINE MANDATE. Trying to end the British Mandate and bring about ISRAEL's independence, it performed such terrorist acts as blowing up the King David Hotel in JERUSALEM.

IRON AGE. The stage in the development of civilization marked by the use of iron in weapons and tools. The Iron Age reached EGYPT by about 1500 BCE.

ISLAM. The monotheistic religion founded by MUHAMMED in the seventh century CE. Islam means "submission" to the will of God. Its Scripture, the QURAN, reveres the PATRIARCHS and prophets of the HEBREW SCRIPTURES, as well as JESUS CHRIST, as PROPHETS who were leading humans toward an understanding of God but teaches that the Prophet MUHAMMED has been given the final revelation. Islam is the world's second most widespread religion and currently the fastest-growing.

ISLAMIC JIHAD. A militant Palestinian organization founded in the **GAZA STRIP** during the 1970s. It is committed to the creation of an Islamic Palestinian state and the destruction of **ISRAEL** through a **HOLY WAR** (See **JIHAD**). It also opposes moderate Arab governments that it believes have been tainted by Western secularism.

ISLAMISM. An ideology that demands complete adherence to the **QURAN** and rejects, as much as possible, outside influence, with some exceptions (such as access to military and medical technology). It is imbued with a deep antagonism towards non-Muslims and has a particular hostility toward **THE WEST**.

JENIN MASSACRE. Israeli armed incursion into Jenin early in 2002, following a suicide bombing with heavy loss of life. In the fighting in Jenin, some 80 persons were killed, of whom 32 were civilians. Widely inflated reports of 500 civilians massacred were later discredited by UN investigators.

JEREMIAH, BOOK OF. The book of the **OLD TESTAMENT** named after the **PROPHET** who lived in **JERUSALEM** prior to and during the fall of **JUDAH** to the **BABYLONIANS** (ca 620 – 587 BCE). He was frequently in danger from the political and religious leaders who were angry because of his prophetic messages of the coming catastrophe. **JEREMIAH** was not taken to **BABYLON**, and it is thought that he died in **EGYPT**.

JEWISH LOBBY. The formal and informal attempts by American Jewish citizens to influence public policy in favor of **ISRAEL**. The most powerful lobbying group is the American Israel Public Affairs Committee.

JEWISH REVOLT. A revolt of large numbers of **JEWS** against Roman Rule, from 66-70 CE. Except for the holdout on **MASADA**, the revolt ended with the destruction of the **TEMPLE** in **JERUSALEM** in 70 CE.

JEWISH SCRIPTURES. See **HEBREW SCRIPTURES**.

JIHAD. An Arabic word meaning "struggle," it can refer both to the continuing internal struggle of humans for personal betterment and to the struggle of **MUSLIMS** against unbelievers. In the latter context, a Jihad is considered to be a **HOLY WAR**, invoked by **FUNDAMENTALIST MUSLIMS** against the leaders of modernizing **ARAB STATES**, or against **ISRAEL** or its supporters.

JIZYA. A head tax required until recent times of all **CHRISTIANS** and **JEWS** (**PEOPLE OF THE BOOK**) living in **MUSLIM** lands. (See **DHIMMI**).

JOHN, GOSPEL OF. The fourth book of the **NEW TESTAMENT**, one of the four **GOSPELS** that narrate the life and teachings of **JESUS CHRIST**. It differs in many respects from the other three Gospels and is probably based on sources different from those used by the authors of **MATTHEW**, **MARK**, and **LUKE**. Scholars assert that the Gospel of John, in its present form, dates from about 100 CE.

JUDAISM. The oldest of the three monotheistic faiths, Judaism derives its name from the tribe of **JUDAH**, whose descendents were taken to **BABYLON** and later returned to rebuild **THE TEMPLE**. As a result of this formative experience, the spiritual leaders of the returnees oversaw the final compilation of the **HEBREW SCRIPTURES** and put their stamp on Jewish worship practices. Judaism survived the **DIASPORA**. Today Judaism as understood and practiced has reformed, conservative, and ORTHODOX factions.

KAABAH. The large cubic structure, covered with a black cloth, in the center of MECCA, SAUDI ARABIA. A black meteorite, in pre-Islamic times thought to be the abode of the god AL-LAH, is encompassed within the Kaabah. The Kaabah, and in particular the meteorite, is the geographic center of Islamic worship. MUSLIMS all over the world face the Kaabah when they pray.

KAFFIYEH. A traditional BEDOUIN head covering worn by many Arab men, including YASSER ARAFAT. (See ARAFAT, YASSER).

KIBBUTZ. (Plural Kibbutzim) A type of collective farm introduced into ISRAEL by ZIONIST settlers from RUSSIA during the latter part of the nineteenth century. On a kibbutz, members share land ownership, most possessions, work responsibilities, and profit. Less than one percent of ISRAELIS now live on kibbutzim.

KNESSET. The Israeli Parliament, housed in JERUSALEM.

LADINO. A language and culture retained by SEPHARDIM, which blended Spanish and Arabic elements.

LAND-FOR-PEACE. The basis for the OSLO ACCORD by which ISRAEL would surrender to a Palestinian state all land taken in the 1967 SIX-DAY WAR, including the WEST BANK and GAZA. ISRAELIS who agree with the Land-for-Peace concept do not agree that it includes EAST JERUSALEM. PALESTINIANS insist that East Jerusalem is an essential part of Land-for-Peace.

LEAGUE OF NATIONS. An international organization established after World War I. Although its demise came with World War II, many of the concepts that underlie its structure were incorporated within its successor organization, the UNITED NATIONS. The headquarters of the League of Nations was in Geneva, Switzerland.

LEVITICUS, BOOK OF. The third book of the TORAH and the PENTATEUCH and subsequently of the OLD TESTAMENT.

LINGUA FRANCA. A common language by which people of different linguistic groups can communicate. A lingua franca often originates as a trade or administrative language. In the HOLY LAND during the time of JESUS CHRIST, both ARAMAIC and Greek were used as common languages.

LUKE, GOSPEL OF. The third book of the NEW TESTAMENT, and one of the SYNOPTIC GOSPELS, it includes many of the instances in JESUS CHRIST'S life related by MATTHEW (See MATTHEW, GOSPEL OF) and MARK (See MARK, GOSPEL OF) but also relates additional material. For this reason, it is thought that the writer of the Gospel of Luke had access to a source unknown to Matthew and Mark. Luke's Gospel, written in the seventh or eighth decade of the first century, is considered to be the first part of a narrative continued in the BOOK OF ACTS. (See ACTS, BOOK OF).

MACCABEAN REVOLT. An uprising of Jewish militants against the SELEUCID ruler King Antiochus IV Epiphanes, led by the sons of a priestly family known as the HASMONEANS, beginning in 167 BCE. The term MACCABEES comes from a HEBREW word meaning "hammer."

MACCABEES, BOOKS OF. Two books of the APOCRYPHA which tell the story of the MACCABEAN REVOLT and ISRAEL under the HASMONEAN KINGDOM.

MADABA MAP. A mosaic map, covering all the territory from MESOPOTAMIA to the Nile, set into the floor of a BYZANTINE church in MADABA (JORDAN) during the sixth century. Much of the map survived subsequent earthquakes and attempts at reconstruction. Its jewel for historians is a representation of JERUSALEM at the time, showing the street plan imposed by the Romans in the second century.

MADRASA. A religious school, usually associated with a MOSQUE, in which boys learn to recite the QURAN. In developing countries with limited public education, madrasas often provide the only schooling available for poor families.

MANDATE. A temporary rule over a territory lost by Axis powers (Germany and TURKEY) during World War I and assigned by the LEAGUE OF NATIONS to Britain or France for the purpose of leading the mandate to self-government.

MARK, GOSPEL OF. The second book of the NEW TESTAMENT and oldest of the four GOSPELS, Mark may have been written as early as 64 CE. With similarities to the GOSPELS of MATTHEW (See MATTHEW, GOSPEL OF) and LUKE (See LUKE, GOSPEL OF), it is one of the three SYNOPTIC GOSPELS.

MARTYR. A person who dies or is killed because of his/her faith.

MASADA. A knoll rising 1500 feet above the shores of the DEAD SEA, Masada is the most visited of all archaeological sites in ISRAEL. Masada was built as a fortified resort for Roman rulers in JUDEA. In 70 CE, during the JEWISH REVOLT against the Romans, Masada was captured by a small group of JEWS known as the ZEALOTS, who held out until 73 CE when the Romans finally breached the fortress. All of the Masada defenders committed suicide rather than submit to the Romans.

MASORITIC TEXT. The accepted HEBREW text that forms the basis of both the Jewish Scriptures and (for PROTESTANTS) the OLD TESTAMENT. (ROMAN CATHOLICS rely on the Latin translation of Jerome based on the Greek SEPTUAGINT). Masoritic comes from the word *Masora*, which usually refers to the notes printed beside the HEBREW text by Jewish scribes and scholars. Until recently, the oldest existing manuscripts of the HEBREW BIBLE dated from the ninth century CE and onward. However, the DEAD SEA SCROLLS provide manuscripts that predate the previous manuscripts by about 1,000 years. A large number of the DEAD SEA SCROLL manuscripts agree with the Masoritic Text.

MATTHEW, GOSPEL OF. The first book of the NEW TESTAMENT, it is one of the four GOSPELS that records the life and ministry of JESUS CHRIST. Scholars think that the author of Matthew had access to the GOSPEL OF MARK (See MARK, GOSPEL OF), as well as an additional source now lost. With similarities to the Gospels of Mark and LUKE (See LUKE, GOSPEL OF), Matthew is considered one of the three SYNOPTIC GOSPELS. The Gospel of Matthew was probably composed in the seventh or eighth decade of the first century. It was addressed primarily to the community of Jewish CHRISTIANS in the DIASPORA.

MESSIAH. A HEBREW word meaning "anointed one" and referring to a person who will deliver his people from oppression. OLD TESTAMENT prophets foretold that a messiah would come into the world to save the Jewish people. The GOSPEL accounts imply that during JESUS CHRIST's lifetime many people who heard him thought that Jesus was the promised Messiah who would save them from the oppression of the Romans.

MIDDLE AGES. A loosely used term that covers the period in Europe from about 1000 CE to the beginning of the **RENAISSANCE** about 1400 CE.

MILLENNIALISM. Christian **FUNDAMENTALIST** teachings based on literal interpretations of prophecies in the Biblical **BOOK OF REVELATION** (See **REVELATION, BOOK OF**) about the coming of a new millennium, when evil will be vanquished and true believers will enter a thousand-year period of peace and harmony marking the return of Christ to earth. (See **PRE-MILLENIALISM**).

MISHNA. A collection of commentary on the **TALMUD**. Mishna and **TALMUD**, together with the **TORAH** and the rest of the **HEBREW SCRIPTURES**, form the core of **JUDAISM** as a religion and of Jewish life and thought.

MODUS VIVENDI. A way of living together.

MONOTHEISM. The concept that there is only One God, almighty and all-powerful. **JUDAISM** came earliest to this understanding. **CHRISTIANITY** developed the concept of the Trinity (Father, Son, and Holy Spirit) in one Unity. In rejecting the Christian understanding, **ISLAM** developed a concept of One God that is closer to that of **JUDAISM**.

MOSAIC LAW. The laws given to **MOSES** on **MOUNT SINAI** (See **SINAI, MOUNT**) and incorporated within the **TORAH**.

MOSHAV. A type of cooperative farm unit in **ISRAEL** that allows some private holding of property. A moshav arrangement is halfway between the collectively owned **KIBBUTZ** and a privately owned farm.

MOSQUE. A building in which **MUSLIMS** worship. Traditionally, a **MOSQUE** includes an outer courtyard with a water fountain for prescribed ablution. The exact direction, or the qibla, of the **KAABAH** in **MECCA** is always indicated in a mosque by a niche called a mihrab. A mosque always contains a large open area where worshippers pray, facing the mihrab.

MUNICH OLYMPICS. Olympic venue in 1972, where Palestinian terrorists assassinated almost the entire Israeli Olympic team.

MYRRH. A gummy substance that flows from the bark of a low, thorny tree found in **ARABIA** and Somalia. It has been used since ancient times as an ingredient in incense and perfume. Liquefied, it was the holy oil used in **HEBREW** ceremonies.

NEHEMIAH, BOOK OF. The book of the **OLD TESTAMENT** that tells of the rebuilding of the walls of **JERUSALEM** and the reform of **JUDAISM** in the middle of the fifth century, as led by the Jewish governor **NEHEMIAH**, who was appointed by the Persian king. (See **EZRA, BOOK OF; EZRA**).

NEW TESTAMENT. The portion of the Christian **BIBLE** that tells of the birth, ministry, death, **RESURRECTION**, and **ASCENSION** of **JESUS CHRIST** (the Gospels of **MATTHEW, MARK, LUKE,** and **JOHN**); chronicles the spread of the early church in the first century (See **ACTS, BOOK OF**); preserves the letters of **PAUL** and other missionaries to early Christian congregations (including Ephesians, Corinthians, Romans); and concludes with the vision of John, a mystic exiled to the island of Patmos. (See **REVELATION, BOOK OF**).

NIGHT VISIT, THE. The tradition, not directly mentioned in the **QURAN**, that **MUHAMMED** traveled at night from **MECCA** to **MOUNT MORIAH** (See **MORIAH, MOUNT**) in **JERUSALEM**, and there (from the **ROCK OF ABRAHAM**) ascended to heaven to meet **ABRAHAM, MOSES,** and **JESUS CHRIST**. Muhammed then returned to Mecca that same night. The site of the Night Visit is memorialized in the **DOME OF THE ROCK**.

NOBEL PEACE PRIZE. A prize awarded each year under the terms of the will of Swedish philanthropist Alfred Nobel to the person or persons who have made the greatest contributions to World Peace.

NORTHERN KINGDOM. The kingdom that was formed in 927 BCE by the **HEBREW** tribes that lived in **GALILEE** and **SAMARIA** following the split that occurred after the death of **SOLOMON**. The **NORTHERN KINGDOM** was often referred to as **ISRAEL**, in contrast with the **SOUTHERN KINGDOM**, termed **JUDAH**. In 721, the **ASSYRIANS** defeated the **NORTHERN KINGDOM** and deported almost all of its population, after which the descendants of the northern tribes disappeared from history.

NUMBERS, BOOK OF. The fourth of the five books of the **TORAH** and the **PENTATEUCH**. The fourth book of the **OLD TESTAMENT**.

OCCUPIED TERRITORIES. See **PLACES: OCCUPIED TERRITORIES**.

OLD TESTAMENT. The first part of the Christian **BIBLE**, based on the books of the **HEBREW SCRIPTURES**, slightly rearranged. For Catholics and Anglicans, the canon of the Old Testament (including the **APOCRYPHA**) is based partly on the **SEPTUAGINT**; for **PROTESTANTS**, the Old Testament canon is identical to that of the **HEBREW** Scriptures, using the **MASORITIC TEXT**.

OMAYYAD CALIPHATE. The period (661-750 CE) when the Arab Empire was ruled from **DAMASCUS**.

ORTHODOX. Religious or political convictions that hue to original or standard interpretations. Orthodox Christian churches, sometimes called Eastern Orthodox churches, have their roots in the rituals and conventions that evolved when the Christian church was headquartered in **CONSTANTINOPLE**.

ORTHODOX CHRISTIANITY. The eastern (Eastern Orthodox) branch of Christianity, with rituals and conventions that developed during the period of **BYZANTINE** rule from **CONSTANTINOPLE**. Sometimes called Orthodox Catholic to differentiate it from **ROMAN CATHOLIC**. The Eastern Orthodox and Roman Catholic branches of Christianity split in the eleventh century CE. Among Eastern Orthodox churches today that trace their origin to **CONSTANTINOPLE** are those with ecclesial headquarters in Athens (Greek Orthodox), Erevan (Armenian Orthodox), **ANTIOCH** (Syrian Orthodox), Bucharest (Romanian Orthodox), and Moscow (Russian Orthodox). (See **ULTRA-ORTHODOX**).

OSLO ACCORD. A **LAND-FOR-PEACE** understanding between **ISRAEL**, represented by former Prime Minister **YITZHAK RABIN** (See **RABIN, YITZHAK**), and the **PALESTINE LIBERATION ORGANIZATION**, represented by **YASSER ARAFAT** (See **ARAFAT, YASSER**), reached in Oslo in 1993, reinforced in the Oslo II Accord signed in Washington in 1995, and first implemented in the **OCCUPIED TERRITORIES** in the that same year. The Accord created the **PALESTINIAN AUTHORITY**, but portions of the Accord dealing with the cessation of settlement-building by **ISRAELIS** and cessation of terrorism by **PALESTINIANS** were never implemented.

OTTOMAN EMPIRE. The Empire ruled by the **TURKS** from about 1450 to 1918. After Sultan **MEHMET II** captured **CONSTANTINOPLE** in 1453, the Ottoman Sultans ruled from the former **BYZANTINE** capital, which they renamed Istanbul. The most famous Ottoman sultan was **SULEIMAN THE MAGNIFICENT**, who ruled in the sixteenth century. At its height in the eighteenth and nineteenth centuries, the territory of the Ottoman Empire included North Africa, southeastern Europe, western **ARABIA**, the **HOLY LAND**, **SYRIA**, and **MESOPOTAMIA**.

PALESTINE LIBERATION ORGANIZATION (PLO). Founded in 1964, the PLO joined **FATAH**, the Popular Front for the Liberation of Palestine (PFLP), and other organizations that shared the goals of helping **PALESTINIANS** to "recover their usurped homes" and replacing **ISRAEL** with a secular Palestinian state. **YASSER ARAFAT** (See **ARAFAT, YASSER**) has headed the PLO since 1968. Its headquarters were in **JORDAN** before 1971, in **LEBANON** until 1982, and in **TUNISIA** until 1995. Since the beginnings of the **PALESTINIAN AUTHORITY** in 1995, PLO headquarters have been in **RAMALLAH**.

PALESTINE MANDATE. The temporary rule of the former **OTTOMAN** province of **PALESTINE** awarded to Britain by the **LEAGUE OF NATIONS**. British rule was *de facto* as of the end of World War I but was ratified by the League in 1923. The Mandate extended east of the **JORDAN**, where it was termed the **TRANS-JORDAN MANDATE**. The League intended that Britain prepare the Mandate for self-government, which for Palestine became an impossible task. The British Palestine Mandate ended on May 14, 1948, at the same time that **ISRAEL** declared its independence.

PALESTINIAN AUTHORITY. Established under terms of the **OSLO ACCORD**, it exercises self-government in urban areas of the **WEST BANK** and **GAZA**. Under terms of the **SHARM EL-SHEIKH AGREEMENT**, the Palestinian Authority has total control of about eighteen percent of the **OCCUPIED TERRITORIES** and shares control with **ISRAEL** of another fifty-eight percent.

PASSOVER. An ancient **HEBREW** celebration commemorating the **EXODUS** of the **ISRAELITES** from **EGYPT**. The term "Passover" signifies that the Angel of Death, who was to kill all first-born males, passed over the homes of the Israelites, whose door frames were smeared with the blood of a newly slaughtered lamb or goat.

PAX ROMANA. The stable conditions that accompanied Roman rule, allowing commerce to flow freely on well-maintained roads.

PENTATEUCH. The Greek word for the five books of the **TORAH**, which came into use after the translation of the **HEBREW SCRIPTURES** into Greek (See **SEPTUAGINT**). Often used to refer to the first five books of the **OLD TESTAMENT**.

PENTECOST. An ancient **HEBREW** first-fruits festival celebrating the harvest of winter wheat, it was usually held fifty days after **PASSOVER**. It also became a celebration of the giving of the Law on **MOUNT SINAI** (See **SINAI, MOUNT**), traditionally fifty days after the escape from **EGYPT**. Fifty days after the first Easter, **JEWS** from all parts of the **DIASPORA** were assembled in **JERUSALEM**

to celebrate the festival that by this time had acquired the Greek name of Pentecost. At this festival, by tradition the Apostles were able to tell the story of the resurrected **JESUS CHRIST** to the assembled crowd, each hearing it in his/her own language. Pentecost has since become a leading Christian festival.

PEOPLE OF THE BOOK. A term that includes **JEWS**, **CHRISTIANS**, and **MUSLIMS**, whose Scriptures share the same **PATRIARCHS** and **PROPHETS**. During the Arab conquests, most conquerors acknowledged that the **QURAN** grants special dispensation to **PEOPLE OF THE BOOK** that is not to be extended to "unbelievers."

PERSIAN EMPIRE. From the mid-sixth century until the time of **ALEXANDER THE GREAT** (ca 560 to 330 BCE), the most extensive Empire the world had yet known, extending far east of **MESOPOTAMIA**, almost to India, and far west of the Nile River in North Africa. In one of history's turning points, the Persian advance was stopped by the Greeks at the battles of Marathon and Salamis.

PFLP. Acronym for the Popular Front for the Liberation of Palestine, one of the constituent groups of the **PALESTINE LIBERATION ORGANIZATION** (PLO). It is second in size and influence to Arafat's **FATAH**.

PILGRIMAGE. A journey to a site holy or meaningful to one's faith.

PILLARS OF ISLAM. The five duties required of every **MUSLIM**: To acknowledge that there is only One God and that **MUHAMMED** is his **PROPHET**, to pray five times daily in the direction of the **KAABAH**, to perform acts of charity, to observe a total fast from sunup to sundown during the month of **RAMADAN**, and (if physically and financially able) to make a **PILGRIMAGE** to **MECCA**.

POGROM. A systematic and politically sanctioned persecution of **JEWS**, carried out particularly in cities and towns of Eastern Europe and **RUSSIA** in the nineteenth and early twentieth centuries.

POLYTHEISM. The worship of or belief in the existence of many gods.

PRE-MILLENNIALISM. The variant of **MILLENNIALISM** that posits a series of events that must precede the **SECOND COMING OF CHRIST**: the return of **JEWS** to the **HOLY LAND**, Jewish rule in the Holy Land, the rebuilding of **THE TEMPLE**, the deception of the Anti-Christ, the mustering of forces of evil from all parts of the world, the period of **TRIBULATION**, the **RAPTURE** of believing **CHRISTIANS**, the climactic battle of **ARMAGEDDON** in which almost all people on earth will be killed, and the conversion of 144,000 **JEWS**.

PROMISED LAND. The Land of **CANAAN**, promised to **ABRAHAM** and his descendents, as recorded in the **BOOK OF GENESIS** (See **GENESIS, BOOK OF**). It is roughly equivalent in area to present-day **ISRAEL** plus the **OCCUPIED TERRITORIES**.

PROPHET. A man or woman with unusual abilities to predict the future or speak as a messenger of God. In the **OLD TESTAMENT**, prophets were chosen by God to bring his messages to the rulers. All of the **OLD TESTAMENT** prophets, as well as **JESUS CHRIST**, are accepted as prophets by **MUSLIMS**, who believe that the last of the prophets to whom God revealed truth directly was **MUHAMMED**.

PROTESTANT. Branches of **CHRISTIANITY** that developed during and subsequent to the **REFORMATION**. As religious leaders broke from Catholicism, new churches formed. Offshoots from these churches formed in turn. As a group all churches that are neither **ROMAN CATHOLIC** nor **ORTHODOX** are called Protestant.

PROTESTANT REFORMATION. See **REFORMATION, THE.**

PSALMS. Poems and songs recorded in the Book of Psalms of the **HEBREW BIBLE** (the **OLD TESTAMENT**) distilling the relationship of humans to God. It is thought that some of the Psalms were composed by **DAVID** as early as 1000 CE. For others, the date of composition varies. Many were written during the **BABYLONIAN CAPTIVITY** or later.

PTOLEMAIC EMPIRE. Empire ruled by the **PTOLEMYS**, the descendents of the general to whom was given the rule of Egypt and adjacent lands following the death of **ALEXANDER THE GREAT** in 323 BCE. The Ptolemaic Empire originally included also much of **PALESTINE** and **TRANS-JORDAN**, but by 200 the Ptolemys had lost control of Palestine to the **SELEUCID EMPIRE**, based in **SYRIA**.

PURIM, FEAST OF. A Jewish festival celebrating the victory of Queen **ESTHER**, wife of a Persian king, over the villainous court minister **HAMAN**, who had given orders for the mass slaying of **JEWS** in the Empire. The event, dating to the latter years of the **BABYLONIAN CAPTIVITY**, is narrated in the **OLD TESTAMENT BOOK OF ESTHER**. (See **ESTHER, BOOK OF; PEOPLE: ESTHER**).

QURAN. The Holy Book of **ISLAM**. The **QURAN** was revealed by the Angel **GABRIEL** to **MUHAMMED** over a 22-year period from 610 to 632 CE, first in **MECCA** and after 622 in **MEDINA**. Because, by tradition, Muhammed could neither read nor write, it is assumed that he dictated the revelations to scribes, who recorded them in Arabic. Although the Quran has been translated into many languages, believers prefer to recite it in Arabic. The Quran is divided into 114 **SURAS**, or Chapters, of varying length.

RAIN SHADOW. An area that is cut off from rain-bearing winds.

RAMADAN. A month-long period of spiritual renewal required of all **MUSLIMS** (See **PILLARS OF ISLAM**). Set according to the lunar calendar, its date varies. During Ramadan, Muslims must abstain from food and drink from sunup to sundown, which can be an especially trying discipline when Ramadan falls during the heat of the summer.

RAPTURE, THE. A **PRE-MILLENNIALIST** belief that just before the period of **TRIBULATION**, which will precede the **SECOND COMING OF CHRIST**, **CHRISTIANS** will be raptured, or taken directly to heaven, thus being spared the horrors of the Tribulation and **ARMAGEDDON**. After Armageddon, the raptured **CHRISTIANS** will return to earth with the Second Coming and will experience his millennial reign.

RECONQUISTA. The 600-year period during which Christian rulers and armies slowly wrested the **IBERIAN PENINSULA** (**SPAIN** and **PORTUGAL**) from Islamic control. The Reconquista (reconquest) ended in 1492 with the defeat of the last **MUSLIM** ruler in southern Spain.

REFORMATION, THE. A period in European history, during the sixteenth century, when the absolute authority of the **ROMAN CATHOLIC** Church was questioned by reformers such as Martin Luther and John Calvin. Translations of Scripture into the vernacular were made widely available through the medium of the newly invented printing press. (See **PROTESTANT; COUNTER-REFORMATION**).

Reformed Judaism. The most liberal branch of **Judaism**, widely followed especially among **Jews** in the United States.

Refugee. A person who has been expelled from his home or can no longer live there and has migrated to what he perceives to be a safer haven.

Registered Refugee. A **refugee** who seeks **United Nations** assistance.

Renaissance. A period of cultural awakening and renewal in Europe, beginning in the fourteenth century in Italy and spreading rapidly to all parts of the continent. As the writings of the ancient Greeks came to be known through Arab translation, and Arab advances in mathematics and the sciences also reached Europe, European writers and artists began to tap sources of knowledge and cultural inspiration that had been "lost" during the long period following the fall of the **Roman Empire**.

Resurrection. The act of coming back to life after death. **Christians** believe that on the third day after his burial, **Jesus Christ** rose from the dead. An account of the Resurrection of Jesus is given in each of the four **Gospels**.

Revelation, Book of. The last book of the **New Testament**, written by John (not the writer of the **Gospel of John** (See **John, Gospel of**)) while living in exile on the Greek island of Patmos in the Ionian Sea towards the end of the first century. Difficulties in interpreting the symbolism in John's images delayed the acceptance of the Book of Revelation in the **New Testament** canon until the end of the fifth century. Some **Christians** look to Revelation for a literal prediction of end-time events. (See **Pre-Millennialism**).

Rift Valley. A geological term indicating the down-thrust that occurs between two block-fault mountains. In the case of **palestine**, the hills to the east and west of the **jordan river**, rising to 3,000 feet, are separated by the rift valley occupied by the river. The rift valley continues southward, where it is occupied by the **dead sea**, the **wadi arabah**, and the **gulf of aqaba**.

Rock of Abraham. By tradition, the stone altar on **Mount Moriah** (See **Moriah, Mount**) on which **Abraham** laid his son Isaac (**Ishmael** by **Muslim** tradition) to be sacrificed, before the actual sacrifice was stopped by divine intervention. Traditionally, both the **Holy of Holies** in **Solomon's Temple** and the **Dome of the Rock** were built on this site.

Roman Catholic. The worldwide branch of Christendom tracing its founding to mid-first century in **Rome** and governed by an ecclesiastical hierarchy headed by the Bishop of Rome, who serves as Pope. (See **Orthodox**; **Reformation**; **Counter-reformation**).

Salaam. An Arabic greeting meaning "Peace!" Its equivalent in **Hebrew** is **Shalom**.

Samaritan Heresy. The belief held by Jewish leaders, following their return from captivity in **Babylon** (See **Babylonian Captivity**) in the late sixth century BCE, that the people of **Samaria** had strayed from the truth in their religious beliefs and were to be shunned. (See **Samaritans**).

Second Coming of Christ. A Christian belief with many variations, ranging from the view that the Second Coming is an ongoing spiritual occurrence in human lives to the literal interpretation of portions of Scripture that associate the Second Coming with predictable cataclysmic events. (See **Pre-Millennialism**).

Second Temple. The **Temple** built by the **Jews** who returned from **Babylon** on the site of **Solomon's Temple**. Completed in 515 BCE. Greatly enlarged by **Herod the Great** in the last two decades of the first century BCE. Destroyed by the Romans in 70 CE.

Security Barrier. The 425 mile long barrier, part fence and part wall, being built by **Israel** to separate itself from the **West Bank** and to funnel all Palestinian trans-barrier movement through secure entry points.

Seder. The commemorative meal by which **Jews** everywhere celebrate the **Passover.**

Seleucids. The generals who inherited the northern portion of **Alexander The Great**'s Empire and their descendents. The **Seleucids**, who ruled from what is now **Syria**, extended their domain into **Palestine** by the beginning of the second century.

Semitic. A subdivision of the Caucasian grouping of early peoples, with links that are primarily linguistic. Semitic languages can be grouped into a northern branch—including Akkadian (also called Assyro-Babylonian), Assyrian, **Aramaic** (including Syriac), Moabite, **Hebrew**, and **Phoenician** (now a dead language)—and a southern branch, which includes Arabic, Sabaean, and Ethiopic (Amharic). All Semitic languages are written from right to left except Amharic and Assyrian, which are written from left to right.

Septuagint. A translation of the **Hebrew Scriptures** into Greek, authorized by Ptolemaic rulers (See **Ptolemaic Empire**) in Alexandria about 200 BCE but supplemented by additional material during the succeeding hundred and fifty years. It contains books not in the **Hebrew** Scriptures. Together, these books are called the **Apocrypha.**

Settlements, Jewish. Communities in the **Occupied Territories** planned by the Israeli government and settled by **Israelis.**

Shalom. A **Hebrew** word meaning "Peace!" The equivalent in Arabic is **salaam.**

Sharia. The body of rules laid down in the **Quran** that are the basis for a civil code in certain **Muslim** countries. The Sharia contains the rules by which a **Muslim** society is organized and governed, and it provides the means to resolve conflicts among individuals and between the individual and the state. Countries presently ruled by Quranic law are **Saudi Arabia**, Sudan, **Iran**, and the northern provinces of Nigeria.

Sharif. A regional or tribal ruler in Arab society.

Sharm el-Sheikh Agreement. An understanding reached in Israeli/Palestinian negotiations in 1999 at **Sharm el-Sheikh** resort at the southern tip of the **Sinai Peninsula.** Implemented in early 2000, the agreement increased the percentage of land in the **West Bank** over which the **Palestinian Authority** has sovereignty.

Shi'a Islam. A branch of **Islam** whose adherents are primarily in **Iran** but also in scattered communities throughout the **Middle East** and North Africa. Shi'a broke early with the dominant **Sunni** (See **Sunni Islam**) faction over the issue of succession. Shi'ites believe that **Muhammed** should have been succeeded by his cousin and son-in-law, Ali. (See **Ali ibn Abu Talib**).

Six-Day War. War initiated by **Israelis** in 1967 in response to **Egypt**'s closing of the **Straits of Tiran** (See **Tiran, Straits of**), **Syria**'s bombardment of Israeli towns from the **Golan Heights**, and Arab guerrilla attacks on Israeli rural communities. After six days a **United Nations**-brokered armistice brought the war to an end, but not before **Israel** had won control of the **Sinai Peninsula**, the **Golan Heights**, the **West Bank**, the **Gaza Strip**, and **East Jerusalem**.

Solomon's Temple. The first Temple to be built on the **Temple Mount** in **Jerusalem**, about 950 BCE.

Southern Kingdom. The remnant of the kingdom of **Solomon** after the northern tribes seceded to form the **Northern Kingdom** in 927 BCE. The **Southern Kingdom** was called **Judah**, the name of the largest of its two tribes. The other tribe that made up the **Southern Kingdom** was **Benjamin**. The **Southern Kingdom** lasted until 586 BCE, when it was destroyed by the **Babylonians**.

Stations of the Cross. A form of devotion that commemorates the Passion and death of **Jesus Christ**. Each of the stations stands for an event that occurred, either as recorded in Scripture or by tradition. As early as 400 CE, pilgrims in **Jerusalem** were walking the **Via Dolorosa** and halting to pray at each marked Station.

Suleiman's Wall. The wall surrounding the **Old City of Jerusalem**, as altered and repaired by **Suleiman the Magnificent** in the sixteenth century.

Sunni Islam. The largest and most numerous of the two major divisions of **Islam**, which early split over the issue of succession. **Sunnis** were those who endorsed the elected leader, **Abu Bakr**. (See **Shi'a Islam**).

Sura. A chapter, or section, of the **Quran**. There are 114 separate Suras in the Quran, each divided by numbered verses.

Synagogue. A place of worship for **Jews**.

Synoptic Gospels. The first three **Gospels**, **Matthew**, **Mark**, and **Luke**, whose accounts of the life of **Jesus Christ** have strong concurrences and may have been taken from similar early sources, now lost.

Talmud. A collection of rabbinical studies of the **Torah**, which date from the second century CE. (See **Mishna**).

Tanzim. The militant armed wing of Arafat's **Fatah Party**.

Tell. An archaeological term indicating a mound or low hill formed by the debris of an ancient settlement.

Temple, The. The historic center of Jewish worship, built on a rise once known as **Mount Moriah** (See **Moriah, Mount**) in **Jerusalem**. According to accounts in the Jewish Scriptures (the **Old Testament**), the Temple was built by **Solomon** in the tenth century BCE, was destroyed by the **Chaldeans** in 586 BCE, rebuilt by the **Jews** in the latter part of the sixth century, and renovated and enlarged by **Herod the Great** toward the end of the first century. The Temple was destroyed by the Romans in 70 CE. (See **Second Temple**; **Solomon's Temple**).

TEMPLE MOUNT. The natural rise within the city of JERUSALEM where by tradition ABRAHAM once offered ISAAC (for MUSLIMS, ISHMAEL) for sacrifice. Originally known as MOUNT MORIAH (See MORIAH, MOUNT), the rise was used by SOLOMON as a platform on which to build his Temple. The Temple Mount was the center of Jewish worship from 950 to 586 BCE (See SOLOMON'S TEMPLE) and from 515 BCE to 70 CE (See SECOND TEMPLE). The Romans, who destroyed THE TEMPLE in 70 CE, later placed religious statues on the Temple Mount. During BYZANTINE times the site had little significance. With the coming of ISLAM, the site became the HARAM AL-SHARIF, its present designation. Over the former site of the TEMPLE, the MUSLIM conquerors built the DOME OF THE ROCK and facing it the AL-AQSA MOSQUE.

TEN COMMANDMENTS. The ten laws given to MOSES on MOUNT SINAI (See SINAI, MOUNT), as recorded in the books of EXODUS and DEUTERONOMY.

TORAH. The first five books of the HEBREW SCRIPTURES as well as the Christian OLD TESTAMENT (where they are designated as the Pentateuch). Included are the books of GENESIS, EXODUS, LEVITICUS, NUMBERS, and DEUTERONOMY.

TRANS-JORDAN MANDATE. The part of the BRITISH MANDATE OF PALESTINE that was east of the JORDAN RIVER. In 1946, the TRANS-JORDAN MANDATE became the independent HASHEMITE KINGDOM OF JORDAN.

TRIBULATION, THE. According to the ESCHATOLOGY of PRE-MILLENNIALISM, the period of warfare and natural disasters that will come to a climax in the Battle of ARMAGEDDON.

ULTRA-ORTHODOX. A collective term applied to all who believe in living according to a literal interpretation of their scriptures. In ISRAEL there are numbers of ultra-Orthodox groups, some highly political and influential in setting Israeli policy, and others with no political involvement. (See HAREDIM).

UMMA. The community of all MUSLIMS everywhere, united in faith.

UNITED KINGDOM (BIBLICAL). The kingdom called ISRAEL, under SAUL (ca 1050-1010 BCE), DAVID (ca 1010-970 BCE), and SOLOMON (ca 970-930 BCE), that united the HEBREW tribes who had settled in the Land of CANAAN. Ended with the breakup (927 BCE) into a NORTHERN KINGDOM, called Israel, and a SOUTHERN KINGDOM, called JUDAH.

UNITED NATIONS. An international organization founded in 1945 as a successor to the LEAGUE OF NATIONS. The UN is headquartered in New York City, but many of its agencies are based in Geneva, Switzerland.

UNDOF (UNITED NATIONS Disengagement Observer Force). A force stationed along the eastern border of the GOLAN HEIGHTS to keep peace between ISRAEL and SYRIA. Since 1974, it has successfully carried out its mission.

UNRWA (UNITED NATIONS Relief and Works Agency). The agency responsible for the welfare of refugees. A separate branch, titled UNRWA for PALESTINE Refugees in the Near East, is devoted exclusively to the maintenance of camps and welfare programs for PALESTINIAN REFUGEES.

UN RESOLUTION 242. Signed following the end of the SIX-DAY WAR in 1967, Resolution 242 calls for the withdrawal of Israeli military forces from all territory occupied in that war and the diplomatic recognition of ISRAEL by all ARAB

263

STATES.

URDU. An Indo-European language spoken by the majority of people in PAKISTAN.

VIA DOLOROSA. The route followed by JESUS CHRIST from the ANTONIA FORTRESS to GOLGOTHA, the place of execution. It is a PILGRIMAGE route from early Christian times. (See STATIONS OF THE CROSS).

WADI. A valley in a desert area. Usually dry, it can hold a torrent of water after a sudden rain.

WAHABBI. An ultra conservative religious faction of SUNNI ISLAM that emerged in ARABIA in the eighteenth century. WAHABBI was embraced by ABDULAZIZ IBN SAUD (See IBN SAUD, ABDULAZIZ) as he fought for control of the ARABIAN PENINSULA in the early part of the twentieth century and established the kingdom of SAUDI ARABIA. Wahabbi teachings are followed by the ruling family and by most MUSLIM clerics in Saudi Arabia today.

WESTERN WALL. Built under the direction of HEROD THE GREAT as a retaining wall for the refurbished SECOND TEMPLE, the Western Wall is the only portion of the TEMPLE that escaped destruction in 70 AD. Ever since, the Western Wall has been a destination for Jewish pilgrims. After 1967, when ISRAEL again had control of EAST JERUSALEM, the Western Wall once more became available to JEWS who wish to pray there.

WMD. Acronym for Weapons of Mass Destruction, referring especially to nuclear, chemical, and biological weapons.

YAD VASHEM HOLOCAUST MUSEUM. Located on the Mount of Remembrance in JERUSALEM, the museum exists so that the world will never forget the horrors and cruelty of the HOLOCAUST. Its principal missions are commemorating and documenting the events of the Holocaust; collecting, examining, and publishing testimonies to the Holocaust; and collecting and memorializing the names of Holocaust victims.

YARMULKE. A skullcap worn especially by religiously observant JEWS.

YIDDISH. Language that developed among JEWS in central Europe during the past five hundred years. Combining elements of German, Slavic, and HEBREW, it was spoken by the majority of JEWS both in Germanic and SLAVIC LANDS.

ZIONISM. The idea that PALESTINE should be a homeland for JEWS (See ZION, MOUNT). Throughout the centuries Jews everywhere retained a special attachment to JERUSALEM, the site of its twice-destroyed TEMPLE. But Zionism as an organized movement dates from 19th century Europe. The idea of a Jewish homeland was formalized in 1897 when following the DREYFUS AFFAIR, THEODOR HERZL (See HERZL, THEODOR) organized the World ZIONIST Organization. Since ISRAEL became independent, its national policy has been guided by Zionism.

GLOSSARY: PEOPLE

Abassids. Rulers of the Arab Empire based in **Baghdad**, 750-1258. They ruled in **Palestine** until 909.

Abdullah. Crown Prince of **Saudi Arabia**. Brother of ailing King Fahd and frequently his spokesman.

Abdullah I. King of **Jordan**. First ruler of the **Hashemite Kingdom of Jordan** (1946-1952). Grandfather of King Hussein (1952-1999) and great grandfather of present King **Abdullah II**.

Abdullah II. King of **Jordan** since the death of his father King Hussein in 1999. Great grandson of King **Abdullah I**, **Jordan**'s first king.

Abraham. The first of the **Patriarchs**, considered by both **Jews** and **Muslims** to be the founding father of their nations. (See **Isaac**; **Ishmael**).

Abu Bakr. A Companion of the **Prophet**, Abu Bakr was selected to be the first Caliph, after the death of **Muhammed** in 632 CE. His accession to power is considered valid by **Sunnis** (See **Sunni Islam**), but not by Shi'ites. (See **Shi'a Islam**).

Alexander the Great. Macedonian conqueror who spread Greek culture over the known world, 333-323 BCE. In 332, he marched through **Palestine**, defeating the Persian contingents stationed there.

Ali ibn Abu Talib. Cousin and son-in-law of **Muhammed**. Believed by **Shi'ites** (See **Shi'a Islam**) to be the legitimate successor of Muhammed.

Ammonites. **Semitic** people who occupied the **Trans-Jordan Plateau** of **Moab** and frequently clashed with the **Israelites**.

Amos. A **prophet** in the **Northern Kingdom**, beginning about 750 BCE.

Annas. High priest in **Jerusalem** in the early part of the first century CE. Succeeded in the office by his son **Caiaphas**.

Arabs. A **Semitic** people who from ancient times occupied the **Arabian Peninsula**. Arabs spread northward into **Palestine** and **Mesopotamia** and westward into North Africa in the seventh century CE, following the founding of **Islam**.

Arafat, Yasser. Founder of the **Fatah** Party, head of the **Palestine Liberation Organization**, and leader of the **Palestinian Authority**.

ARMENIANS. People from the Caucasus region of Armenia, among the earliest peoples to convert to **CHRISTIANITY**.

ASHKENAZIM. JEWS who lived for centuries in Western and Eastern Europe.

ASSAD, BASHAR. President of **SYRIA** since the death of his father, **HAFEZ ASSAD**. (See **ASSAD, HAFEZ**).

ASSAD, HAFEZ. Head of the Arab **BA'ATH** Socialist Party and President of **SYRIA** from 1974 until his death in 2000. Succeeded by his son, **BASHAR ASSAD**. (See **ASSAD, BASHAR**).

ASSYRIANS. A **SEMITIC** people whose imperial ascendancy lasted from about 1000 to 600 **BCE**, when they were defeated by the **CHALDEANS**. In 723, the Assyrians overran **ISRAEL's NORTHERN KINGDOM** and scattered its inhabitants. A few pockets of modern-day Assyrians exist today in **IRAQ**, but the largest contingent has immigrated to the United States. They are found mostly in and around Detroit.

ATATURK, KEMAL. Revolutionary leader and founder of modern **TURKEY**, after the demise of the **OTTOMAN EMPIRE**.

BABYLONIANS. A **SEMITIC** people whose empire was centered in **BABYLON** in **MESOPOTAMIA**. Babylonia was an ancient city-state in the **CHALDEAN EMPIRE**. After joining with the **CHALDEANS** to defeat the **ASSYRIANS**, the Babylonians ruled in the **FERTILE CRESCENT** from 600 to 550 **BCE**, a period titled the Neo-Babylonian Empire. During this period they invaded the Kingdom of **JUDAH**, destroyed **JERUSALEM**, and took many of its inhabitants to **BABYLON**.

BAHA'ULLAH. Leader of the **BAHA'I** world religious movement in the 19th century. Exiled from his Iranian homeland, he spent his last years in Ottoman **SYRIA** and is buried in **HAIFA**.

BALFOUR, ARTHUR. Head of the British Foreign Office in 1917. In a letter to **BARON ROTHSCHILD** (See **ROTHSCHILD, BARON LIONEL**), the leader of the Jewish community in Britain, Balfour stated a position in regards to Jewish settlement in **PALESTINE** that later became official British policy. Balfour favored Palestine as a homeland for **JEWS**, providing that Arab rights would not be infringed.

BARAK, EHUD. Prime Minister of **ISRAEL** from 1999-2001; succeeded by **ARIEL SHARON**. (See **SHARON, ARIEL**).

BATHSHEBA. Wife of King **DAVID** and mother of **SOLOMON**. Enamored with Bathsheba, **DAVID** arranged to have her husband, **URIAH**, sent to certain death in an assault on the walls of **RABBOTH AMMON**.

BEDOUIN. ARABS who are nomadic and tribally organized. Bedouin form a small portion (less than five percent) of the total population of Arab countries, but their customs and manner of dress have been broadly adopted by villagers and even by many city-dwellers.

BEGIN, MENACHEM. Israeli Prime Minister who signed a peace treaty with **EGYPT's ANWAR SADAT** (See **SADAT, ANWAR**) at **CAMP DAVID**, 1979, for which both statesmen received the **NOBEL PEACE PRIZE**.

BENJAMIN. Youngest son of **JACOB**, as well as the name of the tribe formed by his descendents. The tribe of Benjamin settled an area north of **JUDAH** and joined with Judah in forming the **SOUTHERN KINGDOM**.

Bin Laden, Osama. Saudi engineer and radical **Islamist** who joined Afghans in ousting the Soviets. With the approval of **Afghanistan**'s **Taliban** rulers, he stayed to organize **Al-Qaeda**, an international training program for terrorists. Bin Laden's group planned the World Trade Center bombing on September 11, 2001. A target of the International War on Terrorism, he is probably still alive and giving direction to Al Qaeda at this writing.

Caesar Augustas. Born in 63 BCE, Octavian was named Caesar Augustus, the first emperor of **Rome**, in the year 27 and ruled until his death in 14 CE. He was the ruler of Rome at the time of the birth of **Jesus Christ**.

Caiaphas. The High Priest in **Jerusalem** before whom **Jesus Christ** was brought for a hearing. Caiaphas remanded him to **Pontius Pilate**. (See **Pilate, Pontius**).

Caleb. One of two named spies sent by **Moses** to assess circumstances in **Canaan** during the **Israelite**'s period of wandering in the desert.

Carter, President Jimmy. President of the United States 1976-1980; subsequently involved in world wide peace-making efforts.

Canaanites. A **Semitic** people living in the plateau country between the Mediterranean Sea and the **Jordan River** at the time when the **Israelites** arrived (about 1260 BCE).

Chaldeans. A **Semitic** people of lower **Mesopotamia** who formed an empire that defeated the **Assyrians** about 600 BCE. **Babylon** was a city-state within the **Chaldean Empire**, and the name Babylonian is thus often given to the **Chaldean Empire**.

Children of Israel. According to tradition as recorded in the **Book of Genesis** (See **Genesis, Book of**), descendants of **Abraham** through his son **Isaac** and his grandson **Jacob**, who was also named **Israel**.

Christ. See **Jesus Christ**.

Christians. Followers of the teachings of **Jesus Christ**. Divided among **Roman Catholic**, **Protestant**, and **Eastern Orthodox** branches.

Christian Zionists. **Christians** who believe that **Palestine** should be a homeland for **Jews** because the land was promised by God to **Abraham** and his successors. Some Christian **Zionists** participate in organized movements to support **Israel**.

Constantine. Roman emperor who in 313 CE made **Christianity** the official state religion. In 325, he moved the capital of his empire to **Byzantium**, renaming the city **Constantinople**.

Crusaders. European knights who attempted to reclaim the **Holy Land** for Christendom. They remained in the Holy Land from 1096 to 1290, but were ultimately defeated by the **Seljuk Turks** under **Saladdin**.

Cyrus the Great. Founder and first ruler of the **Persian Empire** (580-529 BCE), formed by uniting the two original Iranian tribes, the Medes and the Persians. Under his rule, the **Jews** in **Babylon** were freed and allowed to return to **Jerusalem**.

David. Ruler of the **United Kingdom** of **Israel** from ca 1010–970 BCE. Writer of many **Psalms**, cherished by **Jews** and **Christians** alike. David was the first

Israelite ruler to make **Jerusalem** his capital. His son **Solomon** succeeded him.

Dayan, Moshe. Israeli soldier/statesman who, as defense minister during the **Six-Day War**, formulated the agreement by which **Muslims** would keep control of the **Haram al-Sharif** in return for guaranteeing open access to all.

Dreyfus, Alfred. Jewish French army captain unjustly accused of treason in 1894 and sent to Devil's Island. The **Dreyfus Affair**, in which his freedom was ultimately won by the author **Emile Zola** (See **Zola, Emile**), triggered the organized beginning of the **Zionist** Movement. (See **Herzl, Theodor; Zionism**).

Druze. Members of an offshoot sect of **Shi'a Islam** who trace their beginnings to **Fatimid** rule in Egypt in the 10th century CE. About four percent of **Israelis** are Druze.

Edomites. A tribal people on the plateau east of the **Dead Sea** with whom the **Israelites** contended as they worked their way north during their wanderings. By tradition, the Edomites are descendants of **Esau**.

Esau. Oldest son of **Isaac** and twin brother of **Jacob**. Esau, a hunter, is cheated out of his inheritance by Jacob and his mother. After, he goes to live in **Edom** and becomes the father of the **Edomites**.

Essenes. A reformist community of **Jews** in the third century BCE and later who lived in separate communities isolated from others in order to practice their understanding of the Law. Knowledge of the Essenes has come from the **Dead Sea Scrolls**.

Esther. As told in the **Old Testament** in the **Book of Esther**, a Jewish Queen in the court of a Persian ruler, who saves her people from the persecutions planned by a wicked court minister named **Haman**. Her story is commemorated in the **Feast of Purim**. (See **Purim, Feast of**).

Ethiopian Jews. A community of some 30,000 **Jews** in **Israel**, representing an ancient community of **Jews** in highland **Ethiopia** whose origins are obscure. It is thought that they may be descendants of **Jews** who fled **Israel** for **Egypt** after the destruction of the first **Temple** in 586 BCE and eventually settled in Ethiopia.

Ezra. A Jewish priest and scholar living in **Persia** who led a large company of Jewish exiles back to **Jerusalem** in ca 458 BCE, receiving substantial Persian assistance in the undertaking. In **Israel**, he instituted reforms that changed the course of **Judaism**. Jewish tradition, unsubstantiated by modern scholarship, credits him with establishing the canon of the **Hebrew Scriptures** and with the authorship of the books of **Ezra, Nehemiah**, and Chronicles.

Fatimids. Shi'ite (See **Shi'a Islam**) rulers from North Africa who conquered the **Sunni** (See **Sunni Islam**) **Abassids** in **Palestine** in 909 CE. Their desecration of the **Church of the Holy Sepulcher** (See **Holy Sepulcher, Church of the**) helped to precipitate the **Crusades**. Defeated in **Palestine** by Crusaders in 1098.

Four Evangelists. The writers of the four **Gospels**, the first books of the **New Testament**, by tradition **Matthew, Mark, Luke, and John**.

Franciscans. Members of the clerical order established by Saint Francis of

Assisi. Since shortly before the end of the CRUSADES, the Franciscans have had responsibility for maintaining many HOLY LAND PILGRIMAGE sites, a responsibility they continue today.

FRANKS. Name used in the MIDDLE AGES to designate the people who would later be called French. Among ARABS in twelfth-century PALESTINE, it was used as a general name to designate the CRUSADERS.

FUNDAMENTALISTS. Persons whose religious beliefs are based on strict and literal interpretation of the writings in their Holy Book.

GABRIEL. Angel in both CHRISTIAN and MUSLIM traditions who brings messages from God. Gabriel appears to MARY (See MARY, MOTHER OF JESUS) to announce that she would be the mother of JESUS CHRIST, to Zacharias (father of JOHN THE BAPTIST), and to MUHAMMED as the bearer of messages that are recorded in the QURAN.

GADARENES. People living within the territory under the jurisdiction of the DECAPOLIS city of GADARA.

GLADSTONE, WILLIAM. British Prime Minister 1868-74 and 1880-85, during the reign of Queen Victoria. Ardent advocate of ZIONISM.

GOD-FEARERS. Gentiles attracted to JUDAISM in the ROMAN EMPIRE of the first century. So-named because they did not partake in the full range of Jewish customs and rituals but nevertheless worshipped at synagogues.

HAGAR. Servant of ABRAHAM and mother of his first-born son ISHMAEL. Later exiled by ABRAHAM, she goes to live in ARABIA, where ARABS believe her son becomes the father of the Arab nation.

HAMAN. Persian court minister whose edict against the JEWS is foiled by Queen ESTHER.

HAREDIM. Members of Jewish ULTRA-ORTHODOX communities in ISRAEL. (See HASSIDIM).

HASMONEANS. A priestly family who rebelled against the SELEUCIDS and established an independent kingdom in the HOLY LAND (167-63 BCE). (See MACCABEES)

HASSIDIM. HAREDIM who trace their beginnings to a spiritual movement within JUDAISM in eighteenth century Eastern Europe and RUSSIA. The Hassidic movement revived Judaism in those areas, and afterwards spread throughout the world. Hassidim in ISRAEL are among the most conservative of religious JEWS and have a strong influence on right-wing political parties in the KNESSET.

HEBREWS. The name given by the Egyptians to the CHILDREN OF ISRAEL (that is, the descendents of the twelve sons of JACOB) during the four hundred years they were in EGYPT. A somewhat pejorative name, it could have meant both "foreigners" and "swarthy ones." On their return from Egypt, the ISRAELITES retained this name, which also became attached to the language they spoke.

HELENA. The mother of Emperor CONSTANTINE. By tradition, her journey to the HOLY LAND in 324 established the sites of places connected with the life of JESUS CHRIST.

HEROD ANTIPAS. Son of HEROD THE GREAT. Roman tetrarch in the province of GALILEE and the TRANS-JORDAN province of PEREA. Herod Antipas imprisoned JOHN THE BAPTIST and had him beheaded. During the week of PASSOVER, Herod

Antipas was in JERUSALEM, and PONTIUS PILATE (See PILATE, PONTIUS) sent JESUS CHRIST to Herod Antipas for questioning.

HEROD THE GREAT. Appointed King of JUDEA by the Roman Senate. Reigned for more than thirty years until his death, either in 6 or 4 BCE. Enlarged and refurbished the TEMPLE, built amphitheaters and baths, and established the port of CAESAREA. At the time of the birth of JESUS CHRIST, he ordered the death of all males in the kingdom less than two years of age.

HERZL, THEODOR. Austrian Jewish playwright and reporter who was present in Paris during the DREYFUS AFFAIR. His subsequent call for ZIONISM was articulated in *The Jewish State: A Modern Solution to the Jewish Question* (1895). Herzl is considered the founder of the organized ZIONIST movement.

HITTITES. People of the Hittite Empire, based in central ANATOLIA, who vied with EGYPT for control of the FERTILE CRESCENT during the latter part of the second millennium BCE. As individuals, Hittites are mentioned frequently in the OLD TESTAMENT.

HOSEA. PROPHET in the NORTHERN KINGDOM in the eighth century BCE. Successor to the PROPHET AMOS.

HUSSEIN, KING OF JORDAN. Ruler of the HASHEMITE KINGDOM OF JORDAN from 1952 to his death in 1999. (See ABDULLAH).

HUSSEIN, SADDAM. Ba'athist military ruler of IRAQ from 1979 until 2003. A tyrant, he used chemical warfare against the KURDS and the SHI'ITES (See SHI'A ISLAM) in IRAQ and controlled his country through the exercise of terror. At this writing he is a captive of the Coalition Forces who invaded Iraq in 2003 to overthrow him. (See BA'ATH PARTY).

IBN SAUD, ABDULAZIZ. Over a thirty year period beginning in 1902, Ibn Saud united various desert tribes of the ARABIAN PENINSULA to found the kingdom of SAUDI ARABIA. He reigned as king until his death in 1953. During his reign he oversaw the transformation of an impoverished tribal society into a major oil exporter on the threshold of becoming a modern state.

ISAAC. One of the PATRIARCHS, son of ABRAHAM and SARAH in their old age and half-brother of ISHMAEL. By Jewish tradition as recorded in the BOOK OF GENESIS (See GENESIS, BOOK OF), Isaac was offered by Abraham for sacrifice on MOUNT MORIAH (See MORIAH, MOUNT), but at the last moment an angel stayed Abraham's hand. A thousand years later, about 950 BCE, the traditional place of sacrifice became the site of SOLOMON'S TEMPLE.

ISAIAH. PROPHET in JUDAH, the SOUTHERN KINGDOM, beginning about 740 BCE. CHRISTIANS read Isaiah's prophesies as foretelling the birth and mission of JESUS CHRIST.

ISHMAEL. (In Arabic, Ismail) Son of ABRAHAM by his servant-woman HAGAR and half-brother of ISAAC. Sent away from ABRAHAM's family at the insistence of SARAH, Ishmael and his mother flee southward into ARABIA. There, by tradition, he becomes the father of the Arab nation. MUSLIMS believe that it is Ishmael, not ISAAC, who is offered for sacrifice on MT. MORIAH. (See ISAAC; DOME OF THE ROCK; MORIAH, MOUNT)

ISLAMISTS. MUSLIMS of a FUNDAMENTALIST bent who take literally the injunctions in the QURAN against CHRISTIANS and JEWS and the call of MUHAMMED for JIHAD.

ISRAELIS. Citizens of the country of ISRAEL. Seventy-six percent of Israelis are JEWS, twenty percent are ARABS, and four percent are DRUZE.

ISRAELITES. Name given to the descendents of the twelve sons of JACOB. According to the BOOK OF EXODUS, after spending four hundred years in EGYPT, part of the time in slavery, they then escape to wander in the wilderness for forty years before entering CANAAN, the land promised to their ancestors by God.

JACOB. Third in the line of PATRIARCHS, son of Isaac, grandson of ABRAHAM. He went from the HOLY LAND to HARAN to find a wife, stayed there twenty years, fathered twelve sons (eleven of them born in Haran). Wrestling with an angel in a dream, he realizes that the angel was really God, who tells him that henceforth he shall also be called "ISRAEL," a name meaning "to strive with God."

JEREMIAH. PROPHET in JUDAH before and during the Babylonian conquest and deportation. He foretold the destruction of JERUSALEM and the coming years of exile. It is thought that he died in EGYPT.

JESUS CHRIST. The name Jesus is a Greek version of the HEBREW name JOSHUA, which means "one who saves his people." The name Christ is Greek for the HEBREW word "MESSIAH." Jesus lived in PALESTINE for about thirty-three years until his death by CRUCIFIXION, his RESURRECTION, and his ASCENSION, about the year 29 CE. CHRISTIANS believe that Jesus was the son of God, sent to redeem all people from the burden of sin. JEWS acknowledge that Jesus probably lived, and was a great teacher, but was not the Messiah promised in the HEBREW SCRIPTURES. MUSLIMS consider Jesus the most important of the prophets next to MUHAMMED but reject his divinity.

JEWS. Name derived from JUDEANS, the exiles from JUDAH living in BABYLON in the sixth century BCE. When the exiles return, and thereafter, the descendents of the remnant of the CHILDREN OF ISRAEL (the tribe of Judah, the tribe of BENJAMIN, and the Levites) are called Judeans, which eventually is shortened to "Jews." Scattered world wide, Jews live in almost every country today. Of the world's 14 million Jews, 5.8 million live in the United States, 4.8 million in ISRAEL. Other countries where Jews number more than 100,000 are Australia, Canada, France, RUSSIA, South Africa, the United Kingdom, and Ukraine.

JOHN PAUL II. Pope of the ROMAN CATHOLIC Church since 1978, he is the most traveled Pope in the history of CATHOLICISM. He was born Karol Joseph Wojtyla in Poland in 1920. In the year 2000, he spent ten days on a personal PILGRIMAGE to the HOLY LAND.

JOHN THE BAPTIST. Probably a member of the ESSENES, John lived frugally and was a wandering preacher and mystic at the time when JESUS CHRIST began his ministry. A cousin of Jesus, and of the same age, John baptized Jesus in the JORDAN RIVER. A year later he was imprisoned and later beheaded by HEROD ANTIPAS.

JOHN THE EVANGELIST. One of JESUS CHRIST's disciples, John is credited with writing the fourth GOSPEL. By tradition, in later life John took MARY, MOTHER OF JESUS, to live in EPHESUS in ASIA MINOR. (See JOHN, GOSPEL OF).

JORDANIANS. Citizens of the **HASHEMITE KINGDOM OF JORDAN.** Nearly half are **PALESTINIANS.**

JOSEPH. Eleventh son of **JACOB,** first son of his mother, **RACHEL;** his father's favorite son. Sold by his brothers into Egyptian slavery, he rises to be a chief minister of Pharaoh and brings his father and brothers to live in **EGYPT.**

JOSEPH OF ARIMATHAEA. Man who gave his family's tomb as a burial place for **JESUS CHRIST** after the **CRUCIFIXION.**

JOSEPH, FATHER OF JESUS. Carpenter in **NAZARETH (GALILEE),** a **JUDEAN** from **BETHLEHEM** by birth, and husband of **MARY, MOTHER OF JESUS.** (See **JESUS CHRIST**).

JOSEPHUS, FLAVIUS. Jewish historian writing after 70 **CE** for a Roman audience. He mentions **JESUS CHRIST** in his *Antiquities of the Jews.*

JOSHUA. One of the two named spies sent by **MOSES** to assess the fertility of the **PROMISED LAND.** Appointed by **MOSES** to assume leadership of the **ISRAELITES,** he leads them into battle against the **CANAANITES,** about 1260 **BCE.** His exploits and the conquest of **CANAAN** are narrated in the Book of Joshua, probably written at least five hundred years later.

JUDAH. One of the sons of **JACOB** and subsequently ancestor of the largest of the **TWELVE TRIBES** of the **ISRAELITES.** The territory allotted to Judah dominated the southern part of the **PROMISED LAND** and included **JERUSALEM.** King **DAVID** was of the tribe of Judah. Together with the tribe of **BENJAMIN,** Judah formed the Kingdom of Judah, the remnant of the once **UNITED KINGDOM** of David and **SOLOMON** after the northern tribes seceded. Judah was conquered by the **BABYLONIANS** in 587 BCE. (See **SOUTHERN KINGDOM**).

JUDEANS. Term derived from "**JUDAH**" and first used by the **BABYLONIANS** and **PERSIANS** to characterize the exiles. Later it came to mean the people who lived in the region known as **JUDEA.** (See **JEWS; JUDAH; JUDEA; BABYLONIAN CAPTIVITY**).

KENYON, KATHLEEN. Oxford archaeologist whose discoveries concerning the age of **JERICHO** and the location of the probable site of the **CRUCIFIXION** and burial of **JESUS CHRIST** are documented in her book *Archaeology in the Holy Land,* 1970.

KHADIJA. Wife of **MUHAMMED,** a strong supporter, and the first to believe in his revelations.

KHAZARS. Turkic peoples from Central **ASIA** who in prehistoric times wandered westward to found the Khazar Kingdom on the steppes north of the Black Sea. In the 9th century a Khazar king converted to **JUDAISM.** That **KHAZARS** introduced **JUDAISM** to the Slavs is probable, but the extent of Khazar influence is disputed.

KURDS. An Indo-European people, formerly nomadic, who early settled in the region now occupied by eastern **TURKEY,** northern **IRAQ,** and northern **IRAN.** Conquered in the eleventh century by advancing **TURKS,** and converted to **ISLAM,** the Kurds have never had their own country

LAWRENCE, T. E. British army officer who played a significant role in gaining the support of **ARABS** of the **HEJAZ** (western **ARABIA**) in Britain's war against the **Ottoman Turks** during World War I. Known as Lawrence of **Arabia**.

Lazarus. Friend of **Jesus Christ** in the town of **Bethany**, brother of **Mary** and **Martha**. In one of his miracles, **Jesus Christ** raised Lazarus back to life after he had been dead four days. (See **Mary of Bethany; Martha of Bethany**).

Leah. The less-attractive sister of the woman whom **Jacob** preferred as his wife. His uncle Laban gave Leah to Jacob, then required him to work an additional seven years for **Rachel**, Leah's sister.

Lebanese. The people of **Lebanon**, Arabic-speaking, about one-third of whom are Christian, two-thirds **Muslim**.

Lost Tribes. The descendents of the **Hebrew** tribes that once occupied the regions known as **Samaria** and **Galilee**. From north to south, they included **Dan**, Naphtali, Asher, Zebulun, Issachar, the half-tribe of Manasseh, Ephraim, and (in **Trans-Jordan**) Gad, the half-tribe of Manasseh and Reuben. Allied in the **Northern Kingdom**, they were conquered by the **Assyrians** in 723 BCE and dispersed throughout the Assyrian Empire, subsequently losing their identity. A tenth tribe that has also disappeared, but was not among those captured by the Assyrians, was Simeon, whose original territory was in the northern reaches of the **Negev Desert**.

Lot. The nephew of **Abraham**, who accompanied him on his wanderings and who settled in the vicinity of the two eventually doomed cities of **Sodom** and **Gomorrah**.

Luke the Evangelist. The writer of the third **gospel** and also of the Acts of the Apostles (See **Acts, Book of**). He may be the same Luke who was with **Paul** both in **Caesarea** and **Rome**, but there is no evidence to substantiate this. (See **Luke, Gospel of**).

Maccabees. The leaders of the **Hasmonean** priestly family who led the **Maccabean Revolt** beginning in 167 BCE. Maccabee is from an **Aramaic** word meaning "hammer."

Maccabeus, Judas. Renowned for his generalship in the **Maccabean Revolt** against the **Seleucids**, as well as his subsequent skill at governing.

Maimonides, Moses. Famed Jewish physician and philosopher (1135-1204 BCE) who was forced to leave **Spain** during the rule of the Almohads and subsequently moved to **Egypt**.

Mameluks. Rulers of the **Holy Land** during two centuries following the end of the **Crusades**. Created as a warrior caste by **Saladdin**, the Mameluks were Caucasians purchased or captured as infants and trained as superior soldiers who owed allegiance only to their ruler. Eventually they took power and, based in **Egypt**, created a strong state, defeating the **Crusaders** and keeping the Mongols out of **Palestine**. They were incorporated into the **Ottoman Empire** in 1517 but continued to hold positions of power under the **Turks**.

Mark the Evangelist. Writer of the second of the four **Gospels** that begin the **New Testament**. May have been the Mark who was with the crowd on **Pentecost**, and the Mark who accompanied **Paul** on one of his missionary trips. (See **Mark, Gospel of**).

Maronites. Members of a Syrian Christian community whose ties are to the **Roman Catholic** Church in **Rome**. Several thousand Maronite **Christians**, most all of them Arab **PALESTINIANS**, live in **ISRAEL**.

MARTHA OF BETHANY. Friend of **JESUS CHRIST** living in a town near **JERUSALEM**; sister of **MARY OF BETHANY** and **LAZARUS**.

MARY OF BETHANY. Friend of **JESUS CHRIST** living in a town near **JERUSALEM**; sister of **MARTHA OF BETHANY** and **LAZARUS**.

MARY OF MAGDALA. Woman from the Galilean town of **MAGDALA**, whom **JESUS CHRIST** healed of a mental illness. She became a loyal follower, was present at the **CRUCIFIXION**, and was among those who found the empty tomb on Easter morning.

MARY, MOTHER OF JESUS. Woman of **NAZARETH** who as a virgin learns that she is to become the mother of **JESUS CHRIST**. She gives birth in **BETHLEHEM**. Mary is mentioned many times in the **GOSPELS**, most notably at the wedding of **CANA** and as a witness of the **CRUCIFIXION**. Jesus assigned her care to **JOHN** (See **JOHN THE EVANGELIST**), and by tradition at the end of her life, Mary lived in **EPHESUS**.

MATTHEW THE EVANGELIST. Writer of the first of the four **GOSPELS** that begin the **NEW TESTAMENT**. (See **MATTHEW, GOSPEL OF**).

MEHMET II. Early Ottoman ruler, skilled warrior and builder, who in 1453 captured **CONSTANTINOPLE**, changed its name to Istanbul, and made it the capital of the **OTTOMAN EMPIRE**.

MELKITES. Syrian Catholics in communion with the **ROMAN CATHOLIC** Church who nevertheless follow **BYZANTINE** worship traditions. Melkite clergy are free to marry. A Melkite community of several thousand Palestinian **ARABS** lives in **ISRAEL**, chiefly in **GALILEE**.

MESSIAH, THE. The savior whom the **OLD TESTAMENT** prophets foretold would come into the world to save the Jewish people. The prophecies were variously understood so that some of the **JEWS** looked for a Messiah who would rescue them from political tyranny, while others waited expectantly for a spiritual reformer. **JESUS CHRIST** was considered the Messiah by many Jews during his lifetime but opposed by many as well.

MESSIANIC JEWS. JEWS of present times who have converted to **CHRISTIANITY** but who, nevertheless, hue to many **OLD TESTAMENT** Jewish traditions.

MESSIANISTS. Name given to **JEWS** in the first century **CE** who believed **JESUS CHRIST** was the promised **MESSIAH**. Eventually Messianists were called **CHRISTIANS**.

MICAH. PROPHET in the **SOUTHERN KINGDOM** in the middle of the eighth century **BCE**.

MOSES. Chosen by God to lead the **CHILDREN OF ISRAEL** out of Egyptian captivity, Moses later received the **TEN COMMANDMENTS** on **MOUNT SINAI** (See **SINAI, MOUNT**). He led the **HEBREW** tribes during the forty years they wandered in the desert but died without entering the **PROMISED LAND**. He is revered alike by **JEWS**, **CHRISTIANS**, and **MUSLIMS**.

MUHAMMED. Founder of the monotheistic religion called **ISLAM**. Muhammed is called "**THE PROPHET**" by his followers, who are known as **MUSLIMS**. Born in **MECCA** in 578 **CE**, Muhammed was a trader who, by tradition, could neither read nor write. Over a 22-year period, from 610 until his death, he received revelations that were written down by his followers. The revelations have been preserved in the **QURAN**, the Holy Book of **ISLAM**. His flight from Mecca to **MEDINA**, known as the **HEGIRA**, marks the beginning of the Islamic calendar.

MUSLIMS. The name given to the followers of **ISLAM**.

NABATEANS. A **SEMITIC** people who established a wealthy kingdom in the southern desert area of what is now **JORDAN** (See **PETRA**). For four centuries (200 **BCE** to ca 200 **CE**), the Nabateans profited from trade between **ARABIA**, **PALESTINE**, and the **FERTILE CRESCENT**. Their kingdom was conquered by the Romans in the late first century, but they continued to function as traders.

NASSER, GAMAL ABDEL. Egyptian army officer who secured **EGYPT**'s independence from **GREAT BRITAIN** in 1952, and subsequently became Egypt's president. In 1956 Nasser nationalized the **SUEZ CANAL**.

NATHAN. A **PROPHET** who lived in the court of King **DAVID**.

NEBUCHADNEZZAR. King of **BABYLON** from 605–562. Under his reign, the **SOUTHERN KINGDOM** was conquered and **JUDEANS** were taken as captives to **BABYLON**. Nebuchadnezzar built the famous Hanging Gardens of **BABYLON**.

NEHEMIAH. Jewish leader in the service of the Persian king in **SUSA**. Learning of the sorry state of affairs in **JERUSALEM**, Nehemiah asked and received permission to go to Jerusalem in 445 **BCE**. He supervised the repair of the walls, introduced law and order, and reformed abuses; he returned to **PERSIA** in 443 but soon after came back to Jerusalem and continued with his reforms. (See **EZRA**).

OMAYYADS. The caliphs who ruled the Arab Empire from **DAMASCUS** from 661 to 750 **CE**.

ORIENTAL JEWS. Term no longer in favor to designate the 600,000 Arab-speaking **JEWS** who immigrated to **ISRAEL** from Arab countries in North Africa and the **MIDDLE EAST** after 1948. (See **ASHKENAZI**; **SEPHARDIM**).

OTTOMAN TURKS. The rulers of the **OTTOMAN EMPIRE**, centered in Istanbul, from ca 1453 to 1918.

PALESTINIAN REFUGEES. PALESTINIANS who were displaced by **ISRAELIS** as the new state of **ISRAEL** was being formed (1946–1948) and after the **SIX-DAY WAR** in 1967.

PALESTINIANS. Persons whose homeland is **PALESTINE**. Under the British **PALESTINIAN MANDATE**, both **JEWS** and **ARABS** considered themselves to be Palestinians. After the declaration of the country of **ISRAEL** in 1948, the term Palestinian came to be identified solely with the Arab-speaking community. Arab Palestinians are a blend of all the **SEMITIC** and other peoples who have lived in the **HOLY LAND** from earliest times. After the coming of **ISLAM** in the seventh century, most of the people of **PALESTINE** adopted Arabic as their spoken and written language.

PATRIARCHS, THE. Founding Fathers of both **JUDAISM** and **ISLAM**, and revered also by **CHRISTIANS** because of **OLD TESTAMENT** accounts. Included are **ABRAHAM**; his two sons, **ISAAC** and **ISHMAEL**; Isaac's two sons, **JACOB** and **ESAU**; and Jacob's Twelve Sons, the progenitors of the **TWELVE TRIBES** of **ISRAEL**.

According to tradition, Abraham is the founder of both the Jewish and Arab nations, the former through Isaac, the latter through Ishmael.

PAUL. Leading early Christian missionary who founded churches throughout **ASIA MINOR** and traveled widely in the Mediterranean world. A Roman citizen from Tarsus, **PAUL** was also a Jew schooled in theology. Most of the letters to Christian churches found in the **NEW TESTAMENT** were written by Paul. Tradition says that Paul was executed during the reign of the Emperor Nero in 67 CE.

PEOPLE OF THE BOOK. A designation that includes **JEWS**, **CHRISTIANS**, and **MUSLIMS**, all of whose faith is grounded in Holy Books that revere the same prophets.

PHILISTINES. The "Sea Peoples" whom the Egyptians encountered on the coastlands of the eastern Mediterranean about 1450 BCE. Many scholars think they were remnants of the Minoan civilization. Technologically more advanced than the **ISRAELITES** who settled on the plateau, the Philistines maintained their supremacy until they were annihilated by the **ASSYRIANS** in 723.

PHOENICIANS. A **SEMITIC** people who settled in the northern coastlands of the eastern Mediterranean, they developed a maritime empire that expanded to outposts in North Africa and **SPAIN**. By the time the **ASSYRIANS** defeated the Phoenicians in the eastern Mediterranean, their center had already shifted to **CARTHAGE**, where they founded the Carthaginian Empire.

PILATE, PONTIUS. The Roman legate under Tiberius Caesar in command of **PALESTINE** from 26 to 36 CE. After telling the assembled crowd that he found **JESUS CHRIST** innocent, he nevertheless acceded to their demands and sentenced him to be crucified. Tiberius later recalled him, and he was banished by Caligula to the Danube provinces, where he died in 43 CE.

PROPHET, THE. Name often used by **MUSLIMS** when speaking of **MUHAMMED**.

PTOLEMYS. The line of kings who ruled in **EGYPT** upon the breakup of **ALEXANDER THE GREAT**'s Empire, beginning after 310 BCE. For the next 100 years, they fought with the **SELEUCIDS** for control of **PALESTINE**.

QURAYSH. Arab tribe in control of trade in **MECCA** and its surrounding area at the time of **MUHAMMED**. Muhammed was a member of a minor branch of the Quraysh. Although the Quraysh early rejected Muhammed's message, leading him to flee to **MEDINA**, by 630 they had become converts and eventually played a leading role in the **OMAYYAD CALIPHATE**.

RABIN, YITZHAK. Prime Minister of **ISRAEL** whose negotiations with **YASSER ARAFAT** (See **ARAFAT, YASSER**) resulted in the **OSLO ACCORD** in 1993, for which both were awarded the **NOBEL PEACE PRIZE**. Rabin was subsequently assassinated by an **ULTRA-ORTHODOX** Israeli.

RACHEL. Wife for whom **JACOB** worked an extra seven years in **HARAN**, in servitude to his uncle Laban. Mother of **JOSEPH**, born in Haran, and **BENJAMIN**, born in **HEBRON**. She died giving birth to Benjamin.

RAMSES II. Pharaoh whose building projects in the Nile Delta required the labor of many slaves, including the **ISRAELITES**. It is thought that Ramses II was Pharaoh at the time of the **EXODUS**.

ROTHSCHILD, BARON LIONEL. Leader of Jewish community in England whose request in 1917 to Foreign Secretary **ARTHUR BALFOUR** (See **BALFOUR, ARTHUR**) for clarification of British policy toward Jewish settlement in **PALESTINE** led to a reply that subsequently framed British Palestine policy. (See **BALFOUR DECLARATION**).

SADAT, ANWAR. President of **EGYPT** who at the invitation of **PRESIDENT JIMMY CARTER** (See **CARTER, PRESIDENT JIMMY**) met with Prime Minister **MENACHEM BEGIN** (See **BEGIN, MENACHEM**) of **ISRAEL** at **CAMP DAVID** in 1979. The outcome was peace between the two countries, for which both received the **NOBEL PEACE PRIZE**. Sadat was later assassinated by an Egyptian **ISLAMIST** militant.

SALADDIN. Crusader transliteration for Salah al-Din, the commander of the **SELJUK TURKS** who successfully captured most of the Christian forts in **PALESTINE** in the mid-thirteenth century CE. Saladdin was a **KURD**, member of a tribal group conquered by the Seljuks. The **CRUSADERS** never recovered from the blows inflicted by Saladdin.

SAMARITANS. The people who emerged in the **HILL COUNTRY** between **GALILEE** and **JUDEA** after the **ASSYRIAN** defeat and dispersion of most of the people of northern **ISRAEL** in 723 BCE and subsequent resettlement of the area with peoples from other parts of the Assyrian Empire. The Samaritans adopted a version of **JUDAISM** that the exiles, on their return from **BABYLON**, refused to acknowledge.

SAMUEL. The **PROPHET** who in the eleventh century BCE picked **SAUL** to begin to unite the **ISRAELITE** tribes and subsequently anointed the shepherd boy **DAVID** as **SAUL**'s successor.

SARAH. Wife of **ABRAHAM** and mother (in her old age) of **ISAAC**, her only child.

SAUDIS. The citizens of **SAUDI ARABIA**.

SAUL. The first king who tried to unite **ISRAEL** (1020-1000 BCE). He was killed in a battle with the **PHILISTINES** on **MOUNT GILBOA** (See **GILBOA, MOUNT**) near **BEIT SHA'AN**.

SCYTHIANS. Horsemen from the plains north of the Black Sea who served the ancient Egyptians as mercenaries. (See **SCYTHOPOLIS**).

SEA PEOPLES. Name given by the Egyptians to the maritime invaders, the **PHILISTINES**, who reached the eastern Mediterranean coast in the mid-fifteenth century BCE.

SELEUCIDS. Rulers descended from Seleusus, the general who received much of **MESOPOTAMIA**, **SYRIA**, and **ASIA MINOR** as his share to rule following the breakup of **ALEXANDER THE GREAT**'s Empire. In the third and second centuries, the **SELEUCIDS** struggled with the **PTOLEMYS** for control of **PALESTINE**. They gained the ascendancy at the beginning of the second century but were subsequently defeated by the **MACCABEANS**.

SELJUK TURKS. A Turkic people from central Asia who moved westward to occupy the **ANATOLIAN PENINSULA** in the tenth and eleventh centuries, becoming strong enough to defeat the **FATIMIDS** in the **HOLY LAND** before the arrival of the **CRUSADERS**. The Seljuks delivered crushing blows to the Crusaders in the middle of the 13th century but were themselves defeated and replaced by the

MAMELUKS. (See TURKS; SALADDIN).

SEMITES. The term applied to a groups of peoples closely related in language whose common origin is southwest ASIA. The term "Semite" derives from the name of Noah's son Shem (Genesis 10). (See SEMITIC).

SEPHARDIM. Descendents of the JEWS who were expelled from SPAIN in 1492 and settled primarily in the lands surrounding the Mediterranean Sea. Many retained Spanish language and culture throughout the following centuries. SEPHARDIM comprise a portion of those who immigrated to ISRAEL in the past fifty years. (See LADINO).

SHARON, ARIEL. Prime Minister of ISRAEL, representing the Likud party, since 2001. Prior positions included Defense Minister, Minister of SETTLEMENTS (See JEWISH SETTLEMENTS), and General in the Army.

SHI'ITES. MUSLIMS who believe that the successor to MUHAMMED should have been his cousin ALI IBN ABU TALIB. (See SHI'A ISLAM).

SOLOMON. Son of DAVID and last ruler (970-930 BCE) of the kingdom that united the TWELVE TRIBES of ISRAEL. Under SOLOMON, the kingdom expanded in all directions and wealth poured into the capital in JERUSALEM. SOLOMON built the first Temple. (See SOLOMON'S TEMPLE; TEMPLE).

SULEIMAN THE MAGNIFICENT. Sultan of the OTTOMAN EMPIRE, 1520-1566. His rule was noted for opulence. In JERUSALEM, he repaired the DOME OF THE ROCK and built a new wall around the city, the one still standing today.

SUNNIS. MUSLIMS who belong to the largest branch of ISLAM. With the exception of the people of southern IRAQ, most ARABS are SUNNIS. (See SHI'A ISLAM, SUNNI ISLAM).

SYRIANS. Citizens of SYRIA, which is both a modern country and an ancient Greek and Roman province.

TALIBAN. MUSLIM FUNDAMENTALIST rulers of AFGHANISTAN who allowed BIN LADEN'S AL QAEDA movement to train and operate within their country. Defeated by United States and Coalition forces following the events of September 11, 2001, the Taliban now operates covertly to try to destabilize the present government of Afghanistan.

TURKS. Citizens of TURKEY. Descendents of Central Asian Turkic peoples who first began to occupy the ANATOLIAN PENINSULA in the eleventh century. Under their leader SALADDIN, the SELJUK TURKS were successful in defeating the CRUSADERS. The OTTOMAN Turks came later to power.

TWELVE TRIBES. The descendents of the twelve sons of JACOB, also called the CHILDREN OF ISRAEL, who following the escape from EGYPT and the subsequent wanderings in the desert, came to occupy parts of the PROMISED LAND (the Land of CANAAN) allotted by MOSES to each. (See LOST TRIBES).

UNIATES. Members of eastern churches affiliated with the ROMAN CATHOLIC church. They follow rites derived from ancient traditions of Christian churches in the East, rather than Roman rites. (See MELKITES, MARONITES).

URIAH. A HITTITE, husband of BATHSHEBA. Sent by DAVID to die in the assault on the walls of RABBOTH AMMON.

WALLENBERG, RAOUL. Diplomat in southeastern Europe during World War

II who was able to use his diplomatic privilege to save hundreds, perhaps thousands, of **Jews** from being sent to concentration camps. He was captured and eventually executed by Russians.

ZEALOTS. Zealots are those who care passionately about their cause and are willing to go to great lengths to defend it. From 70 to 73 **CE** a group of **Jews** known as the Zealots captured and held the Roman fortress of **MASADA**.

ZIONISTS. Those who are motivated by **ZIONISM**.

ZOLA, EMILE. French author who played a leading role in the **DREYFUS AFFAIR**.

GLOSSARY: PLACES

ABILA. Northernmost of the **DECAPOLIS** archaeological sites in **JORDAN**.

ACCO. City in **ISRAEL**, north of **HAIFA**. Ancient Mediterranean port called Ptolemais during the period when the **PTOLEMYS** occupied **PALESTINE**. Called **ACRE** by **CRUSADERS**. An archaeological site as well as a modern town. Pop. 46,000.

ACRE. See **ACCO**.

ADEN. Arabian Sea port in **YEMEN**, Pop. 510,00.

AELIA CAPITOLINA. Roman name for **JERUSALEM** after 135 **BCE**.

AFGHANISTAN. Islamic country bordered on the east by **PAKISTAN**, on the west by **IRAN**, and on the north by Uzbekistan. Its recent former rulers, the **TALIBAN** (ousted by Coalition troops in 2002), gave shelter to **OSAMA BIN LADEN** (See **BIN LADEN, OSAMA**) and his **AL QAEDA** training camps. Afghanistan is now attempting to establish a democratic government in its capital of Kabul, representative of its many different ethnic groups. Pop. 28.7 mil.

AL-AQSA MOSQUE. See **TERMS: AL-AQSA MOSQUE**.

ALEXANDRIA. City in western part of **EGYPT**'s Nile delta, founded by **ALEXANDER THE GREAT**. Pop. 4.3 million.

AL-HARAM AL-SHARIF. See **HARAM AL-SHARIF**.

AMMAN. Capital of **JORDAN**, located in the central west portion of the country. Called **PHILADELPHIA** in Graeco-Roman times. Pop. 4.3 million.

AMMON. Ancient kingdom east of the **JORDAN RIVER** within the plateau area known as **MOAB**. Known in the **OLD TESTAMENT** as **RABBOTH AMMON**. Site of present-day **AMMAN**.

ANATOLIA. Name for the area included within the **ANATOLIAN PENINSULA**.

ANATOLIAN PENINSULA. Westernmost peninsula of **ASIA**, bordered by the Black, Ionian, and Mediterranean Seas. Also known as **ASIA MINOR**. Occupied by the modern country of **TURKEY**.

ANTIOCH (ANTAKYA). City in southeastern **TURKEY** on Syrian border. Roman administrative city and early Christian center. Pop. 156,000.

AQABA. **JORDAN** port city located on the **GULF OF AQABA**. Pop. 96,000.

ARAB MIDDLE EAST. Includes the Arab-speaking countries of the **MIDDLE EAST**: **EGYPT, JORDAN, LEBANON, SYRIA, IRAQ, YEMEN, SAUDI ARABIA, OMAN, QATAR, BAHRAIN,** and the **UNITED ARAB EMIRATES.** Excludes **ISRAEL, TURKEY, IRAN,** and **CYPRUS.**

ARAB QUARTER. Arab section of the **OLD CITY OF JERUSALEM.**

ARAB STATES. Countries where Arabic is the chief spoken language. In addition to the **ARAB MIDDLE EAST,** Arab States include Libya, Tunisia, Algeria, Morocco, Mauritania, and Sudan.

ARABIA. Loosely defined in ancient times to include all desert areas south and west of the **FERTILE CRESCENT** and east of the better-watered **TRANS-JORDAN PLATEAU** areas.

ARABIAN DESERT. The area of very low rainfall extending from the **RED SEA** to the **PERSIAN GULF.** The highlands of **YEMEN** are excluded from the "desert" designation.

ARABIAN PENINSULA. Area bordered by the **RED SEA** on the west, the Arabian Sea on the south, and the **PERSIAN GULF** on the east. Occupied by the countries of **SAUDI ARABIA, KUWAIT, QATAR,** the **UNITED ARAB EMIRATES, OMAN,** and **YEMEN.**

ARAFAT'S ISLANDS. Term sometimes used to designate the noncontiguous urban areas over which the **PALESTINIAN AUTHORITY** has complete control.

ARAM. Ancient kingdom within the **FERTILE CRESCENT,** north and east of **DAMASCUS.**

ARMENIAN QUARTER. Smallest of the four sections of the **OLD CITY OF JERUSALEM.**

ASHDOD. Israeli port city, south of **TEL AVIV.** Site of ancient Philistine port. Pop. 206,000.

ASHKELON. Israeli port city, south of **TEL AVIV.** Archaeological site revealing bronze and iron age Egyptian and Philistine occupation. Pop. 111,200.

ASIA. As distinguished from Europe, all the land east of the Dardanelles, the **BOSPORUS,** and the Sea of Marmara. The **MIDDLE EAST** is sometimes designated as Southwest Asia.

ASIA MINOR. The **ANATOLIAN PENINSULA.**

ASSYRIA. Ancient kingdom centered in northern **MESOPOTAMIA** with its capital at Nineveh.

BABYLON. Ancient city-state on the **EUPHRATES RIVER** that expanded into the **BABYLONIAN EMPIRE** and the Neo-Babylonian or **CHALDEAN EMPIRE** (See **BABYLONIANS; CHALDEANS**).

BAGHDAD. City on the **TIGRIS RIVER.** Capital of **IRAQ.** Seat of the **ABBASSID CALIPHATE.** Pop. 6.4 million.

BAHRAIN. Island in the **PERSIAN GULF** off the coast of **SAUDI ARABIA**; a sovereign country whose territory is Bahrain Island.

BALKAN LANDS. Countries of the mountainous peninsula of southeastern Europe known as the Balkans. Present day countries include Slovenia, Croatia, Serbia,

Macedonia, Bosnia, Albania, and Bulgaria. The Balkan appellation does not usually include Greece.

BANIAS. Part of an Israeli national park on the lower slopes of **MOUNT HERMON** (See **HERMON, MOUNT**) in far northern **ISRAEL**. Springs in Banias are one of the sources of the **JORDAN RIVER**. Called **CAESAREA PHILIPPI** during Roman times.

BEATITUDES, MOUNT OF THE. A hillside near **CAPERNAUM**, on the northern shore of the **SEA OF GALILEE**, where **JESUS CHRIST** preached his Sermon on the Mount, which included the Beatitudes (Blessed are…) as well as the Lord's Prayer.

BEERSHEBA. A town in the **NEGEV DESERT**, west of the **DEAD SEA**, occupying an ancient site of the same name. Pop. 191,000.

BEIRUT. The capital of **LEBANON**, located on the Mediterranean Sea. Pop. 1.2 million.

BEIT SHA'AN. Town south of **SEA OF GALILEE** occupying strategic position in **JEZREEL VALLEY** between **JORDAN RIVER** and Mediterranean coast. A **DECAPOLIS** city in Graeco-Roman times, when it was known as **SCYTHOPOLIS**. Important archaeological site. Pop. 16,000.

BETHANY. Village east of **JERUSALEM** on the way to **JERICHO**.

BETHLEHEM. WEST BANK town about ten miles south of **JERUSALEM**. Birthplace of **JESUS CHRIST**. Pop. 170,000.

BIBLICAL PROMISED LAND. The territory promised to the descendents of **ABRAHAM**: from the southern slopes of **MOUNT HERMON** (See **HERMON, MOUNT**) in the north to the **NEGEV DESERT** in the south, and from the Mediterranean Sea in the west to the **JORDAN RIVER** and the **DEAD SEA** in the east.

BITHYNIA. Roman province in the northern part of **ANATOLIA**.

BOSPORUS. Strait separating Europe from **ASIA**, and **TURKEY**'s European provinces from its Asiatic mainland. Istanbul is on the west side of the strait.

BYZANTIUM. Greek name for the city on the west side of the **BOSPORUS** that became **CONSTANTINOPLE** in 315 CE and Istanbul in 1453.

CAESAREA. Roman port city and administrative center on the Mediterranean Sea. Now an archaeological site, about twenty miles south of **HAIFA**.

CAESAREA PHILIPPI. Resort in far northern **GALILEE** built by the son of **HEROD THE GREAT**. Now known as **BANIAS** and included within an Israeli national park.

CAIRO. Capital of **EGYPT**, located on the lower Nile River. Pop. 15.5 million.

CAMP DAVID. Presidential retreat in Maryland frequently used as a site of international conferences.

CANA. Village three miles north of **NAZARETH** where **JESUS CHRIST** performed his first miracle. Now the Arab town of Kafr Kanna. Pop. 12,000.

CANAAN. See **BIBLICAL PROMISED LAND**.

CAPERNAUM. Village on the northern shore of the **SEA OF GALILEE** around which **JESUS CHRIST**'s ministry was centered. Now an archaeological site.

CAPPADOCIA. Early Christian site in central **ANATOLIA**. Included within the modern region in **TURKEY** known as Kapadokia.

CARMEL, MOUNT. A ridge, rather than a mount, that marks the south side of the **JEZREEL VALLEY** and terminates in **HAIFA.**

CARTHAGE. Phoenician colony on the coast of North Africa in what is now **TUNISIA.** Chief city of the Carthagenian Empire and later a Roman city. Ancient Carthage was destroyed by the Romans during the Punic Wars 146 BCE.

CENTRAL HIGHLANDS. HILL COUNTRY between the Mediterranean Sea and the **JORDAN VALLEY.**

CHALDEA. The area in the southern part of **MESOPOTAMIA** inhabited by the **CHALDEANS** in the early part of the first millennium BCE. Its chief city was **BABYLON.**

CHALDEAN EMPIRE. Synonymous with the Neo-Babylonian Empire. (See **BABYLON**).

CHRISTIAN QUARTER. Section of the **OLD CITY OF JERUSALEM** that contains the Church of the Holy Sepulcher. (See **HOLY SEPULCHER, CHURCH OF THE**).

CONSTANTINOPLE. Known until 330 CE as **BYZANTIUM,** Constantinople was chosen by the Roman Emperor **CONSTANTINE** as his capital. After **ROME** weakened, it became the capital of the **BYZANTINE EMPIRE.** Following its defeat by the Ottoman **TURKS** in 1453, its name was changed to Istanbul. Located on the western or European side of the **BOSPORUS** in what is now **TURKEY.**

CORDOBA. City in southern **SPAIN** that was once an Arab city of culture and learning. Pop. 325,000.

CORINTH. City in ancient Greece and site of an early Christian community.

CYPRUS. Large island in the eastern Mediterranean. Inhabited by both Greeks and **TURKS.**

DAMASCUS. Capital of **SYRIA.** An ancient city located on the **FERTILE CRESCENT** trade route. Population 4.0 million.

DAN. The northernmost location in **ANCIENT ISRAEL** (See **ISRAEL, ANCIENT**), on the lower slopes of **MOUNT HERMON.** (See **HERMON, MOUNT**).

DEAD SEA. Lowest surface on earth, 1,290 ft. below sea level, occupying a geological trough that also includes the **SEA OF GALILEE, JORDAN RIVER, WADI ARABAH, GULF OF AQABA,** and **RED SEA.**

DECAPOLIS. A regional name given in Graeco-Roman times to the (mostly) **TRANS-JORDAN** location of the league of ten semi-autonomous trade cities collectively called by that name.

DECAPOLIS CITIES. Of the ten cities that once were considered part of the **DECAPOLIS, AMMAN** (once **PHILADELPHIA**) is now the capital of **JORDAN, DAMASCUS** is the capital of **SYRIA,** and **BEIT SHA'AN** (once **SCYTHOPOLIS**) is a small city in **ISRAEL.** The remainder are archaeological sites: **GERASA (JERASH), PELLA, ABILA,** and **GADARA** in **JORDAN,** Capitolia and Dium in **SYRIA,** and **HIPPOS** in **ISRAEL.**

DIASPORA, JEWISH. Countries or regions where **JEWS** displaced from their homes in **PALESTINE** settled or to which they or their descendents were subsequently scattered. The original **DIASPORA** was to lands surrounding the Mediterranean Sea, the **FERTILE**

CRESCENT, MESOPOTAMIA, and PERSIA. Eventually areas of Jewish settlement included all of Europe and lands settled by Europeans.

DIASPORA, PALESTINIAN. Countries or regions, chiefly in the MIDDLE EAST, where PALESTINIANS displaced from their homes in ISRAEL are now living.

EAST JERUSALEM. The part of JERUSALEM that originally was synonymous with the OLD CITY, which was retained by JORDAN in 1949, following the Arab-Israeli war, but was taken by ISRAEL in the SIX-DAY WAR in 1967. Under Israeli jurisdiction, East JERUSALEM has expanded beyond the old walled city to include adjacent areas of both Arab and Jewish settlement. Israel considers EAST JERUSALEM TO be a part of Israel and includes its population within Israeli statistics. PALESTINIANS insist that East Jerusalem (which includes the HARAM AL-SHARIF) be the capital of the new Palestinian state. Pop. 325,000.

EDOM. Ancient name for the area of the JORDAN PLATEAU south and east of the DEAD SEA.

EGYPT. Country in the northeastern corner of Africa, adjacent (in the SINAI PENINSULA) to ISRAEL. First Arab country to establish diplomatic relations with ISRAEL (1979). Pop. 72.1 million.

EILAT. Israeli port city at the southern tip of the NEGEV DESERT on the GULF OF AQABA. Pop. 45,000.

EPHESUS. Graeco-Roman city on the west coast of ASIA MINOR. An archaeological site today.

ETHIOPIA. Country in the highlands of East Africa, west of the RED SEA. Pop. 71 million.

EUPHRATES RIVER. One of the two rivers that encompass MESOPOTAMIA (the Land between the Rivers). Joins with the TIGRIS RIVER to form a joint mouth flowing into the PERSIAN GULF. Dams on the Euphrates in TURKEY, SYRIA, and IRAQ are now storing water for irrigation.

FERTILE CRESCENT. The ancient route between the PERSIAN GULF and the Mediterranean Sea, beginning in the irrigated lowlands of MESOPOTAMIA and following the grasslands between the mountains to the north and the desert to the south to reach the HILL COUNTRY and coastlands of PALESTINE. The route continues along the MEDITERRANEAN COASTLANDS southward and westward into the Nile Valley.

FEZ. City in northern Morocco. Early Arab center of learning and culture. Pop. 650,000.

GADARA. Archaeological site in northern JORDAN, overlooking the YARMOUK RIVER. Once a DECAPOLIS city.

GALATIA. Roman province in north central ASIA MINOR.

GALILEE. Ancient and traditional name for the northern region of ISRAEL.

GAZA. Chief city of the GAZA STRIP and regional headquarters of the PALESTINIAN AUTHORITY. Pop. 432,000.

GAZA STRIP. The OCCUPIED TERRITORY that borders ISRAEL on the southwest. EGYPT lies to the south. Pop. 1.3 million.

GENNESARET, LAKE OF. One of the names given in the GOSPELS for the SEA

OF GALILEE.

GERASA. A DECAPOLIS city. Now an archaeological site in west central JORDAN. The Arabic name for the site is JERASH.

GERAZIM, MOUNT. Mountain in SAMARIA on which the SAMARITANS built a Temple.

GERMANIC LANDS. Lands on the northern fringe of the ROMAN EMPIRE, occupied by tribes speaking Germanic languages.

GETHSEMANE, GARDEN OF. Located at the base of the MOUNT OF OLIVES (See OLIVES, MOUNT OF), across the Kidron Valley from JERUSALEM. The name, derived from the ancient use of this site, means "Olive Press."

GILBOA, MOUNT. Overlooks the JEZREEL VALLEY, near BEIT SHA'AN.

GOLAN HEIGHTS. Plateau area north and east of LAKE KINNERET (See KINNERET, LAKE). Syrian territory captured by ISRAELIS in 1967 and occupied and settled by ISRAELIS since that date. Population 38,000.

GOLGOTHA. Stated place of the CRUCIFIXION, outside the walls of JERUSALEM. (See JESUS CHRIST).

GOMORRAH. One of two ancient cities (the other SODOM) said to have been located near the southern end of the DEAD SEA.

GOSHEN. Fertile area in the northeast part of the Nile delta.

GRAECO-ROMAN WORLD. Refers to the eastern part of the ROMAN EMPIRE, where the LINGUA FRANCA and culture was Greek.

GREATER SYRIA. In ancient times included LEBANON, northern PALESTINE, and northern TRANS-JORDAN.

GULF OF AQABA. Northward extension of the RED SEA, giving ISRAEL a southern port and JORDAN its only port.

GULF OF EILAT. Name sometimes given by ISRAELIS to the GULF OF AQABA.

GULF OF SUEZ. Extension of the RED SEA into EGYPT. The GULF OF AQABA and the GULF OF SUEZ border the SINAI PENINSULA.

HADRAMAUT. The exceedingly dry southern coast of the ARABIAN PENINSULA, shared by OMAN and YEMEN.

HAIFA. Chief port city of ISRAEL on the Mediterranean Sea. Pop. 283,000.

HARAM AL-SHARIF. An Arabic name meaning "Noble Sanctuary," given by MUSLIMS about 638 CE to the area of JERUSALEM that the JEWS call the TEMPLE MOUNT and until 70 CE was the site of the Jewish Temple. The Haram al-Sharif contains both the DOME OF THE ROCK and the AL-AQSA MOSQUE.

HARAN. Ancient site in the northern part of the FERTILE CRESCENT; now within TURKEY but at the time of ABRAHAM within the kingdom of PADAN ARAM.

HASHEMITE KINGDOM OF JORDAN. Official name of the country to the east of ISRAEL, bounded on the west by the JORDAN RIVER, on the north and east by SYRIA and IRAQ, on the east by SAUDI ARABIA, and extending southward to the GULF OF AQABA. Pop. 5.6 million.

HASMONEAN KINGDOM. The territory, roughly equivalent to the ancient UNITED KINGDOM of ISRAEL, ruled by the HASMONEAN kings from 167 to

63 BCE.

Hebron. City in the southern part of the **West Bank**. The traditional burial site of **Abraham**, **Isaac**, and **Jacob**, Hebron is considered a sacred area by both **Muslims** (85% of the population) and **Jews** (15%). **Israelis** and **Palestinians** divide administration. Pop. 506,000.

Hejaz. Western mountainous region of the **Arabian Peninsula**.

Hellespont. Ancient name for the **Bosporus**, connecting Europe and **Asia**.

Hermon, Mount. Mountain in **Syria**, northeast of the **Golan Heights**. Mount Hermon's lower slopes are within **Israel** and provide a significant source of water that feeds into **Lake Kenneret** (See **Kenneret, Lake**) and the **Jordan River**.

Hill Country. Designation for the rolling plateau country between the Mediterranean Sea and the **Jordan Valley**. The elevation rises to 3,000 feet.

Hippos. A **Decapolis** city on a hill fronting the eastern shore of the **Sea of Galilee**. Now an archaeological site.

Hira, Mount. Mountain near **Mecca** where **Muhammed** received his first revelations.

Holy Land. The land with associations sacred to three world faiths: **Judaism**, **Christianity**, and **Islam**. Geographically, it includes all of present-day **Israel** and also western **Jordan**, southern **Syria** and **Lebanon**, and the **Sinai Peninsula**.

Horeb, Mount. One of the alternate names for **Mount Sinai**. (See **Sinai, Mount**).

Hula Lakes. Small lakes in the lowlands of far northern **Israel** that collect the waters from **Mount Hermon** (See **Hermon, Mount**) and send them southward to the **Sea of Galilee** and the **Jordan River**.

Iberian Peninsula. Peninsula shared today by **Spain** and **Portugal**.

Idumea. Roman province in the northern **Negev Desert**.

Indus River. River that flows southward in **Pakistan** to reach the Arabian Sea.

Iran. Modern name of the country once called **Persia**. Bordered on the west by **Iraq**, on the north by Armenia, Azerbaijan, and Turkmenistan, on the east by **Pakistan**, and on the west by the **Persian Gulf**. Its population is largely Shi'ite **Muslim** (See **Shi'a Islam**), and its current rulers (religious leaders, or ayatollahs) invoke the **Sharia**. Iran has rich petroleum resources. Pop. 66.6 million.

Iraq. Desert country through which flow the **Tigris** and **Euphrates** rivers, creating the fertile region known in ancient times as **Mesopotamia**. Its borders are with **Iran**, **Kuwait**, **Saudi Arabia**, **Jordan**, **Syria**, and **Turkey**. Ethnic groups include Shi'ites (See **Shi'a Islam**) mainly in the south, Sunnis (See **Sunni Islam**) mainly in the center, and **Kurds** in the north. Iraq is rich in petroleum. Pop. 24.2 million. (See **Hussein, Saddam**).

Islamic Lands. The part of the world to which **Islam** has spread. Includes all of North Africa, northern parts of sub-Saharan Africa, all of the **Middle East** except **Israel**, **Afghanistan**, **Pakistan**, a portion of India, Bangladesh,

Malaysia, Indonesia, and the southern Philippines.

ISRAEL, ANCIENT. A name derived from the **CHILDREN OF ISRAEL**, descendents of the patriarch **JACOB**. The name given to the **UNITED KINGDOM** under **DAVID** and **SOLOMON**, and to the **NORTHERN KINGDOM** after 527 BCE.

ISRAEL, MODERN. Israel as a modern state began in 1948. Since 1967, the territory which Israel claims includes the **OCCUPIED TERRITORIES** of the **GAZA STRIP**, the **WEST BANK**, and the **GOLAN HEIGHTS**. Including the **OCCUPIED TERRITORIES**, Israel is bounded on the south and west by **EGYPT**, on the east by **JORDAN**, on the northeast by **SYRIA** on the north by **LEBANON**. Pop. (excluding that of the **OCCUPIED TERRITORIES**) 6.7 million.

JAFFA. Crusader port city, south of **TEL AVIV**. Now incorporated within the larger city as Tel Aviv-Yafo.

JAFFA GATE. The western and most frequented gate in the walls which surround the **OLD CITY OF JERUSALEM**. The Jaffa Gate leads from the western or new part of **JERUSALEM** into the Old City.

JEBEL MUSA. Arabic for "Mount of **MOSES**." An alternate name for **MOUNT SINAI**. (See **SINAI, MOUNT**).

JENIN. City in the northern part of the **WEST BANK**. Pop. 247,000.

JERASH. Arabic name for the archaeological site of **GERASA**. Also the name of the adjacent town. Pop. 26,300.

JERICHO. Ancient city west of the **JORDAN RIVER** near where it empties into the **DEAD SEA**. Now within the **WEST BANK** and governed by the **PALESTINIAN AUTHORITY**. Pop. 33,000.

JERUSALEM. Located in the southern part of the plateau that rises from the **JORDAN VALLEY**, about 25 miles from **JERICHO**, 50 miles from **TEL AVIV**. **ISRAEL**'s capital and largest city. Includes the **OLD CITY** in the eastern part, adjacent Arab and Israeli suburbs, and a modern western part. Population of western and Old City, 708,000. Metropolitan area pop. 1.1 million. (See **EAST JERUSALEM**).

JERUSALEM, OLD CITY OF. See **OLD CITY OF JERUSALEM**.

JEWISH QUARTER. The Jewish section of the **OLD CITY OF JERUSALEM**.

JEWISH SETTLEMENTS. Term referring to Jewish communities in the **OCCUPIED TERRITORIES** that have been established by **ISRAEL** since 1967. Jewish settlements are most numerous in the **WEST BANK** but also exist in **GAZA** and the **GOLAN HEIGHTS**.

JEZREEL VALLEY. Ancient east-west route south of the **SEA OF GALILEE**, leading from the **JORDAN VALLEY** to the Mediterranean Sea.

JOPPA. Ancient **PHILISTINE** port, now known as **JAFFA**, or Yafo. Forms the southern part of **TEL AVIV**.

JORDAN. See **HASHEMITE KINGDOM OF JORDAN**.

JORDAN PLATEAU. Highlands to the east of the **JORDAN VALLEY** and the **DEAD SEA**.

JORDAN RIVER. Flows out of the **SEA OF GALILEE** into the **DEAD SEA**.

Jordan Valley. Broad valley in which the **Jordan River** flows, bordered to east and west by highlands.

MEDITERRANEAN COASTLANDS. Lowlands bordering the Mediterranean Sea.

MESOPOTAMIA. Name given to the fertile land between the **EUPHRATES** and **TIGRIS** Rivers. One of the earliest centers of civilization.

MIDDLE EAST. Term that generally includes the Arab-speaking countries from **EGYPT** to **IRAQ**, plus **TURKEY**, **ISRAEL**, and **IRAN**. Some scholars also include the Arabic-speaking largely-Muslim countries of Sudan, Libya, **TUNISIA**, Algeria, and Morocco in North Africa.

MIDIAN. The southernmost and driest part of the **JORDAN PLATEAU**. An ancient designation, not in current usage.

MOAB. The well-watered part of the **JORDAN PLATEAU** west of the **DEAD SEA**. An ancient designation, not in current usage.

MOAB PLATEAU. See **MOAB**.

MORIAH, MOUNT. Biblical name of the hill to which **ABRAHAM** journeyed for the (aborted) sacrifice of his son **ISAAC** (for **MUSLIMS**, **ISHMAEL**). Located within present-day **JERUSALEM**, it later became the **TEMPLE MOUNT**, then the **HARAM AL-SHARIF**.

MUSLIM WORLD. See **ISLAMIC LANDS**.

NABATEA. Territory in what is now southern **JORDAN** and **ISRAEL**'s **NEGEV DESERT** ruled by the **NABATEANS** from their capital at **PETRA**.

NABLUS. City in the **WEST BANK** that was once knows as **SHECHEM**, Pop. 118,000.

NAZARETH. City south and west of the **SEA OF GALILEE**. Pop. 65,300.

NEBO, MOUNT. Mountain peak in **JORDAN** overlooking the northern edge of the **DEAD SEA**. From this height, **MOSES** got a view of the **PROMISED LAND** before he died. Elevation 2,700 ft.

NEGEV DESERT. The dry area of southern **ISRAEL**, extending roughly from **BEERSHEBA** to **EILAT**.

NETANYA. City in **ISRAEL** on the Mediterranean coast, north of **TEL AVIV**. Pop. 178,000.

NORTHERN KINGDOM. Territory of the tribes who split from the **UNITED KINGDOM**, ruled by **SOLOMON**, in 927 BCE. The territory included all of **GALILEE** and **SAMARIA**.

OCCUPIED TERRITORIES. Territories occupied by **ISRAEL** since the end of the **SIX-DAY WAR**, including the **GAZA STRIP**, the **WEST BANK**, and the **GOLAN HEIGHTS**. (See **EAST JERUSALEM**).

OLD CITY OF JERUSALEM. The eastern portion of the modern city of **JERUSALEM**, contained within the walls built by the **OTTOMAN** ruler **SULEIMAN THE MAGNIFICENT** in the sixteenth century CE. The existing street plan of the Old City was laid out by the Romans in 135 CE (See **MADABA MAP**), but there has been a city on the site for more than 3000 years. The most prominent feature of the Old City is the **HARAM AL-SHARIF**, called by **JEWS** the **TEMPLE MOUNT**.

OLIVES, MOUNT OF. Hill to the east of the **OLD CITY OF JERUSALEM**, from which, according to the account in the **BOOK OF ACTS** (See **ACTS, BOOK OF**), the **ASCENSION** of **JESUS CHRIST** took place.

OMAN. Country occupying the southeast portion of the **ARABIAN PENINSULA.** Pop. 3.2 miliion.

OTTOMAN EMPIRE. Turkish-ruled areas from ca 1450 to 1917 **CE.** At its peak in the eighteenth century the Ottoman Empire held suzerainty over southeastern Europe, **ANATOLIA, PALESTINE,** the **FERTILE CRESCENT, MESOPOTAMIA,** and North Africa from its capital in Istanbul.

PADAN ARAM. Name of the area north and east of **DAMASCUS** controlled by the Arameans from the early part of the second millennium. Subsequently changed to **ARAM.**

PAKISTAN. Islamic country bounded on the west by **AFGHANISTAN** and **IRAN** and on the east by India. Includes within its territory the fertile valley of the **INDUS RIVER.** Pop. 157 mil.

PALESTINA. Name derived from ancient **PHILISTINES** given by Romans in 134 **CE** to their provinces previously known as **JUDEA, SAMARIA,** and **GALILEE.** Subsequently came to be called **PALESTINE.**

PALESTINE. Prior to 1948 the name for the area at the eastern end of the Mediterranean Sea now occupied by **ISRAEL** and the **OCCUPIED TERRITORIES.** Also, the probable name for the new Palestinian state that may emerge out of negotiations between **ISRAEL** and the **PALESTINIANS,** which will include the **WEST BANK** and the **GAZA STRIP.** In popular parlance Palestine has come to mean the land that Palestinian **ARABS** claim for their own. Its boundaries thus vary depending on the views of the person using the term.

PALESTINE MANDATE. The area awarded to Britain by the **LEAGUE OF NATIONS** in 1923 and governed as a mandate until 1948. It included the present areas of **ISRAEL** and the **OCCUPIED TERRITORIES,** plus **JORDAN,** which was later separated as the **TRANS-JORDAN MANDATE.**

PALESTINIAN AUTHORITY. The areas of the **WEST BANK** and **GAZA** over which the Palestinian Authority has total or partial control, under terms of the **OSLO ACCORDS** and the **SHARM EL-SHEIKH** agreements.

PARAN, WILDERNESS OF. Area in the southern part of the **NEGEV DESERT** mentioned in the **EXODUS** account of the wanderings of the **ISRAELITES.**

PELLA. DECAPOLIS city during the Graeco-Roman period, now an archaeological site under restoration in **JORDAN.** Located east of the **JORDAN RIVER** and north of **JERASH (GERASA).**

PEREA. Roman district centered in the **JORDAN VALLEY,** east of the river and north of the **DEAD SEA.**

PERSIA. Empire ruled from **SUSA** in what is now **IRAN,** from ca 550 to 330 **BCE,** extending eastward to the **INDUS** and westward to include the **FERTILE CRESCENT, ASIA MINOR,** portions of Greece, **PALESTINE,** the Nile Valley, and the North African coastlands.

PERSIAN EMPIRE. See **PERSIA.**

PERSIAN GULF. Body of water that separates **ARABIA** from **IRAN** and connects through the Straits of Hormuz with the Arabian Sea.

PETRA. Capital of the Nabatean Empire. Archaeological site in southern

JORDAN.

PHILADELPHIA. Name of **AMMAN** during the Greek and Roman periods of occupancy. A **DECAPOLIS** city.

PHILIPPI. City in the northeastern part of Greece during Graeco-Roman times.

PHILISTIA. Territory on the coastal lowlands and adjacent hill slopes of present-day **ISRAEL** once occupied by the **PHILISTINES** until their defeat by the **ASSYRIANS** ca 723 BCE. Roughly equivalent to the area from the **GAZA STRIP** to **HAIFA.**

PHOENICIA. Territory roughly equivalent to modern **LEBANON** inhabited in the second and first millennia **BCE** by the advanced peoples known as the **PHOENICIANS.** Although Phoenicia was wiped out by the **ASSYRIANS** in the 7th century, by that time the Phoenicians had colonized widely in the Mediterranean. **CARTHAGE** was a Phoenician colony.

POITIERS. City in France that marked the furthest northward advance of Arab conquest. The **ARABS** were turned back at the nearby battle of **TOURS** in 732 CE.

PONTUS. Northeast province of Roman **ASIA MINOR**, with the Black Sea on the north, **CAPPADOCIA** on the south, and **GALATIA** on the west.

PORTUGAL. Country in the western part of the **IBERIAN PENINSULA.** Bordered on the west and south by the Atlantic Ocean, on the east and north by **SPAIN.** Pop. 10.9 million.

PROMISED LAND. See **BIBLICAL PROMISED LAND.**

QATAR. PERSIAN GULF country occupying a small peninsula projecting into the Persian Gulf from **ARABIA.** Pop. 650,000.

QUMRAN. Location of the first site where the **DEAD SEA SCROLLS** were found, in rough, cave-riddled country west of the northern part of the **DEAD SEA.**

QUNEITRA. Town now in **SYRIA** on eastern border of the **GOLAN HEIGHTS**, within territory monitored by the **UNITED NATIONS.** From 1967 to 1974 within territory occupied by **ISRAEL.** Destroyed by **ISRAELIS** in 1974. Pop. 38,000.

RABBOTH AMMON. Ancient walled city of the **AMMONITES.** Site of present-day **AMMAN**, capital of **JORDAN.**

RAFAH. City near the southern border of the **GAZA STRIP.** Pop. 145,000.

RAMALLAH. WEST BANK city, about ten miles north of **JERUSALEM**, serving as headquarters of the **PALESTINIAN AUTHORITY.** Pop. (Metropolitan Area) 145,000.

RED SEA. Body of water separating the **ARABIAN PENINSULA** from Africa.

RIYADH. Capital of **SAUDI ARABIA.** Located in an oasis in the center of the country. One of the world's fastest-growing cities. Pop. 3.8 million.

ROMAN EMPIRE. Extended at its height in the second century CE from Britain and **SPAIN** in the west to **MESOPOTAMIA** and **PALESTINE** in the east, and from the forested region north of the Alps to the edge of the desert in North Africa.

ROMAN PALESTINE. Land from the Mediterranean Sea eastward to the western portions of the **JORDAN PLATEAU**, and from **SYRIA** in the north to **NABATEA**

and the **NEGEV DESERT** in the south.

ROME. The capital of the **ROMAN EMPIRE**, now the capital of Italy, and (in the Vatican) the headquarters of the **ROMAN CATHOLIC** Church. Pop. 3.6 million.

RUSSIA. World's largest country in terms of area. Country of origin of most immigrants to **ISRAEL** in the past two decades. Pop. 146.7 million.

RUSSIAN STEPPES. Grasslands north of the Black Sea. In ancient times, the homeland of mercenary mounted **SCYTHIAN** warriors.

SAINT CATHERINE'S MONASTERY. Located high on a mountainside within view of **MOUNT SINAI** (See **SINAI, MOUNT**), in the southern part of the **SINAI PENINSULA**.

SAMARIA. HILL COUNTRY of central **PALESTINE**. Included within the **WEST BANK** portion of the **OCCUPIED TERRITORIES**. Historically the central of the three regions of the ancient kingdom of **ISRAEL**. Included within the **NORTHERN KINGDOM** after the kingdom of **SOLOMON** was divided.

SAUDI ARABIA. The largest country in the **ARABIAN PENINSULA**. Pop. 23.3 million.

SAYDA. See **SIDON**.

SCYTHIA. The grassland region north of the Black Sea from which **SCYTHIAN** mercenaries were recruited by **HITTITES**, Egyptians, and other ancient empires.

SCYTHOPOLIS. Greek name for **BEIT SHA'AN**. One of two **DECAPOLIS CITIES** in what is now **ISRAEL**.

SEA OF GALILEE. Actually, a lake, receiving the waters flowing southward off the slopes of **MOUNT HERMON** (See **HERMON, MOUNT**) and sending them south in the **JORDAN RIVER** to the **DEAD SEA**. Other names for the Sea of Galilee are the **LAKE OF TIBERIAS** (See **TIBERIAS, LAKE OF**), the **SEA OF GENNESARET** (See **GENNESARET, SEA OF**), and **LAKE KINNERET** (See **KINNERET, LAKE**).

SEA OF REEDS. Swampy area north of the **RED SEA** mistranslated in early **OLD TESTAMENT** sources as the **RED SEA**.

SEPPHORIS. City of hellenized **JEWS**, with evidence of wealth and sophistication, located about four miles north of **NAZARETH** during the time of **JESUS CHRIST**. Now an archaeological site.

SHARM EL-SHEIKH. Egyptian resort at the southern tip of the **SINAI PENINSULA**, built by **ISRAELIS** during the 1970s when they held the Sinai Peninsula. Occasional site of international meetings involving **ISRAEL** and the **PALESTINIAN AUTHORITY**.

SHARON VALLEY. Broad area of the coastal plain of **ISRAEL**, between **TEL AVIV** and **HAIFA**.

SHEBA. Homeland of the Queen who is said to have visited **SOLOMON** in the tenth century **BCE**. Generally assumed to be Saba, the highlands of present-day **YEMEN**. But may possibly have been located in the highlands of **ETHIOPIA**.

SHECHEM. Ancient name for the present **WEST BANK** city of **NABLUS**. Located in the **CENTRAL HIGHLANDS**. **ABRAHAM** stopped in Shechem, and **ISRAEL**'s kings were crowned there.

SICILY. Island portion of Italy separated from the mainland by the Straits of Messina. Its chief city in Graeco-Roman times was Syracuse.

SIDON (SAYDA). Ancient and modern Mediterranean port city in LEBANON. Pop. 151,000.

SILK ROAD. Caravan route that led from the Mediterranean through Central ASIA into China. Lost much of its importance when maritime contacts were established between Europe and the Far East.

SINAI DESERT. A continuation of the ARABIAN DESERT.

SINAI, MOUNT. Mountain peak in the southern part of the SINAI PENINSULA. Also called MOUNT HOREB (See HOREB, MOUNT) and JEBEL MUSA (the Mount of MOSES). Here, by tradition, MOSES received the TEN COMMANDMENTS.

SINAI PENINSULA. Peninsula between the GULF OF SUEZ and the GULF OF AQABA, fronting the Mediterranean Sea on the north, and the RED SEA to the south.

SLAVIC LANDS. Countries where Slavic languages are spoken. These include RUSSIA, Poland, the Czech and Slovak Republics, Serbia, Croatia, Bosnia, Macedonia, and Bulgaria. Serbs, Bulgarians, and Russians use the Cyrillic alphabet, based on Greek and introduced from CONSTANTINOPLE. Most of their population is EASTERN ORTHODOX in religion. Other Slavic countries use the Latin alphabet, and most of their population is ROMAN CATHOLIC.

SODOM. One of two ancient cities (the other GOMORRAH) said to have been located near the southern end of the DEAD SEA.

SOLOMON'S TEMPLE. The first TEMPLE, built in JERUSALEM by SOLOMON in ca 930 BCE and sited on MOUNT MORIAH (See MORIAH, MOUNT). It was destroyed by the BABYLONIANS in 586 BCE.

SOUTHERN KINGDOM. The part of the UNITED KINGDOM that remained when the northern tribes seceded in 927 BCE. Generally called JUDAH, after the larger of the two tribes (the other, BENJAMIN) that occupied the HILL COUNTRY in the southern portion of the UNITED KINGDOM, from the vicinity of JERUSALEM into the northern part of the NEGEV DESERT.

SPAIN. Larger of the two countries that occupy the IBERIAN PENINSULA. Pop. 41.9 million.

SUEZ CANAL. The big ditch (locks are unnecessary) completed in 1869 to connect the Mediterranean Sea and the RED SEA via the GULF OF SUEZ.

SULEIMAN'S WALL. The most recent of the many walls built, modified, or reinforced through the centuries to surround JERUSALEM. SULEIMAN'S WALL dates to the mid-sixteenth century.

SUMER. Most ancient of Mesopotamian civilizations, comprising a number of city-states whose welfare depended on irrigated agriculture and trade. The Sumerian civilization dates to 3500 BCE. It was still in existence at the time of ABRAHAM, about 1850 BCE, when ABRAHAM left the Sumerian city-state of UR. By that time, however, the BABYLONIANS were in ascendancy in the region.

SUSA. Capital of the ancient PERSIAN EMPIRE. Located in western PERSIA, about 75 miles west of the TIGRIS RIVER and about 250 miles north of the

PERSIAN GULF.

SYRIA. In its present configuration, Syria as a country is bordered by LEBANON, TURKEY, ISRAEL, and IRAQ. In SELEUCID and Roman times, it was a region north of PALESTINE with varying boundaries. Pop.19.3 million.

TEL AVIV. Located in the central part of ISRAEL's coastal plain facing the Mediterranean Sea. Tel Aviv is a modern city founded by Jewish settlers in 1909. Offically, Tel Aviv-Yafo, to indicate that the port of JAFFA lies within its southern boundary. Pop. 369,000.

TEMPLE. Structure on the TEMPLE MOUNT built by SOLOMON in the tenth century to house the ARK OF THE COVENANT. Destroyed by the BABYLONIANS in 586 BCE. (See SECOND TEMPLE).

TEMPLE MOUNT. An elevated area in the eastern part of the OLD CITY OF JERUSALEM that once held THE TEMPLE (See MORIAH, MOUNT). Since the MUSLIM conquest in 538 BCE, the site has been known to MUSLIMS as AL-HARAM AL-SHARIF. The total area of the Temple Mount/Haram al-Sharif is about 45 acres.

TIBERIAS. Roman city on the west shore of the SEA OF GALILEE, now a resort city in ISRAEL. Pop. 43,700.

TIBERIAS, LAKE OF. Roman name for the SEA OF GALILEE.

TIGRIS RIVER. The eastern of the two main rivers that bound MESOPOTAMIA. With headwaters in TURKEY, the TIGRIS flows through SYRIA, then IRAQ, to join with the EUPHRATES RIVER before emptying into the PERSIAN GULF.

TIRAN, STRAITS OF. Narrow passageway into the GULF OF AQABA from the RED SEA, between the SINAI PENINSULA and SAUDI ARABIA.

TOURS. City in southern France. Site of the decisive battle in 732 CE that marked the farthest northward push of the ARABS in Western Europe.

TRANS-JORDAN. A general term for the area east of the JORDAN RIVER.

TRANS-JORDAN MANDATE. Portion of the BRITISH PALESTINE MANDATE east of the JORDAN RIVER. The Trans-Jordan Mandate led to the founding of the HASHEMITE KINGDOM OF JORDAN.

TRANS-JORDAN PLATEAU. The plateau that comprises most of the eastern part of JORDAN, rising to 3,000 feet. It presents a sheer face east of the JORDAN RIVER.

TULKARM. Palestinian city in the northern part of the WEST BANK, near its western border. Pop. 163,000.

TUNISIA. Country in North Africa, bound by Libya on the west and Algeria on the east. Site of ancient CARTHAGE. The PALESTINE LIBERATION ORGANIZATION (PLO) was based in TUNISIA from 1982 until 1993. Pop. 9.9 million.

TURKEY. Its capital is Ankara. Turkey became an independent country following the defeat of the OTTOMAN EMPIRE in World War I. Pop. 75.1 million.

TYRE. Ancient Phoenician seaport on the Mediterranean coast of LEBANON. Now a modern city, Pop. 119,000.

UNITED ARAB EMIRATES (UAE). Country occupying a portion of the eastern part of the ARABIAN PENINSULA fronting the southern part of the PERSIAN GULF. Its desert border is with **SAUDI ARABIA** and **OMAN**. The capital of the UAE is Abu Dhabi. Pop. 3.3 million.

VIA DOLOROSA. Route followed by **JESUS** (See **JESUS CHRIST**) as he walked from the **ANTONIA FORTRESS** to **GOLGOTHA**, the place of **CRUCIFIXION**. A pilgrim route since early Christian times, it begins in what is now the **MUSLIM** quarter of the **OLD CITY** and ends at the **CHURCH OF THE HOLY SEPULCHER** (SEE **HOLY SEPULCHER, CHURCH OF THE**).

WADI ARABAH. Southward continuation to the **GULF OF AQABA** of the structural trench occupied by the **SEA OF GALILEE**, **JORDAN RIVER**, and **DEAD SEA**. A route used by both **ISRAEL** and **JORDAN**, it marks a division between the area in southern **ISRAEL** called the **NEGEV DESERT** and the **ARABIAN DESERT** of southern **JORDAN**.

WADI RUM. Area in the desert of southern **JORDAN** of great beauty, where cliffs of black basalt and white and red sandstone overlook a network of wadis that rarely contain water.

WEST BANK. Part of the **OCCUPIED TERRITORY** that **ISRAEL** gained from **JORDAN** in the **SIX-DAY WAR** in 1967. Lies north of the **DEAD SEA**, west of the **JORDAN RIVER**, and south of **LAKE KINNERET** (See **KINNERET, LAKE**) (the **SEA OF GALILEE**). Seventeen percent of the West Bank is occupied by Israeli **SETTLEMENTS** (See **SETTLEMENTS, JEWISH**). Pop. 2.3 mil (excludes Jewish settler population of 207,000).

WEST, THE. A term that includes Europe and the countries once settled by Europeans and embraces the common aspects of the culture evolved from their political, economic, and religious history.

YARMOUK RIVER. River flowing into the **JORDAN RIVER** from the east, forming a boundary between **JORDAN** and **ISRAEL**'s **GOLAN HEIGHTS**. Its deep gorge serves as a barrier to travel. The **BYZANTINE**s lost the battle with the **ARABS** fought at the Yarmouk River in 638, and thereafter **PALESTINE** came under **MUSLIM** domination.

YEMEN. Country in the southwest corner of the **ARABIAN PENINSULA**, bordering **SAUDI ARABIA** and the **RED SEA**. It includes the highest and wettest portion of the Peninsula, with elevations to 8,000 feet. Pop. 16.7 million.

ZIN, WILDERNESS OF. Area in the southern part of the **NEGEV DESERT** mentioned in the **EXODUS** account of the wanderings of the **ISRAELITES**.

ZION. The term Zion was often used to mean **JERUSALEM**, so a return to Zion meant a return to Jerusalem.

ZION. MOUNT. A rise in the topography of the **OLD CITY OF JERUSALEM**, culminating outside the southwest corner of the city's walls. In the **PSALMS** and elsewhere in the **HEBREW SCRIPTURES** (**OLD TESTAMENT**). Mount Zion and **MOUNT MORIAH** (See **MORIAH, MOUNT**) were both part of the low hills on which the city was built.

SOURCES

Achtemeier, Paul J., Editor, *Harper's Bible Dictionary.* HarperCollins, New York, 1985.

Ahmed, Akbar S. *Islam Today: A Short Introduction to the Muslim World.* I.B. Tauris, New York, 2002.

Ajami, Fouad. *The Arab Predicament: Arab Political Thought and Practice since 1967.* Cambridge University Press, New York, 1992.

Armstrong, Karen. *A History of God: The 4000-Year Quest of Judaism, Christianity and Islam.* Ballentine Books, New York, 1993.

Armstrong, Karen. *Islam: A Short History.* Modern Library, New York, 2000.

Armstrong, Karen. *Jerusalem: One City, Three Faiths.* Ballantine Books, New York, 1997.

Cahill, Thomas. *The Gifts of the Jews: How a Tribe of Desert Nomads Changed the Way Everyone Thinks and Feels.* Doubleday, New York, 1998.

Cahill, Thomas. *Desire of the Everlasting Hills: The World Before and After Jesus.* Anchor Books, New York, 1999.

Chacour, Elias. *We Belong to the Land: The Story of a Palestinian Israeli Who Lives for Peace and Reconciliation.* HarperCollins, New York, 1990.

Dimont, Max I. *Jews, God, and History.* Rev. Ed. Penguin Putnam, New York, 1994.

Firestone, Reuven. *The Origin of Holy War in Islam.* Oxford University Press, New York, 1999.

Fox, Edward. *Sacred Geography.* Henry Holt and Company, New York, 2001

Friedman, Thomas L. *From Beirut to Jerusalem.* Farrar, Straus & Giroux, New York, 1990.

Gerber, Jane S. *The Jews of Spain: A History of the Sephardic Experience.* The Free Press, New York, 1992.

Goodwin, Jason. *Lords of the Horizons: A History of the Ottoman Empire.* Henry Holt and Company, New York, 1999.

Gorenberg, Gershom. *The End of Days: Fundamentalism and the Struggle for the Temple Mount.* Oxford University Press, Oxford, 2000.

Lewis, Bernard. *The Middle East: A Brief History of the Last 2000 Years.* Paperback Reprint Edition, Touchstone Books, New York, 1997.

Lewis, Bernard. *Islam and the West.* Oxford University Press, London, 1994.

Lewis, Bernard. *What Went Wrong: Western Impact and Middle Eastern Response.* Oxford University Press, New York, 2001.

Nasr, Sayyed Hossein. *Islam: Religion, History, and Civilization.* Harper, San Francisco, 2002.

Peters, F. E. *The Monotheists: Jews, Christians, and Muslims in Conflict and Competition. Vol I: The Peoples of God.* Princeton University Press, Princeton, 2003.

Peters, Joan. *From Time Immemorial: The Origins of the Arab-Jewish Conflict Over Palestine.* Harper and Row, New York, 1984.

Reuther, Rosemary R. and Reuther, Herman J. *The Wrath of Jonah: The Crisis of Religious Nationalism in the Israeli-Palestinian Conflict.* 2nd Ed. Augsburg Fortress, Minneapolis, 2002.

Said, Edward W. *Orientalism.* Vintage, New York, 1979

Said, Edward W. *The Question of Palestine.* Vintage, New York, 1992

Shipler, David K. *Arab and Jew: Wounded Spirits in a Promised Land.* Random House, New York, 1986.

Weber, Timothy P. "How Evangelicals Became Israel's Best Friend," *Christianity Today*, October 5, 1998.

Wright, Lawrence. "Forcing the End," *New Yorker*, July 20, 1998.

The New Jerusalem Bible. Doubleday, New York, 1985

The New Oxford Annotated Bible. Oxford University Press, New York, 1994.

The Koran Interpreted. Translation by A. J. Arberry. Macmillan, New York, 1955. Touchstone Edition, Simon & Schuster, New York, 1996.

Index

A

E

J

L

N

O

P